CHINA
– BUSINESS OPPORTUNITIES IN
A GLOBALIZING ECONOMY

Editor
Verner Worm

CHINA
– BUSINESS OPPORTUNITIES IN A GLOBALIZING ECONOMY

Copenhagen Business School Press

CHINA
- Business Opportunities in a Globalizing Economy

© Copenhagen Business School Press, 2008
Printed in Denmark by Narayana Press, Gyllling
Cover design by BUSTO | Graphic Design

1st edition 2008

ISBN 978-87-630-0214-1

Distribution:

Scandinavia
DBK, Mimersvej 4
DK-4600 Køge, Denmark
Tel +45 3269 7788
Fax +45 3269 7789

North America
International Specialized Book Services
920 NE 58th Street, Suite 300
Portland, OR 97213-3786
Tel +1 800 944 6190
Fax +1 503 280 8832
Email: orders@isbs.com

Rest of the World
Marston Book Services, P.O. Box 269
Abingdon, Oxfordshire, OX14 4YN, UK
Tel +44 (0) 1235 465500
Fax +44 (0) 1235 465655
Email Direct Customers: direct.order@marston.co.uk
Email Booksellers: trade.order@marston.co.uk

All rights reserved. No part of this publication may be reproduced or used in any form or by any means – graphic, electronic or mechanical including photocopying, recording, taping or information storage or retrieval systems – without permission in writing from Copenhagen Business School Press at www.cbspress.dk

Table of Contents

Introduction 7
VERNER WORM

CHAPTER ONE 13
Virtuous Circles in Chinese Growth – Can it Continue?
NIELS MYGIND

CHAPTER TWO 43
Foreign Direct Investment in China:
Origin, Distribution, and Impact on the Economy
KJELD ERIK BRØDSGAARD

CHAPTER THREE 63
Knowledge Exchange with Offshore R&D Units:
Novo Nordisk, GN Resound, and BenQ Siemens Mobile in China
JULIE MARIE KJERSEM AND PETER GAMMELTOFT

CHAPTER FOUR 91
Subsidiary Influence and its Impact on Role Development:
Three Cases from the Coatings Industry in China
JENS GAMMELGAARD

CHAPTER FIVE 113
Guanxi Capital as a Sustainable Competitive Advantage
METTE BJØRN AND VERNER WORM

CHAPTER SIX 139
Micro-Evidence on Investment Patterns and Motivations of Chinese Multinationals
BERSANT HOBDARI, MARINA PAPANASTASSIOU AND EVIS SINANI

CHAPTER SEVEN 155
Ethnic Chinese Entrepreneurship in Southeast Asia:
Measuring the Economic Impact of Mainland China
MICHAEL JACOBSEN

CHAPTER EIGHT 171
The Danish Seduction of the China Outbound Tourism Market:
New Issues for Tourism Research
CAN-SENG OOI

About the Authors..*193*

Introduction

Verner Worm

Forty years ago, Beijing was closed to the outside world. In 2008, however, Beijing opened up for one of the most celebrated international events – the International Olympic Summer Games.

China's radical transition over the past forty years has surprised the global community – and attracted considerable media attention.

Since 1978, China – with its population of 1.3 billion – has achieved an annual growth rate of almost 10 percent. It is about to overtake Germany as the third largest economy in the world. In 2007 China's economic growth reached 11.4 percent. At current exchange rates, China accounts for approximately 6 percent of global GDP and has 37.5 percent of the world population (Winters and Yusuf 2007).

Despite China's geographically uneven development – with a Gini coefficient of 0,47 in 2006 – one should not forget that China's rapid economic progress has managed to lift an astounding 1.2 million people out of poverty each month since 1990 (Forget the World Bank, Try Wal-Mart, 2006). The World Bank expects the high growth rate will continue until 2030 (Global Economic Prospects 2007).

In terms of purchasing power parity (PPP), China has been the second largest economy since 2005. Often referred to as the "conveyer belt of the world," China has been ranked as the most attractive destination for foreign direct investment (FDI) in the world since 2002 (Foreign Direct Investor Confidence index); 50 percent of all cameras and 25 per cent of washing machines sold in the world originate in China (Ideas are the King, 2007)

With an annual total of approximately US$ 60 billion, China is one of the main recipients of FDI – rather uncommon for a developing country with an estimated annual per capita income of US$ 2000 in 2006 (US$ 7700 in PPP same year).

Roughly one third of China's industrial production is made in foreign-invested companies. As of 2006, these companies account for almost 60 percent of China's foreign trade (Market Profile on Chinese

Mainland). In 2007, China became the world's second largest export nation: behind Germany and ahead of the U.S.A. and Japan. The label "Made in China" is no longer perceived to be substandard – a common perception during China's planned economy era.

According to Global Envision.org, 70 percent of Wal-mart's products are made in China. Scandinavian firms are increasing their production in China. Business with China is not limited to local production, however. Investment also goes in both directions. In March 2008, China held the world's largest foreign currency reserve of more than US$ 1.5 trillion (Market Profile on Chinese Mainland). Outward investment is increasing rapidly and China now ranks eighth in terms of outward FDI. For example, in Kalmar, Sweden 1,100 Chinese firms are now in the process of setting up a "window display" for their products in a 70,000 square meter building. To support this investment, 1,400 apartments for Chinese staff will be built. The "window display" is planned to open in 2008 (Berlingske Tidende, Business, 24 July 2007).With the scale of Chinese outward investment, the EU has begun to take notice. In fact, German Chancellor Angela Merkel recently suggested that the European Union should use public funding to protect strategic industries and companies from buyouts by state-controlled investors from China and other nations with significant foreign reserves (Williamson, 2007). The U.S.A. has similar restrictions against foreign buyouts.

In summary, the above points underline why China has emerged as a focal point for the business community at large, as well as within the field of international business research.

This focus on China has inspired this book. A collaboration between researchers within the Department of International Economics and Management at the Copenhagen Business School and with various external co-authors, the book focuses on different aspects of Chinese FDI: both inward and outward investment.

In the first chapter, Niels Mygind looks at the main causes behind the impressive economic growth in China. Analysis is based on the interactions between Politics, Institutions, and Economy. Niels Mygind discusses not only factors which have contributed over the past 30 years to China's high growth rate, but he also identifies potential threats to this development.

In the second chapter, Kjeld Erik Brødsgaard explores the major role which FDI has played in China's economic development. Based on statistics, Brødsgaard describes the development of FDI over time in terms of amount of investment, geographical location, etc. Brødsgaard discusses how development creates a spillover effects to endogenous companies through the introduction of new technologies and management skills as well as how development generates employment.

In chapter three, Julie Marie Kjersem and Peter Gammeltoft specifically look at FDI in research and development (R&D) in multinational firms. They analyze R&D both from a Chinese and a Western political perspective, they investigate the motives behind these investments from Western companies, and they assess the socio-cultural implications for the international collaboration within R&D. The issues are presented through three case companies – all of which are R&D-intensive firms

Following the case studies of international management of R&D in chapter three, Jens Gammelgaard examines in chapter four the role of foreign-owned subsidiaries' power in China and their dynamics through three cases from the coating industry (i.e. paint). Based on three case companies, Gammelgaard is able to focus his findings within the field of subsidiary-headquarter power relations.

Chapter five, by Mette Bjørn and Verner Worm, develops the concept of *'guanxi'* capital and how it can contribute to sustainable competitive advantage. *'guanxi'* capital as a basis for competitive advantage is developed by combining specific Chinese cultural and structural characteristics with more Western theories of social capital and the resource-based view of business. Recent economic development is discussed in light of the distinction between *'guanxi'* and the increasing amount of corruption in China.

Bersant Hobdari, Marina Papanastassiou, and Evis Sinani turn to outward Chinese FDI in chapter six. Until recently, outward Chinese FDI had been unexplored. Based on a solid empirical data set, however, the authors manage to describe major characteristics of Chinese outward investments: including region, size of investment, form of investment, sector, etc. In conclusion, the authors show that outward Chinese FDI is mainly market- and technology-seeking, which fits well with German Chancellor Angela Merkel's above remarks.

In chapter seven, Michael Jacobsen questions how small- and medium-sized enterprises (SMEs) in Southeast Asia are impacted by Mainland China's economic development. Jacobsen argues convincingly that this question cannot be answered without considering national loyalties and the respective host countries' preferences, since SMEs are forced to follow the rules of the host country. Jacobsen contrasts the SME situation with large, ethnically-Chinese MNCs in Southeast Asia. According to his research, these MNCs are able to penetrate the Chinese market and capitalize from its growth based – at least partly – on cultural affinities. Jacobsen's assertion seems appropriate, since the largest portion of FDI to mainland China stems from surrounding regions.

In the final chapter, Can-Seng Ooi draws a picture of China's outbound tourism by focusing on Chinese tourism to Denmark. Ooi contends that although Chinese tourists seem to like Denmark, the Danish authorities are less enthusiastic about tourism in general and about Chinese tourism in particular. Ooi interviews a local Danish political leader, who states: "Tourists don't vote," and thus they become less important to focus upon from a political and a rights-protection perspective. Ooi's article elucidates how Denmark repackages and rebrands itself as a nation to attract more Chinese tourists, and how Chinese authorities educate their tourists in host-country-appropriate behaviour, Chinese travellers are usually (i.e. 90%) business travellers. This dynamic and complex interaction between host and local (it could be foreign companies as well) are described. This is a perfect chapter to conclude a book focusing on China's economic relations in a globalized world.

Acknowledgement

The editor and all the contributors would like to thank Anne Sluhan-Reich for her meticulous work in getting the English right for this book. Thanks also go to Enrico Canal Bruland and Can-Seng Ooi for their hard and professional work in typesetting the book.

References

Chinese exhibition window in Sweden. 2007 *Berlingske Tidende, Business*, July 24. Foreign Direct Investor Confidence index 2007 http://www.atkearney.com (Accessed November 20, 2007).

"Forget the World Bank, Try Wal-Mart" 2006 http://www.globalenvision.org/library/10/1279/ (Accessed October 3, 2007).

Winters L. and Yusuf, S. (Eds.) 2007 *Dancing with giants. Introduction. Singapore*. The World Bank and the Institute of Policy Studies (Singapore).

How to interpret Gini Coefficient in China 2006 http://en.ce.cn/Insight/200509/13/t20050913_4669147.shtml (Accessed November 20, 2007).

Ideen er konge 2007 (The idea is the King). Mandag Morgen. February 12, 2007.

IMF forecast 2007 *Global Growth Seen at 5.2 pct in 2007* http//www.imf.org/external/pubs/ft/survey/so/2007/NEW0725A.htm (Accessed July 27, 2007).

Market Profile on Chinese Mainland 2007. http://www.tdctrade.com (Accessed February 29, 2008).

Williamson, H. 2007. *Merkel seeks European-wide vetting of foreign acquisitions*. Financial Times July 19.

World Bank 2007. *Global Economic Prospects – managing the next wave of Globalization* http://econ.worldbank.org/ (Accessed November 20, 2007).

CHAPTER ONE

Virtuous Circles in Chinese Growth – Can it Continue?

Niels Mygind

For several centuries China was the largest economy in the world. It even had higher levels of income than Europe from the 5th to the 14th centuries. Later, Europe had a higher per capita income, but because of its significantly larger population, China continued to be a larger economy for several centuries. China's economy collapsed, however, between 1840 and 1940 due to foreign exploitation, military conflicts, and the Japanese attempt at conquest. At the start of the Communist rule in 1949 per capita GDP was less than 75 percent of the level in 1820 (Maddison 2001). During the subsequent Mao period of rule, China's economy began to grow again at rates of 5-6 percent per year. Its growth, however, was not without painful ups and downs – mainly due to political instability. Between 1950 and 1980 education levels in China improved significantly. Life expectancy increased from 40.8 to 67.8 years (Fogel 2006). By the end of the 1970s, China was ready for an economic boom – provided the right institutional changes would be implemented. These changes were apparently made, evidenced by its high and stable growth rates of 8-10 percent per year since 1978. Some scholars have questioned the statistics (Summers and Heston 1994, Young 2003), but even with their suggested revisions, only 1-2 percent would be lost – which does not alter the overall picture of significant growth. According to Goldman Sachs (2003), continuing high growth will make China the largest economy in the world within the next 40 years. Also the World Bank (2007) is optimistic on long run economic growth in China, and forecasts an annual growth rate of 8 percent up to 2030.

This chapter aims to take a broader look at the main causes for China's growth. It will analyze the dynamics from a holistic point of view; the paper not only looks at narrow economic causes, but it bases its analysis on the dynamic interaction between Politics, Institutions, and Economy (PIE). This dynamic can be viewed as a series of virtuous self-enforcing circles amongst the three PIE elements. Thus, the two key research questions for this chapter are:

- What are the main positive self-enforcing circles that have contributed to the exceptionally high and enduring growth in China since 1978?
- Can threats be identified which might break some of these virtuous circles?

The year 1978 marked the shift to market-oriented reforms in China with a gradual introduction of market-oriented prices, a gradual opening up for international trade and FDI, as well as a gradual widening of the scope for private business activities. This process was lead by the political takeover of leading positions in the Communist Party by market-oriented reformers led by Deng Xiaoping. These reformers initiated a process of the gradual build-up of market-oriented institutions. This had a strong – positive – effect on the Chinese economy and thus led to consolidation of the power of the reform-oriented segment of the party.

This *political-institutional* virtuous circle will be described with a focus on how the gradual reform process has reformed economic institutions, how this affected the economy and led to the consolidation of the reform wing. This section will look closer at the threats that may weaken this circle such as social tensions caused by increasing inequality, and on factors that may enhance further growth like continuing reforms and restructuring of the financial sector. As a separate circle, China's interaction with the globalization process will be emphasized in the *openness circle*. These two circles are closely related to the third circle – the *catch-up circle* – because institutional changes create the background for freeing productive resources, in particular the huge Chinese labour-force. Reformed institutions are also important for the high accumulation of capital which, from the time of low level per capita GDP, started a swift process of 'catch up' with developed countries. This swift growth has to a high degree been characterized by *extensive growth* based on high investments and moving labour from agriculture to industry. The questions remain: how long can this catching-up process continue? What are the future prospects for prioritizing *intensive growth* based on increasing total factor productivity? This analysis concludes with a summary of results which stresses the interactions between the three circles in the PIE model. However, before delving into the dynamics and sustainability of these three circles, a short presentation of the theoretical framework of the PIE-model must be made.

The PIE-Framework: Politics – Institutions – Economy

Human beings devise institutions as constraints on human behaviour to shape human interaction (North 1980). The political and economic institutions of a society define the rules of the game for its citizens. In recent years, it has been widely recognized that high institutional quality is a main driver for growth and high per capita GDP (IMF 2005, WEF 2006). This is the reason why *institutions* – both formal and informal – are included as a main box in the model of society given below (see Mygind, 2007 for further details). The *political institutions* define the rules for how the political system functions through the constitution. The *economic institutions* set the framework for the game rules in the economy. The *informal institutions* in the culture 'set' unwritten rules both for politics and for economy. The change of formal institutions is done through the political process – thus, arrows point in both directions between *politics* and *institutions*.

The political process is based on the distribution of power, income, and resources to the citizens. Citizens can be divided into different *social groups* in relation to this distribution. Different cultures can also play a role e.g. in relation to different ethnic or religious groupings so there is also a connection between informal institutions and social groups.

The *economy* is divided in two parts: flow variables, such as GDP, investments, consumption, inflation etc.; and stock variables, such as human resources (i.e. size and quality of the workforce), capital equipment in the production structure, technological quality of this capital, infrastructure, natural resources and geography. The e*conomy* is strongly influenced both by the economic institutions and by the decisions for economic policy determined in the political process. At the same time, the *economy* lays the foundation for distribution between different social groups. The level of development in the *economy* also feeds back to the development of institutions. Therefore, the Figure includes arrows in both directions between the *economy* and the boxes of *politics* and *institutions*.

Figure 1:1 Dynamics of the PIE-Model

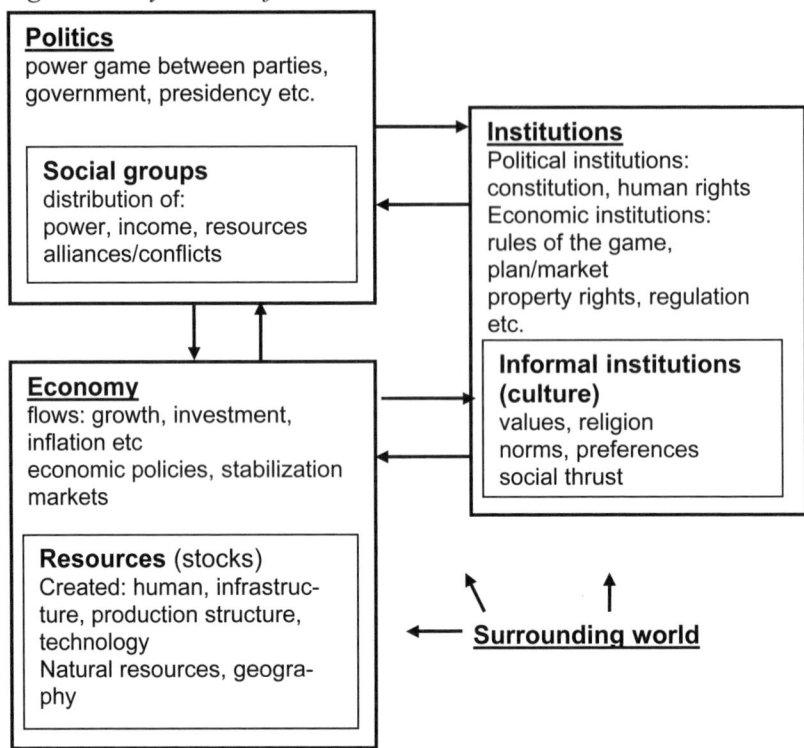

Finally, is it important to include the influence from the *surrounding world* on all three boxes: International coercion and alliances influence *politics*. International pressure, benchmarks, and supervision influence *institutions*. International interaction through trade, FDI, and other types of economic cooperation strongly influences the *economy*. There is a feedback effect – like the effect China's growth has on global oil prices. However, the different links in the model have different weights depending on the specific analysis, as exemplified in the following section.

The Political-Institutional Circle

The political-institutional circle in Figure 1:2 emphasizes the connection from politics to institutional change, then over the effects for the economy, and back to the consolidation of power of the reformers in the political system. This is illustrated by the circle with clockwise direction of the main causality.

Figure 1:2 The Political-Institutional Circle in China

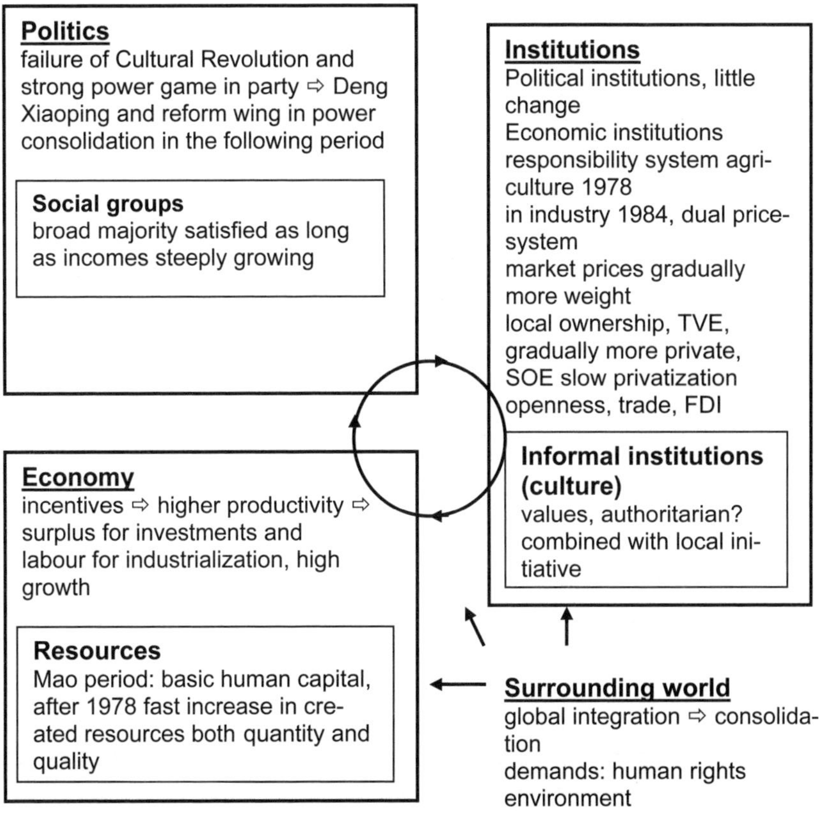

Politics
failure of Cultural Revolution and strong power game in party ⇨ Deng Xiaoping and reform wing in power consolidation in the following period

Social groups
broad majority satisfied as long as incomes steeply growing

Economy
incentives ⇨ higher productivity ⇨ surplus for investments and labour for industrialization, high growth

Resources
Mao period: basic human capital, after 1978 fast increase in created resources both quantity and quality

Institutions
Political institutions, little change
Economic institutions responsibility system agriculture 1978
in industry 1984, dual price-system
market prices gradually more weight
local ownership, TVE, gradually more private, SOE slow privatization
openness, trade, FDI

Informal institutions (culture)
values, authoritarian? combined with local initiative

Surrounding world
global integration ⇨ consolidation
demands: human rights environment

The legitimacy of the communist monopoly of power and political stability to a high degree rests on the increase in living standards for China's population. At the same time political stability has in China supported the continual upgrade of institutions and stable macroeconomic policies which promote high growth.

The disastrous Cultural Revolution which caused several years of low or negative growth was followed by some years of political instability and strong power struggles. This finally led to the consolidation of the position of Deng Xiaoping who promoted a pragmatic and market-oriented change of economic institutions starting with the introduction of *the responsibility system* in agriculture from 1978. The system was based on small family units which, after delivering their production quotas at fixed prices to the state, could sell the residual surplus at market prices. This created a strong motivation for increasing production. In the following years, productivity in agriculture rose steeply together with a rise in the proportion of goods sold at market-based prices. This created a surplus of capital and labour in the local villages and was the foundation for swift industrialization (Naughton and McMillan 1992). The responsibility system was introduced to industry in 1984 and many new semi-private ownership structures – mainly so-called township village enterprises – were established. In the following years, locally owned/semi-private enterprises based on market-oriented incentives made up a high and increasing part of the steeply growing manufacturing sector. The openness policy with increasing foreign trade and FDI (to be analyzed in the next section) is closely connected to this development. The entry of these new companies created increasing competitive pressure on the old state-owned enterprises.

These market elements coexisted with the planned economy with fixed quotas sold at state fixed prices, with a gradual shift in balance toward the market (Naughton 1994). Although state-owned enterprises continued to enjoy a privileged position in relation to the dominant State Owned Commercial Banks, they were forced to some market-oriented restructuring. Late in the restructuring process many small state-owned enterprises were privatized under the principle *'keep the large and let the small ones go.'* With the further transfer of township village enterprises to formal private ownership and with the continuous increase of foreign-owned enterprises, the private sector gained a significant share of production (Sun 2002).

When compared to the transition which took place in Eastern Europe, the Chinese institutional change was slower and more incremental. The Chinese followed the principle *'crossing the river by feeling for the stones under your feet.'* Each step in the reform process was based on experiments of institutional change in a certain region. If successful in one region, the reform was spread to the rest of China or, spread step-by-step throughout the country (e.g. the gradual increase in the number of Development Zones open for foreign investments).

There have been discussions and tensions within the Communist Party about specific institutional changes and the speed of implementation. Around the time of the 1989 massacre in Beijing, a discussion took place about possible democratic-oriented reforms. The hardliners won the struggle, however. Later tensions arose between a group especially focussed on the development in the coast regions – Shanghai – and a more Beijing-oriented group. The Shanghai group – with Jiang Zemin and Zhu Rongji dominated the 1990s. The current Chinese political leaders – Hu Jintao and Wen Jiabao – worked in poorer provinces most of their political careers before consolidating their power in the party at the beginning of the new millennium. They have emphasized regionally-balanced growth with more support to the Western provinces. In spite of these regional differences, there has been general agreement within the communist leadership about the prioritization of institutional changes to promote economic growth. Thus, in the Communist Party the pragmatic line introduced by Deng Xiaoping has dominated since 1978. The party has transitioned from its Maoist communist principles to a more technocratic ideology with economic growth as the highest priority. Party leadership is currently dominated by engineers. In 1982 around 50 percent of the members of the Central Committee had university degrees. In 2002 this number had increased to 99 percent (Fogel 2006).

The pragmatic line has been consolidated during the reform process because institutional changes created incentives that turned out to be successful for China's economic development. The population has been satisfied with the increasing standard of living and, thus, there has been little cause for strong opposition to the ruling Communist party. Tensions within the party have been limited and the faction who supports further reforms in the direction of a private market economy has been clearly dominant. Some of the most recent steps toward a market economy based on private ownership include the 2002 sanction for private company owners – capitalists in Marxist terms – to become party members. In 2004 the constitution was amended to protect private property rights (OECD 2005).

The Communist party controls both the overall development of the economic institutions policies and it controls directly the state owned enterprises and the thereby 'the commanding heights' of the economy. The party exercises its power through the nomenclatura system and the continued existence of party factions in government organs and party cells/groups/branches/committee in enterprises. There have been only small changes in the political institutions over the period, however, Brødsgaard (2004) states that there have been some changes in recent years from a system directed by informal power relationships and processes to a system that is governed by formal rules and power relationships. He argues that China in recent years has undergone a process of institutionalization and normativization that has been continued and perhaps even deepened in the Hu Jintao era.

The question remains today whether there are forces in China's future development which might break the circle of political stability and support for further reforms? Will we see a continuation of the gradual reforms followed by further freeing of the productive potential and continuing high growth and consolidation of the power structure? Threats to this political-institutional self-enforcing circle could include the increasing economic gap between the coastal regions and Western China overlapping with the gaps between rural and urban areas. The ratio between urban and rural incomes declined somewhat in the years after the introduction of the agricultural reforms which gave the rural population a strong lift. However, since the start of the 1980s the proportion has increased from around 2.0 to 3.3 (Shane and Gale 2004). It can be argued that this is not itself a problem since rural areas also experienced a significant increase in living standards, although not as steep an increase as for urban populations. This change is according to Deng's thesis of '*letting some get rich first,*' with the implication that the increased standard of living will spread from the coast to other regions. However, it can be argued that extreme differences between populations will create tension because some groups react against the increasing inequalities.

During this period of development a dilution of the social security system in China – the so-called '*iron rice bowl*' – with secured income, health care, and pensions through the municipality or through the state-owned enterprises has occurred. In the new market system an increasing proportion of the population pays these cost themselves from their own savings. In particular migrant workers – numbering more than 100 million – who travel from rural areas to the coastal growth centres have limited rights according to the *hokou registration system*. Labour unions do not exist in China. This has created a paradox of a state lead by a communist party with weak rights for a large proportion of its workers. The question remains: will this inequality create enough tension to disturb China's political stability and high growth rates?

A possible – negative – scenario could be a social reaction with strikes and riots followed by a political reaction with strengthened state repression and increased regulation including a stop to further privatization and perhaps re-nationalization of some of the private enterprises. There were elements of such a development in 1989. However, in recent years the Communist Party has been rather sensitive to these kinds of social problems. Although there have been cases of repression at the regional level, the central government has reacted with attempting to solve the social problems. Another scenario could be the development of policy with stronger social welfare elements. As noted by Blanchard and Giavazzi (2005), there is room for an expansion of the Chinese public sector with higher levels of spending on health care, education, infrastructure, social security, and pensions. This may result in a fall in private savings, but might not hamper growth if investments are allocated more efficiently, see the following section.

The current Party leadership has given higher priority to development of the inner provinces. In 2000 the Party started a '*develop the West*' campaign to push public and private investment into the poorest western provinces. In 2004, the central government announced that increasing rural incomes should be given top policy priority (Shane and Gale 2004). In October 2006, the government set a 2020 target of building a more '*harmonious society*' by promoting development in rural areas and implementing reforms in health care, education, finance and environmental protection (EIU 2007).

Another threat to the continuing success of gradual institutional reform has been raised by Prasad and Rajan (2006) who argue that slow incremental reform has reached its limits because of the rising market orientation and increasing integration with the world economy. For the remaining upgrading of the institutional system cohesive and consequent reforms are necessary. This is especially the case for the reform of the financial sector and for further privatization and reform of the state-owned enterprises. Such reforms imply that the state must give up the control also of the *commanding heights* of the economy and this may meet resistance within the Communist Party. However, also in the later years, the gradual approach has been successfully continued. The development in the financial sector is a good example. Following accession to the WTO in 2001 China was granted a five year period to reform and further open up the banking sector. From December 2006, foreign banks may be established in China with few restrictions. Since 2001 three of the four big state-owned commercial banks have been intensively reformed. The remaining and most problematic bank, the Agricultural Bank of China, lags behind in this process. Bad loans have been cleared and taken over by Asset Management Companies and the bank has substantial new capital so the share of non-performing-loans has fallen from 19.2 percent in 2004 to 9.5 percent in 2006. Substantial minority holdings have been sold in IPOs. China's biggest bank – ICBC – held the world's largest IPO in history of 19.1 billion USD in October 2006 (DB Research 2006). Foreign banks now own 10-15 percent of this bank. The state has a cap for foreign ownership of 25 percent, however. It is expected that the proportion of loans to the state-owned enterprises will fall and simultaneously the activities of foreign banks will increase steeply. Foreign-owned assets comprise now around 15 percent of the banking sector. Compared to Eastern

Europe's 50-90 percent foreign-owned asset share, China's is relatively low.

Continued deepening of the market, further liberalization of the financial sector, and increased openness to the global economy may bring increased risks of the usual business cycles. The latest development on the Chinese stock and housing markets indicates bubbles and risks of subsequent financial crises. On the other hand, China's firm grip on fiscal and monetary policies (as well as more direct regulation) has thus far avoided overheating and high inflationary pressures. There are no political conflicts that point in the direction of looser policies in the coming years. However, the pressure for an appreciation of the Yuan currency may cause some negative effects of increasing unemployment in certain sectors and thus may have a negative effect on real incomes for farmers selling at world market prices. This point will be further discussed in relation to the openness circle.

The deeply-rooted Chinese network relations continue to play an important role in the judiciary system, which is far from the Western ideal for securing the rule of law. Nepotism and corruption play a strong role in Chinese business relations. However, the still-increasing level of FDI and the high level of internal Chinese investment do not indicate that this creates strong barriers for the continuing development of private business. Still, institutions and public service can certainly be much improved and the continued gradual upgrading of institutions can contribute to future growth.

In summary, threats to the political-institutional circle do not seem to be strong enough to stop the positive effects of a continued gradual transformation of institutions. If China follows the political path of the most developed East Asian economies – South Korea, Taiwan, Singapore, and Malaysia – we may in the long run see a shift from authoritarian regimes towards democracy. If China follows this path, a slightly higher degree of uncertainty and political change will not in themselves threaten the high growth path. Democratization will most likely go hand in hand with the growing wealth and confidence of the middle class; it will probably not be a strong tendency before China's per capita income reaches a higher level. At this point in time, the most important factor for waning growth rates will probably be the end of the 'catch-up' process itself – a stage that is probably decades away. This will be further discussed in a following section, but first, the specific institutional change in relation to liberalization of economic ties to the outside world will be analyzed.

The Openness Circle

An important part of the economic reforms in China has been its gradual opening up to the world. This process is part of the political-institutional circle as the reforms have positively affected economic growth and have consolidated the reformers' political power. This has created space for further reforms. However, there are some particular dynamics connected to the openness circle which will be emphasized in this section.

Like other reforms of economic institutions, the openness process was conducted gradually over a long period of time. Up until 1978, foreign trade was centralized and was minimal. In the 1980s, a gradual liberalization of trade followed, but by 1990, high tariffs were still in effect and about half of Chinese imports were regulated by licenses and quotas (Branstetter and Lardy 2006). During the WTO negotiations in 1992, tariff levels were significantly reduced and the number of firms granted trading rights increased dramatically. The exchange rate regime went from a strictly administratively regulated system with an overvalued currency to a more open system based on a strongly devalued currency from 1995 – de facto fixed to the United States Dollar. FDI liberalization began already in 1979 with new legislation governing joint ventures and establishing four Special Economic Zones with preferential tax and more liberal regulation. From 1984 onward, the number of such development zones increased gradually – especially along the East Coast of China. From 1986 *'foreign invested enterprises'* were eligible for reduced tax throughout China and advantages were especially high for export-oriented and technologically-advanced foreign firms (Branstetter and Lardy 2006). In this way, FDI was gradually allowed into more sectors – including the financial sector in later years. Restrictions on foreign ownership loosened; what in the start could only be joint ventures with strong Chinese participation could later be 100 percent foreign-owned. In general China's opening – especially in relation to the WTO commitments – has been more comprehensive and consequential than for other developing countries (Branstetter and Lardy 2006).

Figure 1:3 The Openness Circle

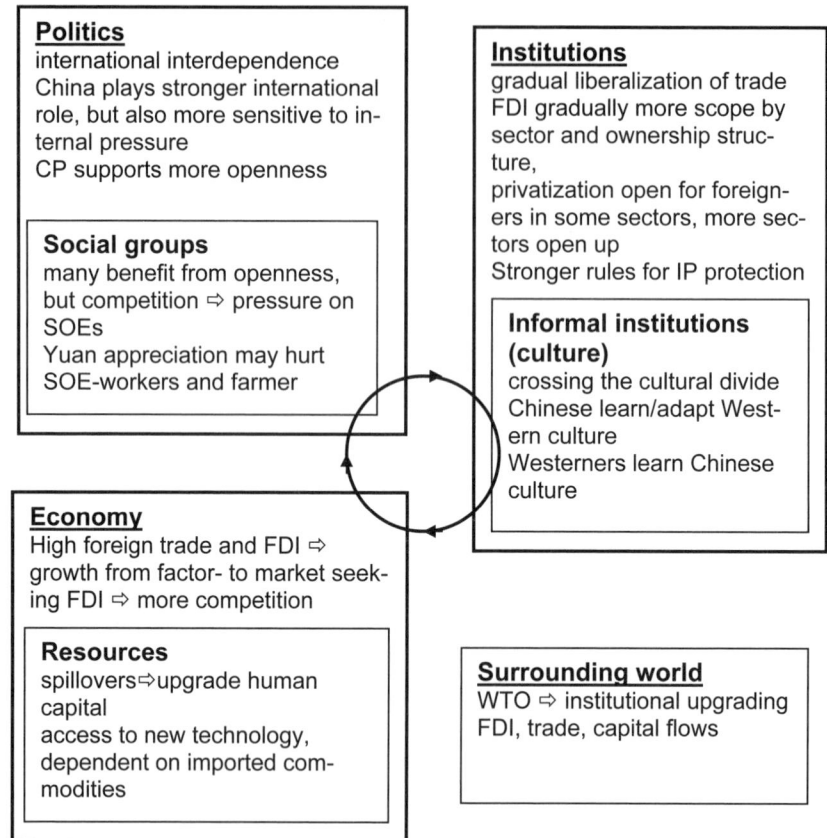

Both exports and imports rose steeply from the start of the 1990s and accelerated further after 2000 with surplus of trade reaching record levels in recent years. In July 2005 China unpegged the Yuan and went into a managed float exchange rate regime. Still, capital movements were under quite strict administrative control and the exchange rate was only allowed to appreciate around 5 percent in relation to USD over the following two years. Inward FDI took off during the 1990s, thus making China the biggest recipient of FDI in 2002. Note, however that as much as 30-50 percent of FDI came from Hong Kong. A considerable part originated from mainland China, but was 'round-tripping' to exploit tax advantages for foreign investments (OECD 2005). Therefore, the numbers for FDI inflows to China are somewhat inflated.

The particular dynamics connected to the openness circle are illustrated in Figure 1:3. The first wave of FDI was factor seeking by targeting the cheap and abundant labour power in China. This can be seen in the steep increase in exports connected to early FDI. Currently 58 percent of exports (China Statistical yearbook 2006) originate from foreign-owned enterprises. With the exception of 1993, China has had a trade surplus every year since 1990 and that surplus has grown in the later years. However, increasing amounts of FDI are oriented toward the steeply-increasing domestic markets e.g. for mobile-phones, cars, etc. So on the one hand, FDI has been an important part of increasing production. On the other hand, more FDI is dependent on the high growth of the Chinese market. In this way the openness circle has its own self-enforcing process.

China's deeper integration into the global economy has also increased the international pressure for upgrading institutions. WTO membership in 2001 was a logical consequence of China's increasing share of world trade. At the same time the process has put pressure on China to open up further for trade and FDI including the liberalization of the financial sector, which was formally opened for foreign ownership in December 2006 following a 5-year adjustment period. The increasing economic integration with the world and the increasing mutual dependency can also be expected to rise some pressure on political institutions. Foreign demands for improved human rights and democratization may eventually affect the Chinese political system. Such institutional convergence may also affect informal institutions. When more goods, capital, and people cross the cultural divide, both sides learn and partially adapt to each others' cultures.

The openness circle is closely related to the 'catch-up' process (to be further analyzed in the next section) since the training of labour used in foreign enterprises helps to upgrade the labour force and helps create technological spill over e.g. in ICT and in the automotive industry: both of which help to upgrade the quality of capital. Productivity has grown most in sectors open to foreign competition (Farrell et al. 2004). The openness circle in this way interacts closely with the catch-up circle by improved competitiveness and increased allocative efficiency. FDI has undoubtedly helped China to expand production into relatively advanced sectors with e.g. a high share of exports in electronics and information technology products (Schott 2006). However, Branstetter and Lardy (2006) and others argue that the advances of Chinese production are not so impressive because most of this production is simple assembly production. This is indicated by the very high volume of imports of intermediate goods in the advanced high export sectors.

On the other hand, there are clear indications that Chinese producers are quickly upgrading. Chinese-owned companies have grown strong in this process, with some firms developing into multinational enterprises. Chinese companies have even been sourcing more developed technology through foreign acquisitions; Chinese-owned *Lenovo's* takeover of IBM's PC division and *Nanjing Automobile*'s purchase of the British *MG Rover* are illustrative examples (Serger and Widman 2006).

The openness circle can also be part of a global growth circle; high growth in China increasingly pushes growth of the world economy. At the same time, Chinese growth is dependent on the access to the large regional markets of the USA and Europe.

Some important threats to the sustainability of the openness growth circle include slowed growth on the Western markets and the risk of Western protective measures. This was illustrated by the protective reactions by the USA and the EU on the end of the last quotas in the Multifiber Agreement which triggered significant growth in Chinese textile exports at the start of 2006. Such developments outside China could be a threat to the continuation of high export-driven growth. This is also closely connected to pressure from the USA and other Western economies for liberalizing the currency exchange rate, which, according to economists and investors, will lead to a further appreciation of the Yuan. Following the 2005 relaxation of the exchange rate, the Yuan experienced a small appreciation. But Chinese politicians have been hesitant to let the Yuan flow freely fearing a significant appreciation which will result in falling competitiveness – especially for some of the less-effective state-owned enterprises – and thus will increase unemployment. However, there is room for a relative fall in exports moving towards external balance of trade. This need not imply more internal imbalance of higher unemployment if the slow down in exports is accompanied of higher growth in consumption for the Chinese population. Such a development can open up for a more balanced world economy and thus more sustainable growth in the long run. There is a risk of political protests from certain groups e.g. of employees in state-owned enterprises and also from Chinese farmers who may experience falling world market prices on certain food commodities measured in an appreciated Yuan. However, more balanced trade, more competitive pressure on the state-owned enterprises, further changes in the production structure with increasing productivity and falling employment in agriculture are all foreseeable elements in the probable growth-path for the Chinese economy. These aspects will be further discussed in the following section: a closer look into the different elements of Chinese growth.

Catch-Up Circle

There is an ongoing discussion concerning the sustainability of Chinese growth in relation to the weight of *extensive* versus *intensive* growth. Growth is *extensive* when it is based on simple addition of factor inputs without improving factor productivity and *intensive* when productivity increases without increasing factor inputs. Krugman (1994) stressed that East Asian growth was to a very high degree based on extensive growth with extremely high investment rates and transfer of labour from low productivity sectors of agriculture to industry. The intensive growth with increases in allocative efficiency and level of technology – the increase in the quality of capital and labour – was, according to Krugman, of limited importance to East Asia. However, newer studies indicate that Chinese growth can be related to strong investments, the increase in labour in high productivity sectors, *as well as* the increase in total factor productivity based on new technology and skill upgrades of the labour force. In certain sectors like ICT one can observe 'leapfrogging' to the most advanced technologies: for example, China's use of the newest types of PC's and mobile phones. Especially in these sectors, in fact, China now leads as a global producer. In this way a high proportion of advanced technology is embodied in investments.

To identify the possible barriers for this type of growth, it is useful to split up the growth in various elements. Expressed in simple terms, growth can be defined as a function of the input of *labour*, the *quality* of this labour input, the input of *capital*, the *quality/technological level* of this capital, *raw material inputs*, and, furthermore, *total factor productivity* based on the efficient use of these inputs. Total factor productivity is often defined including the quality of labour and capital. The allocative efficiency and incentives for investments in physical capital and upgrading of human capital depend on the quality of institutions. In this way, there is a close link to the political-institutional circle.

Each of the growth elements will be discussed separately to consider their development thus far and to assess prospects for the future – including an identification of barriers for the continuation of high growth rates and possible shifts in the weight of the various growth elements.

CHINA – Business Opportunities in a Globalizing Economy

Figure 1:4 The Catch-Up Circle

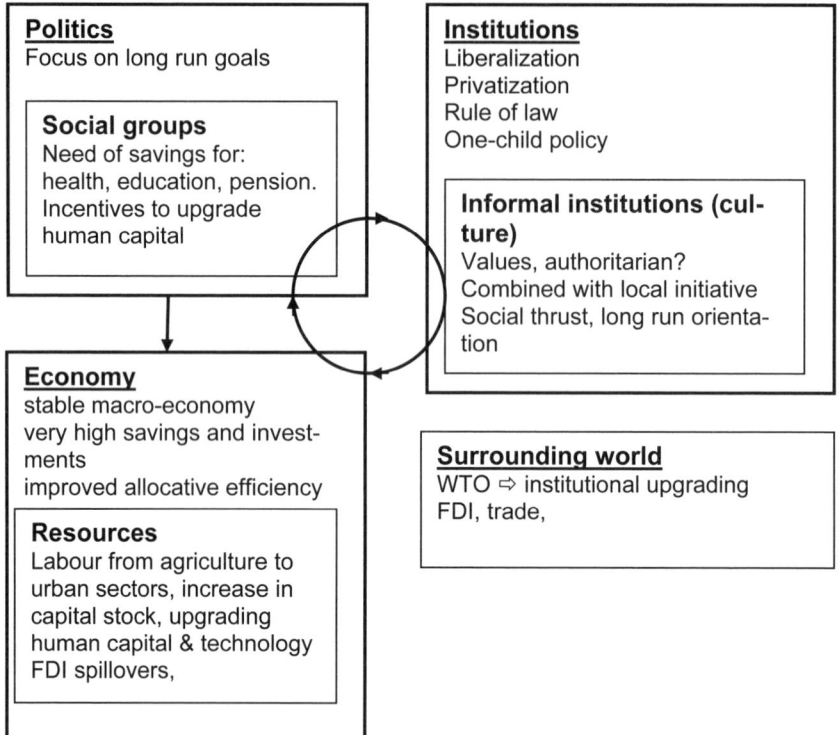

China's population is still relatively young compared to populations of developed economies like the USA, Japan, and Western Europe. The average life expectancy in China steeply increased already during the Mao period. Furthermore, the successful implementation of the one-child policy means that the increase in the working age population will stop around 2010-15 (DB Research 2006). Thus, there will be a steep increase in the dependency rate of the old age population in relation to the working age population. The proportion of the working age population between 15-64 years reaches its maximum in 2010 at 72.2 percent and will then fall to 60.7 percent by 2050. This means that China's high growth rate will face an important barrier in relation to quantity of labour within the next 10 years. The participation rate of the working age population is among the highest in the world (82 percent in 2005) and includes a high participation rate of women (OECD 2007). Thus, unlike the situation in countries such as India and Brazil, it is unlikely that China can mobilize a larger part of the population into the labour market.

Although the total workforce may stagnate, a continued shift from agriculture to industry creates a buffer which can supply labour to manufacturing and services for several years. The share of employment in agriculture declined from 70 percent in 1978 to 45 percent in 2005. The decline was faster in the 1980s and the first half of the 1990s than recently; in fact, the percentage remained constant at around 50 percent from 1996 to 2002 (China Statistical Yearbook 2006). This might be explained by the status of the *hukou-policy* of restrictions for migration to the cities. Currently this policy is being liberalized and the result may be further migration and an additional shift in labour to manufacturing and services (Brooks 2004). This makes room for further growth based on sector shifts – also in the coming decades. The labour reserve of unemployed and underemployed workers in state-owned enterprises adds to China's potential for growth. The official Figures for urban unemployment are low: hovering around 4 percent in recent years. However, these numbers do not include laid-off workers from state-owned enterprises since they are still entitled to social welfare benefits from their company and thus cannot register themselves as unemployed. Surveys from the OECD estimate urban unemployment in the start of the new millennium in China to be around 12 percent (OECD 2005).

Another buffer lies in the potential for upgrading China's *quality of labour*. During Mao's rule, China made a big step forward in primary education; illiteracy all but disappeared. In 1980, China led in gross enrolment ratios for primary school. Enrolment in secondary school has also increased steeply: especially in the 1990s. Tertiary level enrolment has also steeply increased, albeit from a very low enrolment level at the start of the period; it remains relatively low (Fogel 2006). According to OECD (2005) the average length of time spent studying has risen three months every year for the past decade, and the average schooling of new entrants to the labour force rose to eleven years by 2006. At the same time those retiring from the labour force had on average only four years of education. Significant improvements are currently being made at the secondary and tertiary levels. Thus, an increasing quality of labour will contribute to growth over the long term. DB Research (2005) estimates the average number of years of education will increase in China by more than 30 percent from 2005-2020. The expected deceleration in the growth of the quantity of labour could be offset by a continuous increase in the quality of labour.

Similar to other Asian countries, China has maintained a high level of savings both for households and for companies. The savings rate has for many years hovered around 40 percent of GDP. The reasons behind this high level are manifold; other Asian countries have had similar long-term savings rates – some of which may be explained by the long-term perspective inherent in Asian culture. In China the uncertainty and the need to save for pensions, health care, and education create additional reasons for high savings rates. The financial system offers few opportunities for securing financing for housing, cars, and other durable consumer goods. Moreover, it is difficult to secure funding for the entrepreneurial costs of starting new businesses. Thus, consumers must save to get durables and entrepreneurs have to save to start a business and to enjoy the high returns which are possible in a booming economy (Blanchard and Giavazzi 2005). The favourably high proportion of the working-aged population – versus the group of young and old citizens who have negative net savings – also plays an important role in understanding saving patterns in China (DB Research 2006). The swift growth in disposable income can, from a permanent income hypothesis, also be an explanation for high savings levels. Households realize that their permanent long run income has increased only after a certain delay. They increase consumption also after a delay and the result is higher savings. There have been few opportunities for reinvestment of the savings, which implies that nearly all savings have been deposited in banks at relatively low interest rates. However, in the years after 2000 savings have increased even more in China, not because of higher household savings, but because of the high savings taking place in the companies because of booming profits. The share of profit has increased and wages has dropped as a share of GDP from 53 percent in 1998 to 41 percent in 2005 (Kuijs 2006).

The sustainability of the high savings rate can be questioned for several reasons: The future Chinese saver may be more influenced by Western culture and consumerism. The population will age, a diminishing segment of the population will have large amounts of personal savings, and the financial sector will offer better possibilities for loans. Wages may take a bigger share of the pie in the future. However, a slight decrease in savings may be an advantage in the long run for the Chinese economy. In fact there are strong arguments that a slightly lower savings rate can sustain a high growth rate and simultaneously secure long term macroeconomic balances. For several years, Chinese savers have financed excessive-consumption – primarily in the USA. The large US trade deficit to China has primarily been financed by selling US bonds to China. The Chinese current account surplus has risen to 7-8 percent of GDP in the later years resulting in mounting foreign exchange reserves of 1.3 trillion USD in 2007. Thus, there is plenty of room for an increase in domestic Chinese consumption and a turn from growth driven by exports to growth to a higher degree driven by local consumption. This development could also be driven by better social security and pension systems as well as higher public consumption and investment in development of health care, education, and infrastructure as suggested by Blanchard and Giavazzi (2005).

Most of the current savings are transferred to investments in the private, semi-private, and state-owned enterprises. Investments are also made in public infrastructure and public utilities. For several years, the fixed capital formation has maintained a level of around 40 percent of GDP (Shane and Gale 2004). In fact the *quantity* of capital formation has been the most important growth factor in most models for Chinese growth. However, for long term *intensive* growth, the *quality* of the invested capital is very important. Quality relates both to the technological level of the fixed capital and to the efficiency of the allocation of capital. It is difficult both from an analytical and empirical point of view to distinguish between these two factors.

In the industrialization process an important part of growth is due to the flow of labour from low productive agriculture to manufacturing where the invested capital has yielded high returns. It is worth noting that investments in agriculture with better incentives and allocation of capital has also meant increased productivity in this sector (Fogel 2006). This is in fact one of the reasons why so much labour can be transferred from agriculture to other sectors while still increasing food production. However, Kuijs and Wang (2005) have found that sector shifts were important in the 1980s, but have contributed relatively little to the growth since 1993. They find that the bias of the financial system has meant subsidized investments in industry. Because of massive investments in industry, the productivity gap between agriculture and industry has widened, which again explains the increasing inequality of wages between rural and urban sectors. Because of the increase in productivity, the growth in industrial production has only meant relatively low growth in employment in this sector and thus has limited migration to the urban areas in later years. According to China Statistical Yearbook in 2004 manufacturing and construction made up 46.2 percent of GDP, but only 22.5 percent of employment. Kuijs and Wang (2005) suggest that lower subsidies to investment in industry, more encouragement to the service sector, and reduced barriers to labour mobility would mean faster growth in urban employment and would reduce the income gap between rural and urban workers.

Within the discussion on total factor productivity (TFP), Krugman 1993 and Young 2003, indicated heavy emphasis on extensive growth with little increase in TFP. However, many later studies point in the direction of a higher contribution from TFP. There are strong indications that this will be increasingly important in the future. Heytens and Zebregs (2003) find the TFP contribution to growth rates to be between 2 and 3 percent over the period 1971-1998. In calculations decomposing the growth element, IMF staff finds that physical capital accumulation accounted for 3 percent, human capital accumulation for 1 percent, and TFP for 3.5 percent of growth rates from 1979-2005 (IMF September 2006 p. 79). Kuijs and Wang (2005) find TFP contributions of 3.7 percent from 1978-93 and 2.7 percent from 1993-2004. The OECD (2005) finds TFP between 5.6 percent and 2.8 percent of growth rates from 1983-2003, of which the lowest period was 1998-2003.

Still, average labour productivity is quite low in China and there is room for much technological upgrading. In fact, the level of income per capita was much lower at the start of the high growth period in 1979 than was the case for countries like Japan, Hong Kong, South Korea, Singapore, and Taiwan when their economies took off (IMF Sept. 2006 ch. 3). This low starting point leaves space for a longer period of high catch-up growth. First, there is room for much better allocation of capital in connection with continual upgrading of the institutional framework. There is increasing evidence that higher quality institutions support higher TFP (IMF Sept. 2006 p. 91). For China, several studies have shown that the state-owned enterprises in general have lower efficiency than the private and semi-private companies (Desvaux et al. 2004, OECD 2005). However, state-owned enterprises receive a much higher proportion of bank loans than the private sector. This means that continual institutional upgrading, privatization and better allocation of the saved capital can contribute to higher efficiency of capital. There is room for such improvements and thus a possibility that a fall in the physical quantity of capital formation in the future can be substituted by a higher increase in the efficiency of capital.

There will be a point in the future when such institutional upgrading and the technological catch-up will reach its limits. This borderline is the global technological production frontier where the most advanced economies are located. It follows the long run trend growth of the most advanced economies of 2-3 percent per year (IMF 2006). Thus, as China approaches the frontier, growth rates will converge to this level as it happened with Japan in the 1990s. This point of development is, however, several decades ahead for China. In 2005, per capita in PPP terms of China was only 17.4 percent that of the US level. If it is assumed that growth in China would be 8 percent and US growth 3 percent, it would still take approximately 40 years before China would reach the US level. However, Chinese growth rates would level off before this point, but still the high differential can most likely be maintained for the coming 20-30 years.

In recent years, China has increased its effort to develop science and technology to be part of the knowledge economy. Still, Chinese research and development is only 1.3 percent of the GDP compared to EU: 1.9 percent, USA: 2.6 percent, and Japan: 3.2 percent. China has the highest growth rate in research and development and is already ranked number two measured in absolute terms. Also the number of researchers ranks China only second after the USA (Serger and Widman 2006).

Public investments for upgrading infrastructure, education, and health care will contribute to an economic upgrade: both in terms of the quality of physical capital and of labour in the future. There is strong potential for growth especially in the inner provinces of China. Public debt is still low: around 20 percent of GDP (OECD 2005). Thus there is plenty of room for these investments and it can be a strong growth factor to both increase demand and improve the supply side simultaneously.

The final factor to be analyzed – raw materials – is a bottleneck already. The robust growth of the most populous country in the world has put increased pressure on raw materials including energy resources from both inside and outside China (IMF 2006). Higher commodity prices could be a dampening factor, but continued Chinese growth in the later years – despite steeply increasing oil prices – indicate this threat may not be so important.

China has sizeable coal resources and most of the country's energy production is based on coal. According to a June 2007 study by the Netherlands Environmental Assessment Agency, China's carbon dioxide emissions became the largest in the world in 2006. These emissions will increase in the future with continued growth. This is another important reason for the change to a higher degree of intensive growth with increasing efficiency in the use of the different inputs. In relation to energy production, it means higher investment in sustainable energy. Increasing investments in limiting pollution, in wastewater treatment, etc. will be an important part of sustainable growth for the future. However, investments in environmental protection are also part of production. This means another type of growth, but it may not lower the growth level. Moreover, it is important when measuring the resources to include the *human destruction and depletion of natural resources*. The actual growth rates will be less impressive for China when the effects on the environment are accounted for. On the other hand the costs of bringing down pollution and cleaning up for old damages shall not only be taken as reductions of consumption levels. The positive effect on the environment must be added to the production measure. As an example, bringing air pollution down to conformity with WHO standards in the major cities is estimated to generate health benefits of between 3 and 8 percent of GDP (Brajer and Mead 2004). In the later years China has introduced more strict policies to reduce pollution (OECD 2005). It is necessary to further shift to a more sustainable growth path. This may reduce growth measured in traditional GDP terms, but if the positive environmental effects are included such a broader measure of income will probably still show continuing high growth.

The 'catch-up' process can be described as a self-enforcing circle closely related to the political-institutional circle. Institutions play an important role for using the potential of economic resources – for giving the economic agents appropriate incentives to continue high investment levels and to increase the quality of labour and capital inputs. This is especially the case in relation to the financial sector upgrade and reform of state-owned enterprises. The catch-up process should also be seen in relation to the political-institutional circle as the continued high growth is a condition for political stability and continued support for further reforms.

Dynamics of the catch-up circle are concentrated around the *economy* box. The past experience and the potential for quantitative growth in capital and labour inputs – as well as upgrading of these resources – point in the direction of a strong potential for continued growth. Upgrading of capital is both based on improved allocation and on the introduction of more advanced technology. The growth potential is closely related to the relative backwardness at the starting point. Even with a continuation of the very high growth rate, it will take decades before the Chinese per capita level approaches the production frontier borderline of the most advanced countries.

Conclusion

Since 1978, China has experienced an impressive growth process. The PIE model has been introduced to understand this process in a holistic-dynamic framework. The question has been addressed: what are the main elements and what are the threats for a break of the self-enforcing virtuous circles?

The political institutional circle includes the main dynamics of a self-enforcing virtuous circle in the PIE-model. These connections are also relevant for the openness and catch-up circles. However, these two circles are included in the analysis because they add some extra dynamics to the self-enforcing growth process.

Figure 1:5 The Three Self-enforcing Circles in Chinese Growth

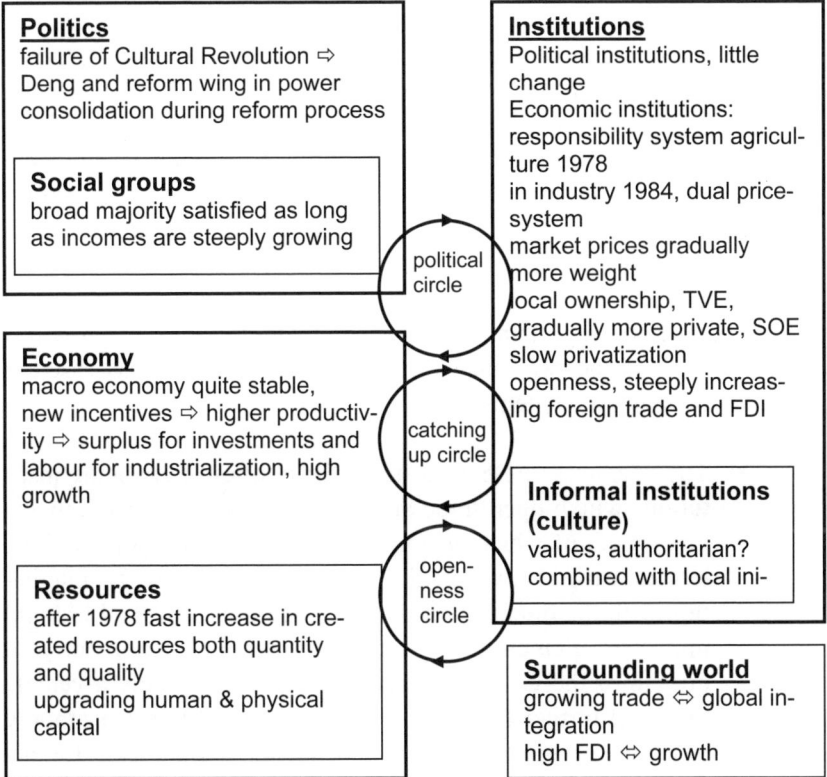

The political-institutional circle emphasizes:

- The political power of leaders is to a high degree determined by the state of the economy. Deng Xiaoping took over after the failure of the Cultural Revolution.
- He started institutional reform with the 'household responsibility' system in agriculture. This included the introduction of

the dual-track price system, which later spread to industry and gradually introduced market prices and market-orientated enterprises with elements of private ownership. The reforms also included gradual liberalization of trade and FDI with increasing openness to the outside world.
- These institutional reforms changed the rules for decision-making, incentives and information flows, and gave a push to economic growth. Productivity rose steeply in agriculture and released labour and capital for a fast industrialization process which was often based on local enterprises with elements of private ownership. These and the foreign-owned enterprises increased the competitive pressure on state-owned enterprises and forced further restructuring.
- Successful economic growth consolidated the power of the reform wing in the Party and reinforced further development of pragmatic market-oriented reforms with a build-up and refinement of market institutions as well as further enhancement of economic growth.

This circle of politics – institutional change – high economic growth is also prevalent in the two other virtuous circles: separately assessed to be able to add extra elements:

- The openness circle is based on the politics of changing institutions which open trade and create access for foreign investors – both of which encouraged growth and consolidated the reform wing. However, this circle also includes the interaction with the outside world. Increasing trade and FDI brought important elements to promote growth in China, but also growth of the Chinese market became increasingly a vehicle to attract further FDI. At the same time the Chinese economy has increasingly developed into an important driver for the global economy – while global growth has a positive feedback on Chinese exports.

The catch-up circle goes deeper into the self-enforcing process within the economy box and between the development of the economy and institutional change. The institutions set the frame for savings and investments, and thus the increase in fixed capital: a main pillar in the high growth in China. Institutions also determine the incentives for upgrading human capital and they set the rules of the game for mobilization and allocation of resources.

The catch-up circle has been based on the high accumulation of capital and high mobilization of labour from relatively low productivity in agriculture to higher productivity in the urban sectors. At the same time, there have been strong increases in productivity within various sectors: especially within industry. This is connected to increased total factor productivity due to better allocation, increasing technological quality, as well as the upgrade of the human capital quality. Self-enforcing elements lie in the high returns on the investments – in new physical capital, in upgraded human capital, and new technology embodied in these investments. These returns support a continuation of the process.

However, there are also important barriers that may break these self-enforcing circles. The main threats for the political-institutional circle are:

- The social and systemic disparity between rural and urban areas. Uncertain conditions for the group of workers losing *the iron rice bowl* when state-owned enterprises and the municipalities are restructured. The risk of increasing social unrest among those groups hurt by the fast restructuring of society and the resulting gaps in social security and health care. This includes the large group of migrant workers with lacking social rights.
- The development of the market economy without the full development of the necessary institutions within finance and corporate governance may cause problems for efficiency.
- Increased market orientation makes the Chinese economy more vulnerable to business cycles, potential bubbles on the stock exchange and real estate markets.

The main threats for the openness circle are:

- Low growth in the main Western export markets of the USA and the EU
- Risks of protective measures toward the strong growth of Chinese exports on these markets

The main threats for the catch-up circle are:

- Stagnant and in the long run shrinking labour force
- Increasing old-age dependency ratio and falling savings rate
- Resource barriers in relation to energy and other raw materials

The answer to the question about the sustainability of the high growth rates depends on how likely and how serious these threats are for breaking the virtuous circles. Closely related to this is the question about counter-measures: to what extent are there political strategies for further institutional changes that can reinforce the self-enforcing cycles? In general the conclusion is that the threats are not insurmountable and there are possible strategies to overcome the problems so growth is likely to continue for decades up to the point where China's per capita GDP comes close to the level of the developed countries.

The increasing inequality is already in the focus of the current Chinese leadership and several policies are developing to push the growth in the poorer rural areas and inner provinces.

Simultaneously, high growth, high savings, high surplus in trade, the relative low state debt, and small fiscal deficits make room for a more active fiscal policy with more weight on developing social security, pensions, health care, and education as well as further upgrading of the infrastructure, especially in inner China. Such policies may lower overall savings, but may at the same time mean a more balanced growth not based on high export surpluses, but rather based on domestic demand. At the same time such policies will probably consolidate the political power giving a more social face to the Party.

Refinement of economic institutions will continue, and the argument that the last stage should be more difficult seems unconvincing. In fact it can be argued that hesitating with the withdrawal of state influence on the economy has been and will for some years continue to be a stabilizing factor for the economy. State regulation is a counterweight to market cycles and bubbles. On the other hand, risks of bubbles e.g. on the stock market and real estate can also be reduced by opening up for more alternatives for placements of the abundant Chinese savings.

A more active fiscal policy may not only increase the domestic demand as driver for growth. Such policies will also make China less dependent on the cycles in the global economy and make China less vulnerable to protective measures from the developed markets.

The barriers for the catch-up circle in relation to the limited total labour supply are in fact not so important when considering the high reserve employed in the relatively low productive rural sectors. There may be temporary bottlenecks in some areas, but there is room for decades of continued transfer of labour from agriculture to industry and services. At the same time China has a large potential in continued training and upgrading of the labour force. The average years of schooling is growing fast and can increase further for several years in the future.

Savings and capital formation is likely to fall somewhat in quantitative terms, but if allocative efficiency continues to be improved and the technological level continues to be upgraded there are possibilities for sustained growth. There is potential to further upgrade institutions as in the financial sector and in relation to privatization of state-owned enterprises and upgrading of the legal system. Gradual institutional improvements are likely to continue and the growth effects of this are likely to follow for a prolonged period of time. The same is true for technological upgrading still from a low level. Plans for increasing Research and Development combined with raising educational levels also promises a release of more of this potential for the coming decades.

Resource barriers and increased pressure for sustainable growth in relation to the environment is an important challenge for the Chinese economy. It may put a barrier on some of the traditional growth elements, but at the same time it can support a new type of growth including investments in environment protection – investments which, in the long run, can increase both GDP and the quality of life for the Chinese people.

The conclusion is that high economic growth is likely to continue for decades in China. There are some important threats, but with wise and pragmatic policies and with further adjustments in the policy of *'crossing the river by feeling for the stones under your feet'*, China will cross that river, and change from a developing to an advanced and leading world economy within the first half of this century.

Acknowledgement
Thanks to my colleagues, the professors, Kjeld Erik Brødsgård, Lars Håkanson and Ole Risager for their constructive comments and suggestions.

References
Blanchard O. J. and G. Francesco 2005. 'Rebalancing growth in China: a three-handed approach.' *CEPR Discussion Paper Series* (5403).

Branstetter, L. and L. Nicholas 2006. 'China's embrace of globalization,' *NBER Working Paper Series* (12373).

Brajer, V. and R. W. Mead, 2004. 'Valuing air pollution Mortality in China's Cities.' *Urban Studies*. 41(8):1567-1585.

Brooks R. 2004. 'Labor market performance and prospects.' In (Prasad ed. 2004) ch. 8:51-64.

Brødsgaard, K. E. 2004. 'Jiang Finally Steps Down.' *The Copenhagen Journal of Asian Studies*. (19):82-88.

China National Bureau of Statistics 2006. *China Statistical yearbook 2006*. Beijing.

Desvaux, G., Wang, M. and D. Xu, 2004. 'Spurring performance in China's state-owned enterprises.' *McKinsey Quarterly*, special edition 2004(4):96-105.

Deutsche Bank Research 2005. 'Current Issues – Global growth centres'. March 23.

Deutsche Bank Research 2006. 'China's pension system.' February 17.

Deutsche Bank Research 2006. 'China's banking sector: Ripe for the next stage?' December 7.

EIU 2007. *Country Profile 2007 – China*. Economist Intelligence Unit, London.

Goldman Sachs (2003): 'Dreaming with BRICs: The path to 2050', *Global Economics Paper*. no 99.

Farrell D., P. Gao and R. G. Orr 2004. 'Making foreign investment work for China', *McKinsey Quarterly*, special edition (4):24-33.

Fogel, R. W. 2006. 'Why China is likely to achieve its growth objectives', *NBER, Working Paper* (12122).

Heytens, P. and H. Zebregs 2003. 'How fast can China grow?' In Wanda Tseng and Markus Rodlauer (eds): *China, Competing in the Global Economy*, IMF, Washington D.C.

IMF 2005. 'Building Institutions' Ch. 3 in *World Economic Outlook*. September. Washington D.C.

IMF 2006. 'Asia Rising: Patterns of economic development and growth', Ch. 3 in *World Economic Outlook*, September. Washington D.C.

Krugman, P. 1994. 'The Myth of Asia's Miracle'. *Foreign Affairs*. 73(6):62-78

Kuijs, L. 2006. 'How will China's Saving-Investment Balance Evolve', *World Bank Policy Research Paper* (3958). July. Washington D.C.

Kuijs, L. and T. Wang 2005. 'China's Pattern of Growth: Moving to Sustainability and Reducing Inequality', *World Bank Policy Research Paper* (3767) November. Washington D.C.

Maddison A. 2001. The World Economy – a millennium perspective. OECD. Paris.

McMillan, J. and B. Naughton 1992. 'How to reform a planned economy: lessons from China', *Oxford Review of Economic Policy* 8(1):130-143.

Mygind N. 2007. 'The PIE-model: Politics – Institutions – Economy.' *CEES working paper series* (67), September. Copenhagen Business School.

Naughton, B. 1994. 'What is Distinctive about China's Economic Transition? State Enterprise Reforms and Overall System Transformation.' *Journal of Comparative Economics* 18:470-490.

North, D. C. 1990. *Institutions, Institutional Change and Economic Performance*, Cambridge University Press, Cambridge.

OECD 2007. Labour markets in the BRICs (Brazil, Russia, India, China). Paris.

OECD 2005. OECD Economic Surveys – China, Paris.

Prasad, E. ed 2004. China's Growth and Integration into the World Economy – Prospects and Challenges, occasional paper (232). IMF. Washington D.C.

Prasad, E. and R. Raghuram 2006. 'Modernizing China's growth paradigm.' *American Economic Review* 96(2):331-336.

Schott, P. K. 2006. 'The relative sophistication of Chinese exports.' NBER Working Paper (12173).

Shane, M. and F. Gale 2004. 'China: A study of Dynamic Growth', United States Department of Agriculture. USDA – WRAS-04-08. Washington D.C.

Serger, S. S. and E. Widman (2006): *Competition from China – opportunities and challenges for Sweden*. Swedish Institution for Growth Studies. Stockholm.

Sun, L. 2002. 'Fading out of local government ownership: recent ownership reform in China's township and village enterprises.' *Economic Systems* 26:249-269.

WEF – World Economic Forum 2006. *The Global Competitiveness Report 2006-2007*. Geneva.

World Bank 2007. Global Economic Prospects 2007 – managing the next wave of globalization, Washington D. C.

Young, A. 2003. 'Gold into Base Metals: Productivity Growth in the People's Republic of China during the Reform Period.' *Journal of Political Economy*. 111(6):1220-1261.

CHAPTER TWO

Foreign Direct Investment in China: Origin, Distribution, and Impact on the Economy

Kjeld Erik Brødsgaard

Since the start of the reforms in 1978, real Chinese GDP growth has averaged 9.5%. Less than ten years ago, China was a middle-sized economy with a foreign trade volume smaller than the Netherlands (Segal 1999). Today, China is the fourth largest economy in the world in nominal terms and the second largest in terms of Purchasing Power Parities (PPP). The non-state sector has grown rapidly and now contributes more to GDP than the traditional state sector. An important driving force for this unparalleled economic growth performance has been the increasing openness of the economy – especially in terms of foreign trade and foreign direct investment.

Foreign Direct Investment (FDI) is an important indicator of the growth and regional distribution of international production. Available statistics show that the developed countries are the largest owners and recipients of FDI, accounting for almost 90 percent of all direct investment outflows and approximately 65 percent of all investment inflows (Dicken 2007; World Bank 2007). For many years, the USA has been the number one source – as well as host – of global investment flows. However, from 2002-2004 China overtook the USA as the single most important recipient of foreign direct investment. This shows that a major change in the pattern of global FDI flows is underway. Since approximately two-thirds of all global investments take place within multinational enterprises, this change indicates that China has become a crucial part of the global value-added chain.

This paper will examine the role of FDI in China's economic development. Firstly, it will provide the empirical background – in terms of the size as well as the regional and sectoral distribution – of FDI. Secondly, there will be a discussion of the country origins of FDI. Thirdly, the paper will look into the role of multinational firms in FDI inflow to China. Fourthly, there will be a discussion of the main determinants of FDI in China; this section will also discuss Hainan as an interesting case of the increased Chinese focus on FDI during the reform era. Finally, we will assess the role of FDI in China's economic development.

A number of works on FDI in China have been published in recent years (Van Den Bulcke et al. 2003; Luo 2000; China Report 2002; Gallagher 2005; Huang 2003; Lardy 1995; Zweig 2002; Zhang and Reinmoeller 2007). Most of these publications emphasize the key role played by foreign investment in China's economic take-off (Guthrie 2006; Lardy 1995). Some argue that China's specific mode of integration with the global economy is closely associated with the competitive pressures created by FDI (Gallagher 2005). This paper aims to add new insight by pointing to the push and pull factors behind FDI inflows to China and by pointing out that although fixed investment in China would have been smaller without the contribution of FDI, the percentage of FDI as a proportion of fixed investment has been reduced in recent years. The empirical material has been culled from recent Chinese statistical publications (Zhongguo tongji nianjian; Zhongguo tongji zhaiyao; Zhongguo waizi tongji) as well as in Western languages (OECD 2003).

The Pattern of FDI Flows to China

FDI inflows to China have grown from almost nil at the outset of the reform period to about 50-55 billion US$ per year in the early 2000s. The surge in FDI began in the early 1990s, following Deng Xiaoping's "Southern Inspection Tour" (*nanxun*), where he pressed for a resumption of economic reforms and a further opening to the outside world. FDI inflows declined slightly during the Asian Financial crisis, but picked up again in 2000 in anticipation of China's WTO accession in 2001 (see Table 2:1). By 2002, China actually surpassed the USA as the most important destination of FDI in the world, accounting for a third of all FDI flows to developing countries and two-thirds of FDI inflows to the Asian developing region. In 2004, China attracted a record of 60.6 billion US$ in FDI, equivalent to 3.7 percent of GDP (Zhongguo tongji zhaiyao 2006). The stock of FDI at the end of the year amounted to 562.2 billion US$ or 34.1 percent of GDP. China's WTO commitments will widen the scope for foreign investment, not only in the manufacturing sector, but also in services and finances sectors.

Table 2:1 FDI Inflow to China, 1979-2004

Year	Projects	Contractual Value (US$ Billion)	Realized Value (US$ Billion)
Total	508,941	1,096.6	562.1
1979-82	920	4.9	1.8
1983	638	1.9	0.9
1984	2,166	2.9	1.4
1985	3,073	6.3	1.9
1986	1,498	3.3	2.2
1987	2.233	3.7	2.3
1988	5,945	5.3	3.2
1989	5,779	5.6	3.4
1990	7,273	6.6	3.5
1991	12,978	11.1	4.4
1992	48,764	58.1	11.1
1993	83,437	111.4	27.5
1994	47,549	82.7	33.8
1995	37,011	91.3	37.5
1996	24,556	73.3	41.7
1997	21,001	51.0	45.3
1998	19,799	52.1	45.5
1999	16,918	41.2	40.3
2000	22,347	62.4	40.7
2001	26,140	69.2	46.9
2002	34,171	82.8	52.7
2003	41,081	115.1	53.5
2004	43,664	153.5	60.6

Source: *Zhongguo waizi tongji 2005: 7.*

As to the sources of FDI in China, important changes have taken place in recent years. During the 1980s and early 1990s, Hong Kong was the most important origin of FDI into China, accounting for about two-thirds of all investment. However, beginning in the mid-1990s, Hong Kong's share began to diminish and in 2004 only amounted to about a third. Taiwan investment has been substantial since the early 1990s and has in recent years hovered around 7-8 percent of total realized FDI value. In 2004, Taiwan's investment fell to 5.14 percent of total FDI to China (see Table 2:2). However, actual investment from Taiwan must be considered much higher, since a significant part of Taiwanese FDI in China is channelled through Hong Kong and especially the Virgin Islands. In 2004, the Virgin Islands accounted for 11.10

percent of total FDI flowing into China (Zhongguo waizi tongji 2005: 16). This placed the Virgin Islands as the second most important source on the list of major investors in China, ahead of South Korea, Japan, the EU and the US. Korea was the third most important investor in China in 2004, accounting for a share of 10.31 percent. In the fourth spot we find Japan (9.0 percent), followed by the EU (7.0 percent) and the USA (6.5 percent). Given the fact that the EU is China's largest foreign trade partner, it is noteworthy that European companies lag behind Korean and Japanese companies in their investments in China. There is a considerable amount of round-tripping of mainland Chinese capital flowing to Hong Kong and back via Hong Kong investment companies. However, even considering that this may inflate Hong Kong investment in mainland China, it is unlikely that it is of magnitude that will alter the basic pattern of Hong Kong being the single most important source of FDI for China (Ash 2008).

Table 2:2 Top 10 Investors in China, 2004

Country/Region	Projects	Realized FDI Value (US$ Billion)	Share in percent
Total	43,664	60.6	100.0
Hong Kong	14,719	18.9	31.3
Virgin Islands	2,641	6.7	11.1
Republic Korea	5,625	6.3	10.3
Japan	3,454	5.5	9.0
EU	2,423	4.2	7.0
USA	3,925	3.9	6.5
Taiwan	4,002	3.1	5.1
Cayman Islands	244	2.0	3.4
Singapore	1,279	2.0	3.3
West Samoa	790	1.1	1.9

Source: *Zhongguo waizi tongji 2005:* 16 and 20.

In terms of regional distribution, the FDI pattern in China shows great disparities. The Eastern provinces (comprising 37 percent of the population) have attracted 86 percent of all FDI to China; the central provinces took up around 9 percent and the western region attracted less than 5 percent of all FDI. In the reform period, from 1979 until end 2003, Guangdong province absorbed more than 129 billion US$ worth of FDI, or about a quarter of the total Chinese FDI stock. Jiangsu has in the same period attracted 14 percent and Shanghai 8 percent; i.e. three Chinese Eastern provinces account for almost half of total FDI (Zhongguo waizi tongji 2004: 31). Poor inner provinces such as Ningxia and Xinjiang only account for 0.04 percent and 0.08 percent, respectively, of total accumulative investment. Even a large, traditionally important province such as Sichuan can only claim 4,729 million US$ of FDI (0.9 percent) for the whole reform period (see Table 2:3).

Table 2:3 FDI Distribution by Province / Selected Municipalities 2003

Province	Realized Value of FDI (in USD Millions)	Share (in percent)
Total	501,470	100
Beijing	20,082	4.00
Tianjian	18,525	3.69
Hebei	9,214	1.84
Shanxi	2,185	0.44
Inner Mongolia	1,013	0.20
Liaoning	23,596	4.71
Dalian	12,454	2.48
Jilin	3,695	0.74
Heilongjiang	4,682	0.93
Shanghai	42,372	8.45
Jiangsu	71,399	14.24
Zhejiang	21,456	4.28
Ningbo	7,260	1.45
Anhui	4,121	0.82
Fujian	43,867	8.75
Xiamen	12,669	2.53
Jiangxi	5,803	1.16
Shandong	35,802	7.06
Qingdao	13,034	2.60
Henan	5,718	1.14
Hubei	10,614	2.12
Hunan	7,972	1.59
Guangdong	129,281	25.78
Shenzhen	23,166	4.62
Guangxi	8,163	1.63
Hainan	7,630	1.52
Chongqing	2,962	0.59
Sichuan	4,729	0.94
Guizhou	534	0.11
Yunnan	1,230	0.25
Tibet	0,030	n.a
Shaanxi	4,090	0.82
Gansu	615	0.12
Qinghai	128	0.03
Ningxia	185	0.04
Xinjiang	424	0.08

Source: *Zhongguo waizi tongji 2004:* 31.

Thus, FDI absorption is heavily skewed in favour of the Eastern provinces to the disadvantage of the inner provinces. Even though the Chinese government in 1999 decided on a policy of "opening the west" (*xibu dakaifa*), this pattern persists. The figures for 2004 show that the Eastern provinces have maintained their share while the central provinces have increased their share at the expense of the Western provinces, testifying to the difficulties in reorienting existing policies. Thus, in 2004, the 12 Western provinces only attracted 2.9 percent of FDI (see Table 2:4).

Table 2:4 FDI Utilized by East, Central and Western Parts of China, 2004

Region	Projects	Realized Value (US$ Million)	Share in percent
Total	43,664	60.6	100
East	37,978	52.2	86.11
Central	3,711	6.7	11.02
West	1,915	1.7	2.88

Note: Eastern Region: Beijing, Tianjin, Hebei, Liaoning, Shanghai, Jiangsu, Zhejiang, Fujian, Shandong, Guangdong, Hainan. Central: Shanxi, Jilin, Heilongjiang, Anhui, Jiangxi, Hubei, Hunan. West region: Inner Mongolia, Guangxi, Sichuan, Chongqing, Guizhou, Yunnan, Shaanxi, Gansu, Qinghai, Ningxia, Xinjiang, Tibet.
Source: *Zhongguo waizi tongji 2005:* 27.

This pattern stems from the FDI policies pursued by the central authorities in China. The reform process has been incremental in nature and has been based on experiments in selected regions and sectors (Brødsgaard 2008). The open door policies started with the establishment of four Special Economic Zones in 1980 in Guangdong and Fujian provinces. Later, 14 coastal cities were given preferential policies in order to attract foreign investment and, in 1988, Hainan Island was turned into a large special economic zone. In Hainan, it was especially the Yangpu Economic Development Zone that was supposed to attract major investment projects from abroad. In the early 1990s, the Pudong New Area was established and soon became the major destination for FDI in the Shanghai region. In 2006 the Tianjian Binhai New Area (TBNA) was singled out as a new national development project similar to Shenzhen and Pudong (Chien 2007). The result of these policies has been a concentration of FDI in the Eastern part of China, which benefit not only from cheap land and labour, but also from a highly-developed infrastructure and a well-educated workforce as well as access to a growing domestic market.

As to sectoral distribution, the main part of FDI has been channelled into manufacturing, which now accounts for about two thirds of total

FDI. The real estate sector follows with around 18 percent, followed by lease and business services at 3 percent. In the manufacturing sector about half of FDI has been directed towards labor-intensive manufacturing. The Pearl River Delta in Guangdong has been converted into a giant shop floor: thousands of small sweatshops with foreign participation, producing everything from shoes to Christmas decorations (Enright et al. 2005). However, an increasing part is being directed towards technology-intensive manufacturing (medicines and pharmaceuticals, electronics, electrical machinery and equipment) and capital-intensive manufacturing (e.g. petroleum refining, chemical materials).

Turning to forms of FDI, equity joint ventures, contractual joint ventures, and wholly foreign-owned enterprises (WFOEs) are the main forms of absorbing FDI into China. In the beginning of the reform period, China only allowed the establishment of joint ventures. It was not until 1986 that the formation of WFOEs was legally allowed. Taking the whole reform period into consideration, joint ventures now represent more than 55 percent of the cumulative realized FDI stock and WFOEs represent 43 percent (see Table 2:5).

Table 2:5 Cumulative FDI by Form, 2004 (US$ Billion)

Form	Projects	Share %	Contractual FDI Value	Share %	Realized FDI Value	Share %
Equity Joint Venture	249,937	49.1	379.4	34.6	222.4	39.6
Contractual Joint Venture	55,855	10.9	178.6	16.3	89.7	15.9
Wholly Foreign-Owned	202,816	39.9	531.4	48.5	239.2	42.6
FDI Shareholding Inc.	110	0.02	2.2	0.2	2.3	0.41
Joint Exploration	191	0.04	4.7	0.43	7.5	1.34
Others	32	0.01	0.2	0.02	0.9	0.16
Total	508,941	100	1,096.6	100	562.1	100

Source: *Zhongguo waizi tongji 2005:* 9.

However, the trend points toward the latter entry form. In 2004, WFOEs were the most important entry mode with 66 percent of all FDI forms. Equity joint ventures only accounted for 27 percent (Zhongguo waizi tongji 2005: 8). There are now about 230,000 foreign-funded enterprises (FFEs) registered and in operation in China

(Zhongguo tongji nianjian 2005). They contribute significantly to China's integration in the world economy, as can be seen in the foreign trade statistics. Since the beginning of the reform period, China's foreign trade has expanded dramatically. In particular the export sector has seen rapid growth in recent years. By the end of 2004 total export value reached US$ 593.33 billion, representing an annual growth rate of 18 percent (Zhongguo tongji nianjian 2006: 740). By the end of 2004 China accounted for 6 percent of world exports, compared to 1 percent in 1980. FFEs have been the driving force behind this upsurge in China's exports. From 1986 to 2004 their share of total exports increased from 1.9 percent to 57.9 percent (Zhang and Reinmoeller 2007). In regards to IT-related and technology-related export, these enterprises account for approximately 88 percent of China's export within these sectors (Zhongguo waizi tongji 2005).

FFEs have not only contributed enormously to the increase in China's foreign trade with the outside world, but they have also been an important driver in the rapid expansion of China's industrial production in recent years. In 1991, the eve of Deng Xiaoping's Southern Inspection Tour, FFEs accounted for 5.29 percent of China's industrial output. This share increased to 31.43 percent in 2003, demonstrating the importance of these companies for China's "wirtschaftwunder" (see Table 2:6).

Foreign companies which invest in China include most of the Fortune 500 companies. According to Chinese sources, at the end of 2003, the number of large-scale foreign-invested companies with a contractual foreign investment of over 10 million US$ totalled 14,562. This accounts for only 3 percent of the total number of FFEs, but represents more than 50 percent of the total foreign investment.

Among the top 500 FFEs in China we find Shanghai Volkswagen Automative, Ltd. with a sales value of 56.708 billion yuan (7.1 billion US$) (Zhongguo waizi tongji 2005); Motorola (China) Electronics with a sales value of 38.639 billion (4.8 billion US$) and Shanghai GM Automobile Co. with a sales value of 34.722 billion (4.3 billion US$). Eight of the top 20 FFEs are based on investment from Western and Japanese multinationals such as VW, General Motors, Hewlett Packard, Dell Computer, Honda, etc. In terms of export value, the top FFEs are almost exclusively in the IT and computer business. This indicates that FFEs in the automotive sector hardly export at all, whereas the enterprises in the IT-sector are strong exporters.

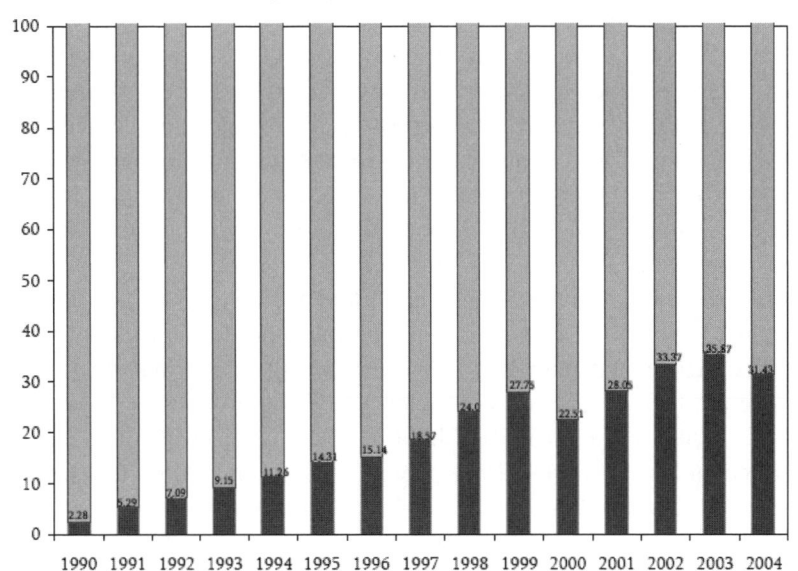

Table 2:6 Industrial Output by FFEs as a Percentage of Total

Year	%
1990	2.28
1991	5.29
1992	7.09
1993	9.15
1994	11.26
1995	14.31
1996	15.14
1997	18.57
1998	24.0
1999	27.75
2000	22.51
2001	28.05
2002	33.37
2003	35.87
2004	31.43

Main Determinants of FDI in China

Based on the above trends, a number of questions arise. How is China able to attract and absorb such large investments? What are the push and pull factors? Clearly, expensive labour and other high costs in their home countries are pushing firms to consider investment in China. The fierce competition taking place as the global big business revolution unfolds also makes it imperative for MNCs to be present in China (Nolan 2001). But what are the pull factors? In general, they can be grouped into three categories: market size and economic structure, preferential investment policies and liberalization, and the cultural and political environment (Tseng and Zebregs 2002).

As for market size, FDI has clearly been attracted by the enormous Chinese market. At the same time, FDI has contributed to rapid economic growth, thereby making it even more attractive to invest in China. It appears that market size (i.e. market-seeking investment) has been more important for European and US investors than for investors from Hong Kong and Taiwan (Klenner 2005). In the first decade and a half of the reform period, a high proportion of FDI flows into China consisted of resource-seeking FDI. Thus Hong Kong enterprises took advantage of low land lease charges and far lower wages in the Pearl River Delta and massively shifted their production capacity to China. From 1989 a similar process began to take place in Taiwan, where whole industries were transferred to China (OECD 2003: 42). Whereas Hong Kong companies have focused on establishing export bases in China, Western companies have been more interested in establishing factories to produce for the local market. Since the mid-1990s, market-seeking FDI has increased in response to the burgeoning Chinese domestic market. This change from resource-seeking investment to market-seeking investment is clearly associated with an alteration in geographical sources of FDI, where FDI from Hong Kong is gradually subsiding, and FDI from OECD countries is increasing in importance. In recent years, an increasingly important factor for Western companies is to use China as a basis for sourcing input to their global value chains. Associated with this is the offshoring of the manufacture of whole products to China (i.e. efficiency-seeking investment). This type of offshoring will increase as China reaches higher levels of education and technology. For global big players an additional important motive for investment is strategic asset-seeking investment, which is a tactical investment to prevent the loss of a resource or potential market to a competitor.

For both Asian as well as Western companies, abundant supply of labour plays a major role. It is probable that low wage costs (i.e. resource-seeking investment) have been a particularly important factor in attracting FDI from Hong Kong and Taiwan, but this is also an increasingly important issue for Western MNCs, as shortages of highly qualified personnel begin to appear.

Infrastructure is a major determinant of FDI decisions for foreign companies in China. The Chinese government has invested heavily in infrastructural projects and has created a road network that is second only to that of the USA. Simultaneously, a number of important railroad projects have been completed. Superior infrastructure is one of the main explanations for the concentration of the FDI in the eastern coastal provinces, particularly in the Special Economic Zones and in the newer development zones that have been created during the 1990s.

Scale effects are also important. The coastal provinces are much larger economies and constitute much bigger markets than the inner provinces. Provinces such as Guangdong, Shandong and Jiangsu have economies that are 10 times larger than those of inner provinces such as Gansu and Guizhou (Zhongguo tongji nianjian 2005: 59). They are also much more oriented towards the outside world in terms of foreign trade. Finally, the combination of scale effects and clustering is important. Once a province has attracted a certain mass of FDI, the effect is that additional capital becomes easier to attract to that region, since foreign investors tend to cluster; clustering allows foreign investors to share information and facilities such as educational and health facilities for expatriates. This pull factor has been particularly advantageous to the coastal provinces and disadvantageous to the inner provinces.

Liberalization and Preferential Policies

FDI in China was a rarity before the beginning of the reform period in 1978-79. But since then, the FDI regime has been gradually liberalized in the typical Chinese fashion of "crossing the river while feeling for the stepping stones." A legal framework was gradually developed during the 1980s to facilitate and regulate FDI. China's accession to the WTO has caused further liberalization.

In 1979, a "Law on Joint Ventures Using Chinese and Foreign Investment" was passed, providing the basic framework for the establishment of foreign-funded enterprises in China. In 1983, "The regulations for the Implementation of the Law on Joint Ventures Using Chinese and Foreign Investment" added more details to the operations and preferential policies for joint ventures. In 1986, a "Law on Enterprises Operated Exclusively with Foreign Capital" formally permitted the establishment of WFOEs in localities outside the Special Economic Zones. In 1986, the "Notices for Further Improvements in the Conditions for the Operation of Foreign Invested Enterprises" and the "Provisions of the State Council for Encouraging Foreign Investment" were published. They were later codified in the 1988 "Cooperative Joint Ventures Law." In 1990, the "Amendments to the Equity Joint Venture Law and Wholly Foreign-Owned Enterprise Implementing Rules" provided an even clearer legal framework for the operation of FFEs. Finally, in 1995, the "Interim Provisions on Guiding Foreign Investment Direction" (revised in 1997) classified the various categories of FDI. In April 2002, following China's accession to the WTO, three revised catalogues for guiding foreign investment were adopted. They covered the three categories of encouraged, restricted, and prohibited investments (OECD 2003).

In the Special Economic Zones the Chinese authorities have added other pull factors such as preferential tax policies, access to land, good infrastructure, etc.

Hainan Case

The Hainan Special Economic Zone is an interesting case of the increased focus on FDI during the 1980s and 1990s. In fact, one of the main goals behind Hainan's establishment as a special economic zone

(SEZ) in 1988 was to make the island a focus for the attraction of foreign investment and for the generation of foreign trade.

In 1991, the Hainan Provincial Government issued a set of regulations which provided the legal framework for the preferential policies adopted to attract foreign investors (Hainan jingji tequ waishang touzi tiaoli 1991). The regulations specified a range of preferential treatments towards foreign investors in terms of tax exemptions, tax deductions, and tax holidays. At the time they were promulgated, they provided the most favorable investment regulations of all economic development zones in China (see Brødsgaard 2008).

Article 31 of the regulations stipulated that foreign-funded enterprises engaged in infrastructure projects such as airports, railroads, power stations, coal mines, and water conservancy facilities scheduled to operate for 15 years or more were exempted from income tax during the first five years of profit-making and allowed a 50 percent tax reduction from the sixth to the tenth years. Those production-based enterprises engaged in industrial production, communications, and transportation which were scheduled to operate for a period of 10 years or more were exempted from income tax during the first two profit-making years and allowed a 50 percent reduction from the third to the fifth years. Those enterprises recognized by the Hainan government as "technically-advanced enterprises" were allowed a further 50 percent tax reduction from the sixth to the eighth years. Foreign-funded enterprises operating in Sanya City, Tongza city, or any autonomous county with national minority population, which were scheduled to operate for 10 years or more, faced even more favourable tax conditions. For the first 10 years of operation, there was a total tax exemption. From the eleventh to the twentieth years, they were granted a 50 percent tax reduction. Products manufactured by foreign-funded enterprises and sold within the Hainan Special Economic Zone were exempt from product tax or value-added tax.

The new regulations also granted foreign-funded enterprises independent decision- and management powers. Thus, article 42 stated that a foreign-funded enterprise had the power to determine the size of its staff and number of its workers, to employ and dismiss senior managers, and to hire and fire staff and workers at its will. Article 43 stipulated that a foreign-funded enterprise could determine its own plans for production, marketing, and financial affairs, and it could also make decisions on its own concerning wages, allowances and bonuses.

Hainan's incentives to foreign investors and business partners also involved long-term leasehold rights of land for up to 70 years. This was longer than in any other SEZ and the suggestion of allowing such leasehold rights for foreigners stirred up considerable debate when it was put forward in connection with plans to establish the Yangpu Development Zone.

In sum, the regulations and associated policies in the form of land leasehold rights created the most liberal tax environment for foreign-funded enterprises that the Chinese authorities had hitherto allowed. Visa procedures for foreign businessmen and employees in joint ventures were more liberal than in any other special economic zone (Liao 1993).

Later, however, other economic development zones were granted some of the same preferential policies so that Hainan gradually lost its special status. In fact, a number of open economic zones such as economic and technology development zones (ETDZs) and high technology development zones (HTDZ) were opened throughout China. Of special importance was the establishment of Pudong New Area in Shanghai in 1990. Pudong has developed into a major showcase for FDI-related economic development in China. With its WTO accession, China has made substantial commitments to further liberalization of trade and investment. These effects will take full effect from 1st January 2007.

The establishment of the various open economic zones in China provided the means for incremental and politically acceptable reform. Reforms were tested in certain localities and, if they were deemed Successful, they were implemented more widely. The most recent experiments in TBNA show that this strategy of incremental reform is still being pursued. TBNA has been declared an experimental zone for comprehensive reform and is allowed to take a number of innovative initiatives within the financial sector such as exploring ways to allow residents and enterprises to buy and sell foreign exchange on a voluntary basis, and allowing foreign banks to develop offshore finance in the TBNA (Chien 2007). Plans are also underway to facilitate Chinese individual investment in the Hong Kong stock-market.

Cultural and Political Environment

Studies on FDI in China have often pointed to the crucial role played by the large overseas Chinese community. Even though Hong Kong's share has dropped substantially in recent years, Hong Kong, Taiwan, and Singapore still account for about half of FDI inflows to China. There is thus no doubt that the Chinese Diaspora continues to provide important sources and channels for investment. A number of studies point out that the shared cultural and ethnic background to a large extent explains the willingness of overseas Chinese capital to invest in mainland China (Yeung 2006; Ip et al. 2000; Weidenbaum and Hughes 1996).

Another factor of paramount importance to Western companies is the assessment of the political stability of the current regime. There is no doubt that China currently faces a host of potentially destabilising problems in terms of growing income inequalities (UNDP China 2005), environmental degradation (Economy 2004), widespread corruption (Yan 2004), etc. In general, however, the political situation seems stable. The transition from the third to the fourth generation of leaders from the 2002-2004 took place without any great factional strife (Brødsgaard 2004). In fact, for the first time since 1949, a full-scale leadership transition took place in a peaceful and orderly manner in conformity with agreed rules and norms. The leadership is clearly eager to continue this process of institutionalization and normativization at all levels of the polity.

At the same time, the regime is engaged in a major overhaul of the cadre corps. New and stricter rules concerning age, educational background, and professional capability have been introduced at all levels of the Chinese bureaucracy (Brødsgaard and Zheng 2004). Present day Chinese cadres are generally much better educated and much younger than they were during Mao's (and even Deng's) time. Currently, education qualifications and professional competencies – rather than political credentials – form the basis for career advancement in the Chinese civil service system. Another important aspect of the upgrading and rejuvenation of the Chinese governing system is the appointment of new ministers who are not members of the Chinese Communist Party (CCP). In April 2007 Wan Gang, a scientist with a German doctorate, was appointed Minister of Science and Technology, and in June 2007 the National People's Congress approved the appointment of yet another non-CCP member of the cabinet: namely Chen Zhu, a Paris-trained scientist. As a consequence of the new focus on formal qualifications and professional competence in leadership appointments, the governing capacity of the Chinese regime has increased considerably. This has had a positive influence on the general business environment – seen from the perspective of Western business executives.

Recently the CCP held its 16 Party Congress. New leaders were elected to the Central Committee and the Politbureau. Moreover two new members from the upcoming fifth generation of leaders were appointed to the Standing Committee of the Politbureau. Both Xin Jiping and Li Keqiang are highly educated (doctorates in social sciences and economics) and relatively young (54 and 52 respectively). Their appointment further underlines the process of institutionalization and regularization in the Chinese political system.

The Impact of FDI on the Chinese Economy

FDI has had a major impact on the Chinese economy. FDI has contributed directly to economic growth through the establishment of FFEs as well as indirectly, by creating spillover effects from FFEs to domestic enterprises, or by incorporating domestic enterprises in their production chains. There are now about 230,000 FFEs registered and operating in China. They account for almost 60% of China's foreign trade and almost 90 percent of China's IT- and technology-related export. FFEs have not only contributed enormously to the increase in China's foreign trade, they have also had a major impact on China's industrial expansion and now contribute almost a third of total industrial production in China. Moreover, FFEs have introduced important new technologies and management skills in crucial sectors of the economy. In this respect EU and other Western investment is of particular importance. Whereas investors from Hong Kong, Taiwan and South Korea have tended to establish production activities in China to take advantage from cheap labour and land (resource-seeking investment), European and American companies have tended to engage in higher value-added, high-tech projects (Ash 2008). European and US investment have in this way contributed to technology transfer and have to a much higher degree than "diaspora" investment had a catalytic impact on Chinas economic development.

However, in terms of FDI per capita, there is still room for expansion. China's per capita FDI is smaller than that received by any OECD member country, with the exception of Turkey. Mexico receives five times as much per capita and even Japan, where FDI accounts for a tiny percentage of GDP, receives seven times China's per capita GDP (OECD 2003). Another noteworthy aspect is that even though OECD countries in general account for almost 90 percent of all FDI flows, they only contribute half of FDI flows into China. Here, there would also be room for considerable expansion. Perhaps even more importantly, while FDI inflows took up an increasing share of fixed capital investment in China during the early 1990s, this share has fallen in recent years. FDI inflows as a proportion of fixed investment peaked in 1994 with a share of 17.1 percent. Since then, this share has gone down and is now 7.2 percent, which is less than the 7.5 percent registered in 1992 when the FDI surge started (see Table 2:7). This is a consequence of the fact that even though FDI in China has grown considerably over the years, internal fixed investment (gross fixed capital formation) has grown even more. Thus, for the past five years the absolute amount of FDI has more or less stabilized, whereas domestic investment has grown rapidly by about 26 percent per year.

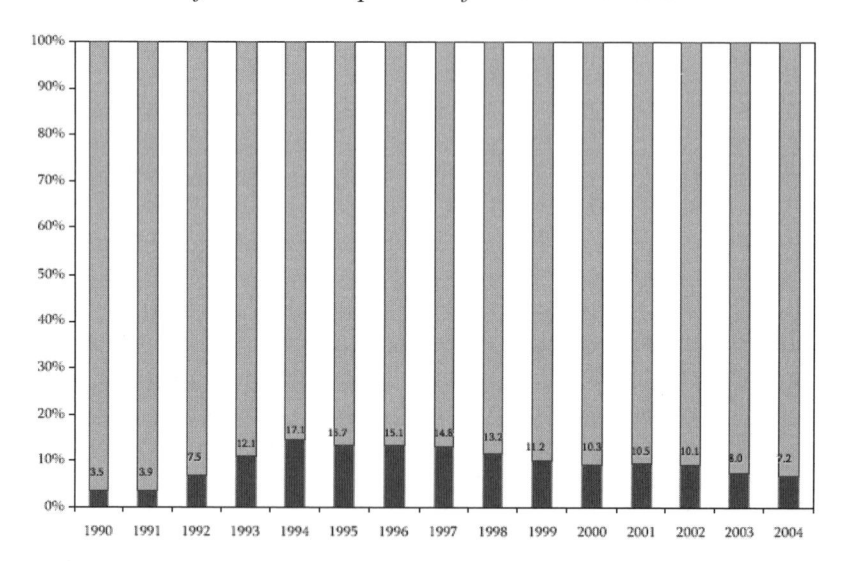

Table 2:7 FDI Inflows as a Proportion of Fixed Investment

Year	%
1990	3.5
1991	3.9
1992	7.5
1993	12.1
1994	17.1
1995	15.7
1996	15.1
1997	14.8
1998	13.2
1999	11.2
2000	10.3
2001	10.5
2002	10.1
2003	8.0
2004	7.2

These figures should caution against maintaining a too optimistic view of the importance of FDI in China's growth (Anderson 2006). Increasingly the main driver of economic growth is domestic investment, stemming from huge savings on the part of households and the major state-owned companies (retained profit). The foreign-funded enterprise sub sector certainly plays an important role, accounting for approximately 30 percent of China's industrial output, but its contribution to China's overall economic growth probably does not exceed 20 percent, even though it is difficult to measure the "catalytic" impact of technology spill-over and the transfer of management practices.

Conclusion

An important background for the Chinese economic hypergrowth since the beginning of the reform era in 1979, has been a steady increase in foreign investments. Annual FDI inflows to China were less than 2 billion US$ in 1986, but they have ballooned to 60.6 billion US$ in 2004.

FFEs now employ 24 million workers and account for approximately 60 percent of China's imports and exports (Nevisky 2006). Overseas investors have brought new technologies, new business practices, better governance, better market knowledge, etc.; these have all had a major impact on China's economy.

During the 1980s and 1990s Hong Kong investment was the most important source of FDI flows into China. Hong Kong enterprises took advantage of the much lower production costs in Southern China and massively shifted their production capacity to the Pearl River Delta (i.e. resource-seeking investment). Although Hong Kong's share of total investment has fallen considerably in recent years, overseas Chinese capital still accounts for more than 50 percent of FDI inflows to China. Japan, the USA, and the EU area only account for approximately 9, 6, and 7 percent, respectively. Since these countries stand for almost 90 percent of global outward investment flows, these are relatively small shares. Thus there should be room for considerable expansion of FDI investment in China on the part of the developed OECD countries. This kind of investment mostly takes place in the form of market-seeking investment or horizontal investment which involves the transfer of production to service the Chinese internal market.

FDI in China has been heavily skewed to the advantage of the developed Eastern provinces and to the disadvantage of the poorer inner provinces, even though the regime has initiated a program of "opening the west." In 2004, the 12 Western provinces only attracted 2.9 percent of total FDI.

Main determinants of FDI in China are market size, preferential policies (in the form of economic development zones), and the cultural and political environment. Of particular importance is the assessment among foreign investors that the present leadership is politically stable and commands considerable legitimacy among the population in spite of numerous social problems and widening income inequalities. This is a major pull factor alongside the size of the Chinese market and the opportunities provided by offshoring whole products or parts of the production chain to China.

In recent years, the absolute amount of FDI inflows has stabilized, while domestic investment has grown steadily. Thus, foreign investment's role as a driver of China's growth seems to be dwindling, although with great variations across sectors and localities. Although there are approximately 230,000 FFEs in China, they now only account for 7 percent of total fixed investment compared to 15 percent 10 years ago. China's economic growth is increasingly driven by internal savings and record high investments. Therefore, one should be careful not to overestimate the role played by FDI in China's "wirtschaftwunder."

Acknowledgement

The paper was first presented at a seminar in the Department of International and Economics, CBS, February 14, 2007. In revising the paper I have benefited from constructive comments and suggestions by Lars Håkanson and Niels Mygind.

References

Anderson, Jonathan 2006. "As If China Really Needed Foreign Investment." *Asian Focus* (13 November).

Ash, Robert F. 2008. "Europe's Commercial Relations with China." In D. Shambaugh et al. (eds). *China-Europe Relations: Perceptions, Policies and Prospects.* London: Routledge 2008: 189-230.

Brødsgaard, Kjeld Erik 2004. "Jiang Finally Steps Down: A Note on Military Personnel Changes and the CCP's Governing Capacity." *The Copenhagen Journal of Asian Studies*, No. 19: 82-88.

Brødsgaard, K.E. and Y. Zheng (eds) 2004. *Bringing the Party Back In: The Role of the CCP in Governing China.* (with Y. Zheng) Singapore: Far Eastern Universities Press.

Brødsgaard, K.E. 2008. *Hainan – State, Society, and Business in a Chinese Province.* London: Routledge, in press.

UNDP China and China Development Research Foundation 2005. *China Human Development Report 2005.* Beijing: China Translation and Publishing Corporation.

China Report 2002. Vol. 38, No. 4 (November) (Special Issue on FDI in China).

Chien S.-S. 2007. "The Tianjin Binhai New Area." *EAI Bulletin* (June): 10.

Dicken, P. 2007. *Global Shift: Mapping the Changing Contours of the World Economy.* London: Sage Publications.

Enright, M. E., E. Scott and K. Chang 2005. *Regional Powerhouse: The Greater Pearl River Delta and the Rise of China.* Singapore: John Wiley & Sons.

Gallagher, M. E. 2005. *Contagious Capitalism: Globalization and the Politics of Labor in China.* Princeton and Oxford: Princeton University Press.

Guthrie, D. 2006. *China and Globalization.* London: Routledge.

Economy, E. 2004. *The River Runs Black: The Environmental Challenge to China's Future.* Ithaca: Cornell University Press.

"Hainan jingji tequ waishang touzi tiaoli" 1992. (Regulations of Hainan Special Economic Zone on Foreign Investment) (Adopted by the Standing Committee of the People's Congress of Hainan Province at its Fifteenth Session on 16 March, 1991). In *Hainan nianjian* 1992: 422-24.

Huang, Y. 2003. *Selling China.* Cambridge: Cambridge University Press.

Ip, D., C. Lever-Tracy and N. Tracy (eds) 2000. *Chinese Business and the Asian Crisis.* Aldershot: Gower Publishing.

Klenner, W. 2005. "Economic Relations Between the EU and China: Evolution of an Exclusive Partnership." China. *An International Journal*, Vol. 3. No. 3 (September): 331-346.

Lardy, N. L. 1995. "The Role of Foreign Trade and Investment in China's Economic Transformation." *The China Quarterly*, No. 144 (December): 1065-1082.

Liao, X. 1993. *Kaifang de chengben.* Haikou: Hainan chubanshe.

Luo, Y. 2000. *Multinational Corporations in China.* Copenhagen: Copenhagen Business School Press.

Nevisky, M. 2006. "Will Super-High Chinese Growth Continue?" *NBER Digest Online* (November).

Nolan, P. 2001. *China and the Big Business Revolution.* Houndmills, Basingstoke: Palgrave.

OECD 2003. *China: Progress and Reform Challenges.* Paris: OECD.

Segal, G. 1999. "Does China Matter?" *Foreign Affairs*, Vol. 78, No. 5 (September/October): 1-13.

Yan S. 2004. *Corruption and Market in Contemporary China.* Ithaca, NY: Cornell University Press.

The World Bank 2007. *World Development Report 2007.* Washington, DC: The World Bank.

Tseng, W. and H. Zebregs 2002. "Foreign Direct Investment in China: Some Lessons for Other Countries." *IMF Policy Discussion Paper* (February).

Van Den Bulcke, D., H. Zhang, and M. do Céu Esteves 2003. *European Union Direct Investment in China: Characteristics, Challenges, and Perspectives.* London and New York: Routledge.

Weidenbaum M. and S. Hughes 1996. *The Bamboo Network: How Expatriate Chinese Entrepreneurs are Creating a New Economic Superpower in Asia.* London: The Free Press.

Zhang, X. and P. Reinmoeller 2007. "Foreign Firms in China: Success by Strategic Choices." In B. Krug et al. *The Chinese Economy in the 21st Century: Enterprise and Business Behaviour*. Cheltenham: Edward Elgar 2007: 42-70.

Yeung, H.W.C. 2006. "Change and Continuity in Southeast Asian Ethnic Chinese Business." *Asia Pacific Journal of Management*, Vol. 23, Issue 3: 229-54.

Zhongguo tongji nianjian 2005. (China Statistical Yearbook 2005) Beijing: Zhongguo tongji chubanshe.

Zhongguo tongji zhaiyao 2006. (China Statistical Abstract 2006) Beijing: Zhongguo tongji chubanshe.

Zhongguo tongji nianjian 2006. (China Statistical Yearbook 2006) Beijing: Zhongguo tongji chubanshe.

Zhongguo waizi tongji 2004. (Statistics on FDI in China) Beijing: Zhonghua Renmin Gongheguo guoshang shangwu.

Zhongguo waizi tongji 2005. (Statistics on FDI in China) Beijing: Zhonghua Renmin Gongheguo guoshang shangwu.

Zweig, D. 2002. *Internationalizing China*. Ithaca, NY: Cornell University Press.

CHAPTER THREE

Knowledge Exchange with Offshore R&D Units: Novo Nordisk, GN Resound, and BenQ Siemens Mobile in China

Julie Marie Kjersem and Peter Gammeltoft

It is well-advertised that China has evolved into a global manufacturing powerhouse. GDP growth rates close to 10 per cent a year have been sustained through a virtuous combination of high domestic savings and investment rates, macro-economic stability, and domestic structural and regulatory reforms on the one hand, and mounting foreign direct investment (FDI) inflows and export volumes on the other. Somewhat less advertised but no less significant is the fact that even though China remains a low-income country in the aggregate, a range of high-tech activities and industries are developing quickly and prospering. These activities are not only targeted and supported by government policies and strategies but they also increasingly attract foreign investment, technology, and R&D activities.

In this chapter we will analyse the emerging phenomenon of foreign investments in R&D in China approached both from the supply side of the constitution of the Chinese system of science, technology and innovation (ST&I), and from the demand side of foreign firms investing in high-tech activities in China. Seen from the perspective of firms, offshoring knowledge-intensive activities to China is not without challenges and more often than not they will encounter unforeseen difficulties in the exchange and protection of knowledge between geographically- and organisationally-dispersed R&D units.

Thus, we approach high-tech investments in China from two angles. First, in connection with the Chinese ST&I system, we will account for its development and constitution. Second, we will account for foreign investments in R&D into China and firms' motives for undertaking them. A particular challenge and concern of companies locating knowledge-intensive activities abroad is to attain effective and efficient exchange of knowledge with other units within the corporate network without risking leakage of proprietary knowledge assets. These issues are discussed through a case analysis of the Chinese R&D labs of Novo Nordisk, GN Resound, and BenQ Siemens Mobile.

The Chinese System of Innovation

Contemporary Chinese policies and strategies reflect a strong determination to become a world-leading nation in science, technology, and industrial innovation. Furthermore, current government policies, strategies, and plans express a sentiment that economic development over the last couple of decades may have come to rely too much on foreign technology and that a shift towards stronger 'indigenous innovation' capability is needed. In the following, a brief review of some conventional innovation input and output indicators confirms that significant progress has indeed been made towards this goal.

Chinese Innovation Systems Reforms

Innovation is generally recognized as taking place within broader 'innovation systems', i.e. within complex networks which span firms, universities, and government organisations. These complex networks form the national innovation system and are influenced by both market and non-market institutions that impact the direction and speed of innovation and technology diffusion (Lundvall 1992). The quantitative strength and qualitative features of a country's innovation system has a defining influence not only on domestic growth and innovation processes, but also on its ability to attract foreign investments in high-tech and knowledge-intensive activities, and the Chinese system of innovation increasingly acts as a pull factor for high-tech investments into China. As we will see, cross-organisational linkages and networks is an area where particular progress has recently been made in China, especially in terms of forward and backward linkages and feedback mechanisms between users and producers of knowledge. Especially the 1990s, saw the increasing interlinkage of the Chinese national innovation system. Chinese ST&I policy making shifted from merely elaborating R&D policies to focusing on a more modern approach to ST&I development by integrating more tightly government ST&I efforts with R&D efforts of foreign and national enterprises. Extensive science and technology system reforms and policies were made with a focus on economic development and technological advancement. Interactions between firms, universities, and research institutes became more frequent. Firms began to play a more active role in technological innovation and became the nucleus of the innovative system (Haiyan and Yuan 2006).

In relation to foreign R&D investments, a number of policies have been put in place in order to encourage the inflow into China. They are focused on support structures such as science parks and incubators; by 2002 over 400 business incubators and 53 high development zones were established at the national level through governmental support (Huang et al. 2004). Thus, one important means by which to attract high technology FDI has been the establishment of high-tech science parks combined with incentives such as free rent, low tenancy cost, favourable lease terms, and tax relief (Gassmann and Han 2004). The Zhongguancun Science Park in Beijing, which is base for 40 universities and 130 research institutes, is one of the more well-established scientific zones (UNCTAD 2005: 142). Given the attractiveness of the Chinese market, the Chinese government is also pursuing a 'technology for market' policy, whereby they encourage foreign investors to transfer technology to China (Gassmann and Han 2004). In other words, while the Chinese government is supporting the national ST&I development through various domestic initiatives, reforms, and policies it is also supporting it by encouraging inflow of foreign high-tech investments through incentives, inducements, and the establishment of attractive high-tech science parks.

In the following sections we will take a closer look at a set of conventional innovation indicators, viz. the educational system and human resources, R&D expenditure, high-tech exports, and patenting, and discuss the intellectual property regime.

Innovation Input Indicators
Human resources is one of the most important inputs to innovation. The educational system and human resources are significant components of the Chinese innovation system. The current 11th Five Year Plan reflects this and it is an area which receives major and increasing attention from the Chinese government. Great strides have already been made in primary education and profound emphasis is placed on developing the higher educational system. One crude indication is the increase in number of universities and institutions of higher education:

there were 1,552 universities and institutions of higher education in 2003, up from 1,396 in 2002 (EIU 2005: 25).

Where the total number of researchers in the country is concerned, relative to the total workforce China lags behind other countries, but China is so populous that it is still home to one of the largest pool of researchers in the world. In 2004, China had the second highest absolute number of researchers in the world with 918,000 behind the United States but ahead of Japan (UNESCO Institute for Statistics).

The number of students in China is also increasing rapidly and, again, due to the sheer size of the population these numbers represent large talent pools. Some 15 million students were enrolled in tertiary education in China in 2002/2003, which is comparable to the USA and to the EU, and China churned out 885,000 university graduates in 2002. Moreover, China has the highest number of students in the world enrolled in science and technology education encompassing approximately 2.6 million (UNCTAD 2005: 296). Even though the number and proportion of students with research training expectedly remains significantly lower than in the USA and the EU, almost 15,000 (1.7%) of the university graduates in 2002 were awarded a PhD degree, a number that rose to 19,000 in 2003 (OECD, 2005: 25). While the Chinese educational system suffers from a number of recognized weaknesses improvements are continuously being made.

China has a large number of students studying abroad: 152,000 Chinese students were enrolled abroad in OECD countries in 2002, accounting for 10 percent of the total number of foreigners enrolled in university education in OECD countries (OECD 2005: 25). The Chinese government is actively trying to attract these students back and educated Chinese abroad are increasingly returning to the mainland as an important supplement to domestic human resources.

Another commonly-deployed innovation input indicator is expenditure on R&D. China's gross domestic expenditure on R&D grew by more than a factor five over the period from 1995 to 2004 to reach 1.23 percent of GDP (OECD 2006).

R&D expenditure can be split into source of funds and sector of performance. In low income countries, business expenditure on R&D is usually relatively low and government carries the bulk of both R&D funding and implementation. The need to economise on scarce resources to achieve scale and scope economies and the need for coordination across different sectors and activities also tends to imply a larger involvement of government. Nevertheless the majority of R&D activities in China today are both funded and performed by business rather than government. This is to a large part explained by reforms of the public S&T system around the turn of the millennium during which previously government-run institutes re-registered their business type. More than 300 institutes were spun into an enterprise, more than 600 became profitable firms by themselves, and a few integrated with universities (Gu and Lundvall 2006). As a consequence, the percentage of R&D performed by business leaped from 49.6 percent in 1999 to 60.3 percent in 2000. In 2004 it reached 67 percent, compared to 70 percent in USA (OECD 2006).

It generated considerable media attention when OECD estimates indicated that China became the world's second largest aggregate R&D spender in 2006, measured in purchasing power parities, thus overtaking Japan. For 2006, R&D intensity was estimated to 1.3% of GDP and spending is projected to increase further to 2.5% of GDP by 2020 in the national 2006-2020 Medium- and Long-Term Program for Science and Technology Development. However, if we look beneath the aggregate numbers, R&D activities are still focused primarily on applied research and development rather than basic research. Compared to the USA and Japan, China still lags behind when it comes to investments in more advanced research. In 2002 a modest 5.7 percent of R&D expenditures were on basic research, 19.2 percent on applied research, and 75.1 percent on experimental development. In comparison, the numbers in the USA were 18.1 percent on basic research, 20.8 percent on applied research, and 61.1 percent on experimental development (OECD 2004).

Innovation Output Indicators

Turning now from innovation input to innovation output indicators, the boom in China's manufactured exports has predominantly been driven by the low cost structure. Nonetheless, the increase in foreign firms located in China has also ensured a continual upgrading of the goods exported by China. Today, most of the world's advanced consumer electronics are manufactured in China. In addition, China is increasingly becoming competitive in a number of important high-tech industries (Walsh 2003), 'high-tech industry' being defined as an industry with high R&D intensity, such as aerospace, computers, pharmaceuticals, scientific instruments, and electrical machinery. One of the indicators is the growing trade in high-tech goods: high-tech goods made up almost 30 percent of the manufactured exports from China in 2004 as compared to 6 percent in 1992. The increase in high-tech exports can, to some extent, be viewed as an indicator for the advancement of the industries in China through science, technology, and innovation improvements. This data should be interpreted with caution, though, since FDI in high-tech industries in developing countries is mostly confined to lower-tech and labour-intensive activities within the value chain and very dependent on imports of intermediate goods, with modest local value-added. Furthermore, in China most of these high-tech exports (as much as 85 percent by some estimates) originate from foreign-invested enterprises highly concentrated in specific geographical locations.

The extent of patenting is often used as an output indicator of innovative activities and over the last decade patenting activity in China has increased significantly, testifying to a strengthening ST&I system. In 2004 354,000 national patent applications were submitted, up from 78,000 in 1994 (Ministry of Science and Technology of the Peoples Republic of China, 2005). Different factors mitigate the record, though; strong formal protection of intellectual property rights is a relatively recent phenomenon in China and thus increases in patenting activity does not exclusively reflect increases in innovative activities but also the transition and tightening of the property rights regime itself. Furthermore, only a minority of applications submitted by domestic companies are for the more advanced 'invention' patents while the large majority is for the simpler 'utility model' or 'design' patents. Applications submitted by foreign companies in China on the other hand were almost exclusively for invention patents in 2004. More generally, a large number of patent applications and grants in China are by foreign rather than domestic companies (Walsh 2003: 67) and between 1999 and 2001 almost half of all domestic inventions were foreign owned.

In terms of international patenting, China's share in patenting at the US Patent and Trademark Office and the European Patent Office is still very small (Schaaper 2004) but there appears to be a greater propensity to register international patents through the World Intellectual Property Organization where China became the tenth largest applicant in 2005 with 1.8 percent of the applications.

China is widely criticized for not sufficiently complying with and enforcing intellectual property laws. Formal legislation is adequate by most accounts while implementation and enforcement of the laws is lacking. Administrative or litigative pursuit of infringements remains a highly complicated and uncertain process. Whether a tight WTO-like IP regime is conducive to economic catch up remains contested, yet awareness is increasing in China that a well-functioning and predictable intellectual property regime is closely connected to accommodation of inward foreign direct investment and smooth integration into the world economy.

Offshoring off R&D to China
As we saw in the previous section, the Chinese innovation system is advancing rapidly, in both quantitative and qualitative terms. Today China attracts not only resource-seeking and labour-intensive investments but increasingly also investments in high-tech activities. In the remainder of this chapter we will focus on the 'demand side' of foreign firms investing in high-tech in China. First we will briefly account for the general motives of companies to do offshore R&D to China, then turn to the analysis of three foreign companies with R&D labs in China.

The motives behind high-tech investments and offshore R&D units can be viewed as more complex in comparison to other forms of FDI (i.e. the relocation of production facilities to low cost countries). Even though motives are many and varied they can be generalized into the generic motives outlined in Table 3:1. They reflect a combination of push and pull factors, resulting from both internal changes and motivations in the firm but also external drivers in the increasingly global arena for conducting business (Gammeltoft 2006). This leads us to the analysis of three companies who have already begun to offshore some of their R&D activities to China.

The Case of Novo Nordisk, GN ReSound and BenQ Siemens Mobile
The following case analysis of three companies with R&D activities in China, Novo Nordisk, GN ReSound and BenQ Siemens Mobile, is based on information collected from the companies' R&D units in both China and Denmark. Accordingly, it provides a fuller and more balanced perspective than most prior analyses of companies' international R&D. Explorative open-ended face-to-face interviews with 38 respondents were conducted in the R&D units in both Denmark and China. All the interviews were conducted in 2005 with interviewees employed that year, thus titles and positions may have changed subsequently (Kjersem 2006).

For each of the three companies we describe and account for the R&D units and their historical evolution. Moreover, we discuss their motives for offshoring R&D to China and the strategic purposes with the R&D units.

Table 3:1 Motives for Internationalising R&D

Market-driven	Exploit existing company-specific assets more widely; motivated by market size and proximity; support local sales, closeness to lead customer, improve responsiveness in terms of both speed and relevance
Production-driven	Supporting local manufacturing operations
Technology driven (pull)	Tapping into foreign S&T resources, technology monitoring (especially competitor analysis), acquire/monitor local expertise, knowledge and technologies
Innovation-driven (push)	Generating new company-specific assets; attaining a faster and more varied flow of new ideas, products and processes; capitalise on location-specific advantages through an international division of labour between R&D labs
Cost-driven	Exploiting factor cost differentials
Policy-driven	National regulatory requirements or incentives, tax differentials, monitoring and exploitation of regulations and technical standards

Source: *Gammeltoft, 2006:* 186.

Novo Nordisk

Novo Nordisk is a focused healthcare company. It is headquartered in Denmark, employs approximately 22,000 full-time employees in 79 countries, and has 99 percent of sales outside of Denmark. Novo Nordisk focuses on four core areas: i.e. diabetes care, haemostasis management, growth hormone therapy, and hormone replacement therapy, and is the global market leader within diabetes care with an insulin volume market share of 50 percent (website of Novo Nordisk).

Globally, more than 3,000 employees are working on R&D activities in Novo Nordisk but R&D activities are mainly located in Denmark. However, the company is commencing on an internationalisation strategy with regards to R&D (Share 2005). They established an R&D unit in China focused on protein expression and purification in bacteria and they have commenced set up of an R&D unit in the USA, focusing on haemostasis management (the stopping of bleeding). The two R&D centres are focused on very different areas, and are not intended to collaborate directly.

Novo Nordisk established its Chinese R&D centre in Beijing in January 2002 and it was the first R&D centre established in China by an international bio-pharmaceutical company with the focus on biotech. The R&D centre moved to greater facilities in the Beijing

Zhongguancun Life Science Park in July 2004, which allows the centre to grow from 25 employees up until about 60 employees in 2008. The R&D centre is an integrated part of the Microbiology Department at Novo Nordisk's Globe Discovery organisation and they take part in various drug discovery projects with teams in Denmark. The Chinese R&D unit takes part in the initial stages of a drug discovery process, before it is developed and tested.

The main motive for Novo Nordisk to offshore R&D to China can be considered policy-driven. The Chinese market is highly attractive for Novo Nordisk, as it is located on Novo Nordisk's top 10 list of sales turnover. In this setting, the policy-driven motive has become particularly important. Mr. Ron Christie, managing director of Novo Nordisk in China, articulates: 'As for the government – it doesn't want foreign companies to use China as a low cost source of labour. If you want to make money here you are expected to give something back' (People 2004: 6).

However, when that is said, Novo Nordisk has chosen a strategy that is based on the technology-driven and innovation-driven motives regarding the R&D unit in China and created an advanced objective for the R&D unit: 'Basically the Chinese government wished for us to set up and R&D unit in China [...]. So my assignment became to set up an R&D unit in China, but we have to get the best out of them and make sure that they seriously contribute to our research' (interview with the Vice President of Microbiology). The company counts on the R&D unit being able to reversibly contribute innovative ideas back to the home-base R&D site in the near future.

The R&D centre has evolved into a centre of excellence, i.e. a uniquely specialised centre within Novo Nordisk, in research in protein expression and purification in the bacteria E. coli. The projects they are involved with centre on a variety of different therapeutic areas such as growth hormone, haemophilia (bleeding disorder), and cancer. It is called R&D but they do not develop drugs in China. The only conduct research, predominantly applied research while the development phase is located in Denmark. Completing a project in the discovery phase requires a team, with input and expertise from many different fields and the Chinese R&D unit works closely with the Novo Nordisk discovery research projects. Thus far, the projects they work on have been initiated in Denmark but the assignments that they receive must be solved independently. The R&D unit is still in its infant stage; however the long-term strategy for the unit is to increasingly contribute to the firm's knowledge base.

Gn ReSound

GN ReSound is a hearing healthcare company; it develops and produces hearing instruments. With headquarters in Denmark, GN ReSound employs approximately 3.800 employees and has production facilities in 5 countries, as well as subsidiaries in 20 countries and distributors in 80 countries. Presently, GN Resound hearing aid division encompasses approximately 200 development engineers.

GN ReSound defines itself as the leading manufacturer of advanced technology hearing instruments. The company offers a full range of hearing instruments, including software-based digital instruments and digitally programmable and traditional analogue products in all sizes and models. Hearing instrument manufacturers are competing in four different price segments: 1) top 2) plus 3) basic, and 4) budget.

Historically GN ReSound came about through a series of mergers and acquisitions and consequently they have obtained a patchwork of R&D units around the world. Today they have units in Copenhagen and Præstø in Denmark, Chicago in the USA, Xiamen in China and a little R&D satellite in Eindhoven in the Netherlands. The R&D functions in GN ReSound are divided into six main areas; digital sound processing technology, audiology, algorithm software, fitting software, product development, and product development services. In China they only focus on development. The satellite centre in Eindhoven is part of the algorithm group. In Chicago they are specialised in development, audiology, and fitting software, whereas they are specialised in all six areas in Denmark.

GN ReSound's R&D unit is located in Xiamen, in the south of China. When the company acquired a manufacturing plant in 1986 in Xiamen, a small R&D unit followed. GN ReSound chose to keep and expand the plant. Initially, the R&D unit functioned as a support and problem-solving unit for production. However, within the last years it has increasingly gained strategic importance. Now the main tasks are to support the manufacturing and to develop low and middle end products. About 30 percent of their work revolves around assisting manufacturing and the rest centres on product development (interview with the R&D manager in China). In 2002, the Chinese R&D unit became part of the global R&D organisation and at present the unit includes 16 employees, with plans to hire up until 30 new employees in 2006.

The main motives for GN ReSound to offshore R&D to China have been cost-driven and production-driven. The Senior Vice President of Research and Core Technology states that: 'First of all we chose China, generally because of cost orientations. It is cheap to develop and it is cheap to produce in China. A great amount of our product production is in China, which also makes it convenient to have a development team nearby the production site'. Furthermore, the market-driven motive is also becoming relevant; the Asian markets are increasingly important for GN ReSound. In addition, the technology-driven motive is depicted in the necessity for GN ReSound to tap into a supplementary pool of human resources (interview with the Vice President of Development).

The Chinese R&D is mainly concentrating on developing products for the plus, basic, and budget segments in the markets, whereas products in the top segment are developed in Denmark and the USA. Thus, GN ReSound seeks to advance the use of their existing technological competencies in the lower cost location of China. Basically, the Chinese unit is re-branding what might have been a top product four years ago, and then they make a derived product for a lower price segment. In this way the unit is to a great extent re-utilising the existing knowledge from the home-base R&D site. The Chinese R&D unit also has its own models to work on so they do not work on cross-border projects with the Danish unit.

BenQ Siemens Mobile
Siemens was one of the first companies in the world to develop mobile phones in 1985. However, the mobile phones division did not prove particularly profitable in 2004. The division sold about 51.1 million handsets during the year, but the mobile phones division posted a loss of 152 million Euros on sales of 4,979 billion Euros (Siemens Annual Report 2004: 60). Consequently, Siemens chose to pay the Taiwanese company BenQ, a company spun off from Acer Group in 2001, to take over their mobile phone division. In order to seal the deal, Siemens management agreed to pay BenQ $300 million and to buy $60 millions worth of stock in BenQ (Time Magazine 2005). BenQ has officially taken over the division in October 2005 and it has taken over all of Siemens Mobile Phones' production sites and R&D facilities. In 2005 BenQ Siemens Mobile was estimated to have a sixth place in the global market with a market share of 5.2 percent (InfoWorld 2005).

BenQ Siemens Mobile has its global headquarters in Munich, Germany, and it serves more than 70 markets around the globe. With the takeover of the Siemens division, BenQ Siemens Mobile employs over 7,000 employees worldwide, among which about 2,500 work in R&D units. Worldwide, BenQ Siemens Mobile encompasses eight main development centres for mobile phones, which were acquired from Siemens. These include R&D units in Aalborg (Denmark), Beijing, Shanghai (China), Kamplintfort, Berlin, Munich, Ulm (Germany), and Manaus (Brazil). For all intents and purposes, then it is the former Siemens R&D network which we are analysing. Moreover, we are particularly focussing on the two R&D units in Denmark and China.

For this analysis it has been chosen to mainly focus on the Java technology R&D units. We chose this specific department because they focus on the most advanced kind of mobile phone development. Therefore, the research is mainly delimited to interviews with key employees in the Java unit in China and in Denmark. The Danish R&D unit is responsible for the advanced Java technology development for the mobile phones, where they collaborate with the Chinese R&D unit. The Chinese R&D unit provides human resources and support for the Java projects that are carried out in Denmark.

The mobile phones R&D unit in Beijing was started in 2000 and it had about 1,000 employees in 2006. The location of the R&D unit is in the north of Beijing. It was chosen because of its proximity to the university and other mobile communication companies, whereby it is easier to attract qualified human resources. Moreover, it is located in the capital of China, close to a large and advanced consumer base. This unit develops products for the Chinese market and it works on present generation mobile phones (whereas the R&D unit in Denmark works on next generation mobile phones). In addition, they provide engineers for cross-border projects. The main motives for establishing an R&D unit in China is market-driven, as the market entails a huge potential for mobile phones companies; the Chinese market is the single largest market for mobile phone subscribers in the world and it is still far from being saturated. Henceforth, it also becomes relevant to customize the products: 'China is a huge market for us and it is not going to be very successful to have German engineers sitting in Germany, trying to figure out what Chinese people want [...] I don't think it would be possible to get the particular Chinese flavour in Germany', explains the Line Manager for the Java Team in China. Moreover, the cost- and technology-driven motives are also present, as the lower cost and the high recruitment potential also have motivated the establishment of an R&D unit in China.

The strategy of the Chinese R&D unit is to take over the GSM and GPRS platform and software. Thereby, the existing platform is being transferred to Beijing. Consequently, the focus in Europe is on the development of a new platform where they will focus on the next 3G and 4G generation mobile phones, which incorporate multimedia features.

In Europe they also develop the high-end products, whereas they in China focus on the lower-end segment.

Cross-Company Analysis: Managing Offshore R&D in China
In this section we focus on the management of offshore R&D in China through analysis of the Danish and Chinese R&D units of Novo Nordisk, GN ReSound, and BenQ Mobile. In alignment with several other scholars, we found the managerial aspects of R&D offshoring to China to be a neglected area of research (von Zedtwitz and Gassmann 2002; von Zedtwitz 2004; Gassmann and Han 2004). To be able to reap the benefits of offshoring R&D to China, knowledge has to be successfully exchanged across borders. Consequently, we will focus on the exchange of knowledge between the geographically dispersed R&D units in Denmark and China.

In order to analyse the exchange of knowledge between the geographically distant R&D units, we have chosen to focus on five dimensions of the knowledge exchange process (see Figure 3:1): the characteristics of the knowledge being exchanged, the Danish unit's motivational disposition towards knowledge sharing, the motivational disposition of the Chinese unit towards knowledge reception, the transmissions channels for exchanging knowledge, and the protection mechanisms associated with knowledge exchange. Finally, we will discuss how the three companies perceived a small set of general features of the Chinese innovation system, which emerged in the interviews as important influences on the knowledge exchange process.

These five dimensions were identified as appropriate to explore in connection with the knowledge exchange process. Since all of the case companies' R&D units in China still can be characterized as young and developing, a great deal of the initial knowledge flows have been directed from Denmark to China, as the Chinese R&D units needed to be developed and upgraded. Obviously this chapter only covers a certain area and does not embrace the many other determinants in the knowledge transfer process, which may very well exist. Moreover, the focus is on the interactive exchange of knowledge rather than on one single delimited transfer.

Knowledge Characteristics and Type of R&D
The knowledge characteristics are important determinants for the transfer of knowledge, as they influence the ease with which it can be exchanged across borders. The difference between tacit and explicit knowledge hinges on whether or not the knowledge can be codified

and transmitted in a documented format. When the knowledge to be transferred is codified its transfer is also simpler and less costly. Conversely, the more tacit the knowledge, the more difficult it is to transfer it (Zander and Kogut 1995; Simonin 1999; Cummings and Teng 2003).

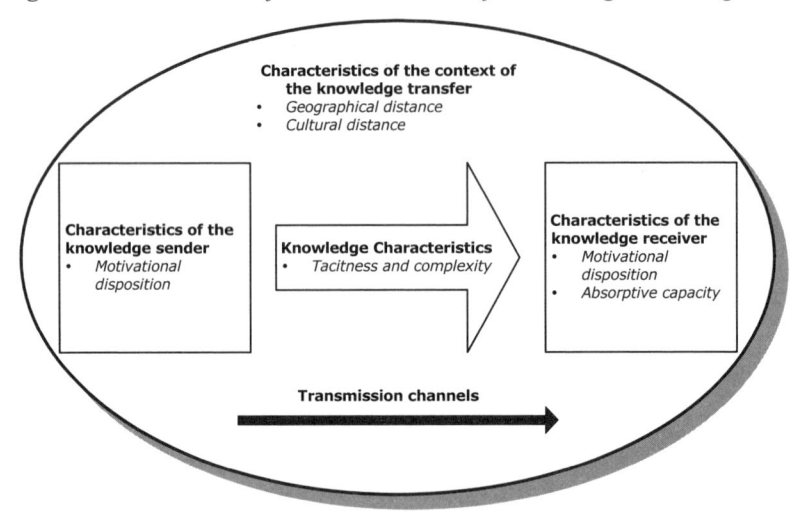

Figure 3:1 Framework for Determinants of Knowledge Exchange

[Figure: Oval containing three boxes connected by an arrow. Top label: "Characteristics of the context of the knowledge transfer — Geographical distance, Cultural distance". Left box: "Characteristics of the knowledge sender — Motivational disposition". Middle arrow box: "Knowledge Characteristics — Tacitness and complexity". Right box: "Characteristics of the knowledge receiver — Motivational disposition, Absorptive capacity". Bottom arrow labeled "Transmission channels".]

Source: *Own Creation based on Szulanski (1996), Simonin (1999), and Gupta & Govindarajan (2000).*

The tacit and codified knowledge characteristics are present to different extents in the case companies. In both the R&D units of GN ReSound and BenQ Siemens Mobile, they work with well-known technology platforms. Moreover, they have an ISO 9000 certification for their development processes. That means that all their work is documented and they follow clearly described and standardized work processes. Within GN ReSound this involves specific information about the procedures, the designs, the measurements, the drawings, and so on. Within BenQ Siemens Mobile the documentation entails writing down all the software code. They have a test department that tests all the documents and software code. Consequently, the work tasks they carry out in both of the R&D units are often very well defined, formalized and to a great extent, documented.

As outlined in the previous section, the Novo Nordisk R&D unit engages in applied research where they are advancing the discovery of new and improved research processes and therapeutic drugs. The work tasks in the R&D unit can best be described as novel and complex. Moreover, there is a great deal of uncertainty connected to the research process. Out of approximately 45 projects in the discovery organisation, only three to four projects will be developed into finished products. Thus, the R&D unit does not engage in extensive documentation: 'We do not have an ISO certificate in the discovery organisation, since we have to operate freely and with so many projects that an ISO certification would kill many forms of creativity and innovation, because the level of documentation for what you are working on will increase rapidly' (interview with Danish scientist). Henceforth, a large part of the knowledge, which is created in the R&D unit in Novo Nordisk is not codified or documented.

Motivation of Danish R&D Units to Share Knowledge

It is noted by many scholars that the behaviour of the knowledge sender with regards to knowledge sharing is key in the knowledge transfer process. The main focus is on the motivation of the sender for transferring knowledge (Szulanski 1996; Simonin 1999; Gupta and Govindarajan 2000). Thus, in this section we focus on the challenges related to the knowledge-sharing propensity of the Danish R&D unit. During the case study a range of obstacles were found. These we have divided into what we identify as the China threat, lack of priority of the Danish colleagues, and diverse levels of skills. On a positive note, however, the Chinese R&D units also bring additional human resources to aid the Danish R&D activities.

The China threat constitutes a challenge for the knowledge sharing propensity of the Danish R&D unit. The choice to utilize human resources at a low cost in China instead of in Denmark can be perceived as a threat to their career prospects by the Danish employees and the conception of the 'China threat' has been an issue in all the case companies. The Danish employees in all three of the Danish R&D units agree that in the beginning they did, to some extent, perceive the Chinese unit as a threat, but not anymore. One of the Danish project leaders from GN ReSound contends that: 'When we started it was difficult to help them, if you were cutting the branch from which you are yourself sitting. But people don't feel like that today.'

Lack of priority of the Danish colleagues is another challenge. From the Chinese R&D units' perspective, it is emphasized that the willingness to share knowledge relies on the individual person in Denmark. Some are better and more willing than others to share their knowledge.

In both of the R&D units it is implied that there may be reluctance in Denmark to spend time on knowledge sharing, which is probably because the Chinese unit is not given a high priority: 'They have so many projects, so we never know when they will finish ours, so we have to wait [...] They don't give our projects such a high priority' one of the Chinese engineers at GN ReSound concludes.

We also found that the *diverse skill levels* create problems for knowledge sharing. It was emphasized that since the colleagues in Denmark often have more experience and knowledge in the area, they find it burdensome to work with colleagues in China that are from a younger R&D unit, and thus they have less experience. One of the Danish scientists from Novo Nordisk states that: 'In the beginning it was annoying that they were not more creative and that they could not come up with better solutions.'

However, the Chinese R&D units also bring *additional resources* with which to conduct R&D activities. In GN ReSound the Chinese R&D unit works on development aspects that are not of high interest for Danish engineers: 'We focus on the top-end products and the Chinese focus on the more standardized products. It is very important for the company that we develop these products, but there are many engineers in Denmark that find that they are not as exciting as the new products [...] The Chinese engineers are extremely good and motivated to make these type of assignments' (interview with the Vice President of Development in GN ReSound). Thus, there is a greater incentive to share knowledge when there is a clear need for the Chinese R&D resources.

Motivation of Chinese R&D Units to Receive Knowledge
The characteristics of the knowledge receiver of the target unit for the knowledge transfer have been found to be of significant relevance. Primarily, the motivation and the ability to absorb new knowledge (absorptive capacity) of the receiver have been the most emphasized impediments to knowledge transfer (Szulanski 1996; Gupta and Govindarajan 2000; Cohen and Levinthal 1990).

The *motivation to receive knowledge* is important in order to get the R&D units up to speed, increase the knowledge base, and accumulate experience. As one of the positive points for conducting R&D in China, all the Danish R&D units described their Chinese colleagues as extremely motivated and eager to learn: 'They are very keen to learn and develop so they can move up the career ladder. Therefore I also think that they are very willing to accept knowledge from other sources or from abroad' (interview with line manager from BenQ Siemens Mobile). Moreover, it is also emphasized that the Chinese employees work very hard and long hours: 'There is not so much 'coffee and cake' in China as in Denmark; they really work hard' one of the Danish scientists at Novo Nordisk stresses.

While the motivation to receive knowledge is high, the *absorptive capacity* of the Chinese R&D unit can constitute a challenge for the exchange of knowledge, since the Chinese employees are lacking the same extent of experience and education as their well-established Danish counterparts. In GN ReSound and BenQ Siemens Mobile it is noted that the Chinese R&D units sometimes take on assignments that they do not yet have the adequate capabilities and experience to carry out. One of the Danish project leaders from BenQ Siemens Mobile states: 'The only thing I actually experience is that they sometimes are a little bit too optimistic. They readily take some assignments that they cannot solve, and then we find out that they could not solve them [...] and then we have to start all over again.' Particularly in the case of GN ReSound, this inequality was perceived to be a challenge: 'If you look at it through the company glass then it is much cheaper to have R&D in China. If you look at the competence situation, then we all would say it is too much hassle. That it will be a hassle until we reach the same level. It requires a huge effort to train the unit' (interview with Danish project leader in GN Resound).

Transmission Channels for Exchanging Knowledge

With the management of innovation around the globe, a firm must be able to coordinate activities and link them in an efficient manner, in order to fully leverage the potential of the offshore R&D unit. Persuad et al. (2002) argue that key challenges within global R&D is about finding the best way to coordinate corporate R&D activities in order to accelerate the pace of innovation. Thus, with significant geographical distance between the R&D units, extensive and efficient coordination mechanisms – particularly within headquarters – become key to make the R&D activities flow and function optimally. The existence and richness of the transmission channels for exchanging knowledge are analysed in terms of formal and informal mechanisms in the case companies.

The *formal transmission channels* centre on formalized structures and institutions. GN ReSound and BenQ Siemens Mobile use advanced computer tools and databases to exchange knowledge between Denmark and China. They utilize resource-planning tools, which help plan the projects across borders from the beginning to end: the activities, the schedule, and the time. Furthermore, the documentation for the work processes are uploaded on shared databases between the R&D sites and the shared intra-web is also utilized for information sharing. At Novo Nordisk, they cannot plan their research in such a stringent manner. It is difficult to evaluate and measure the work. However, the management team makes an overall plan each year with regards to what goals they should reach within the different activities and projects. In all of the case companies, employees hold web meetings or phone meetings with their Danish colleagues once a week to update and keep track on the status of the projects. In addition to emails, they also utilize instant messaging. Thus, the day-to-day exchange of knowledge also takes place through the use of collaborative communication tools: i.e. the internet, databases, web/telephone conferences.

The *informal transmission channels* are not bound by formal contractual agreements and institutions, but encompass a person-oriented mechanism and socialisation. Since the Novo Nordisk R&D unit does not utilize a formal mechanism to exchange knowledge, they rely heavily on informal transmission channels. In Novo Nordisk they make extensive use of both short-term and long-term assignments abroad. The importance of face-to-face meetings was profoundly emphasized both to start-up projects, but also to transfer the work and solve problems. Since they started the R&D unit in China, they have had expatriates stationed there for a year or more. They also make use of wide-ranging rotation programmes and training for the Chinese employees. To keep up with the increasingly-advanced projects, the Chinese employees receive extensive training either by Danish employees who come to China or the Chinese employees will travel to Denmark, typically for three months. BenQ Siemens Mobile also makes use of short-term and long-term assignments, but to a lesser extent. They utilize expatriates widely both in Denmark and in China. In addition, the short-term assignments, usually two weeks in duration, are utilized as a way to enhance the collaborative work and exchange of knowledge. GN ReSound did not place as great an emphasis on the informal channels as the other case companies. They have not engaged in any job rotations or expatriation programmes. They assert it is difficult to get Danish people to go to Xiamen. It is moreover stressed that they do not perceive wide-ranging travelling as a viable solution: 'The idea is that the employees out there teach the new ones. It is about waterfall learning. We are not an educational institution, so if they cannot work independently in China, then much of the point of having them is lost' emphasizes one of the Danish engineers.

Knowledge Protection and Strategies
This section discusses strategies for the protection of knowledge flows between the R&D units. In relation to knowledge exchange between offshore R&D units, concerns about IP infringement may constitute an additional barrier. When a firm's IP is pirated, a major element of its competitive posture and advantage may be jeopardized and the management of IP becomes crucial (Teece 1998).

The IPR system in China has been subject to much scrutiny. Chinese enforcement of IPRs is not yet at the same level as in the West. All the case companies are aware of the difficulty of protecting their IP assets in China. BenQ Siemens Mobile and Novo Nordisk have not experienced any problems, but for GN ReSound it has constituted a real problem. GN ReSound has experienced that employees have left the R&D unit in China to start a low cost company competing with a product which ReSound perceived as too similar to its own. Thus, IPR protection is something upon which the company increasingly focuses its attention. Nevertheless, none of the case companies found their intellectual property to be easy to infringe upon, due to the complexity of their knowledge and products and the experience needed to copy them. In spite of the problems with IP rights, GN Resound did still not perceive IP infringement as a major threat: 'If some take our hearing aids, then it is easy to copy all the mechanical parts, but it is still not easy to make it function, because there are many factors of stability involved in it. So they will still have a good bit of work to make it function', explains one of the Danish engineers.

There are a variety of strategies which the firm can utilize in order to protect the flow of knowledge between the dispersed R&D units. In the following we will focus on IP strategies based on patents, secrecy, lead-time advantage, and complementary assets as outlined by Levin et al. (1987) and Cohen et al. (2000).

All of the three case companies focus on *patents* in general to protect their innovations. However, IPRs may not work in practice as they do in theory, since many patents can be invented around at modest costs. Moreover, they often provide little protection in practice because litigation involves cost and resources (Teece 1998). In Novo Nordisk and BenQ Siemens Mobile they have well-established IPR departments. In GN ReSound their IPR department has just recently been founded (early 2005). Moreover, the Chinese R&D units in Novo

Nordisk and BenQ Siemens Mobile work on filing patents (only abroad), whereas the R&D unit of GN ReSound is not at that point yet. Nonetheless, none of the companies count on utilising the patents in China. They are aimed at the worldwide market as means to block or exchange innovations. BenQ Siemens Mobile and GN ReSound – both companies from industries in which the exchange of complementary innovations is important – utilize the patents as thickets to exchange innovations. 'Patents are of enormous importance to BenQ Siemens Mobile. It is not so much to protect our products, as it is to get access to other things that we would like to have in our product portfolio. So we can trade around' (interview with the line manager from BenQ Siemens Mobile). However, in Novo Nordisk the patents are more used as 'fences' to block the competitors.

Trade secrecy is another way to prevent unwanted appropriation and unintentional technology transfer to rival firms. All of the case companies use secrecy to protect the knowledge and write confidentiality agreements with their employees and suppliers. One of the German project leaders elaborates: 'There are always some holes where information is dropping out, that is why you need to take care that not everybody gets access to everything. We have a single entry point for that.' However, limited access to the knowledge is not just in relation to the Chinese employees. It is also an issue for all the other employees in the case companies. With regards to the more core technologies of the company, the risk of infringement is a challenge in the knowledge exchange. Consequently, the choice in all of the case companies is to keep that strategically close to head quarters.

Lead-time advantage does, to a great extent, depend on the industry characteristics and it refers to a firm having a first mover advantage and engaging in frequent technical improvements in order to stay ahead, whereby the competitors should be left behind in the innovation process. Particularly for the mobile phone industry, and for a company like BenQ Siemens Mobile that develops 35 new phones a year, lead-time advantage is seen as pivotal to sustain the competitive advantage: 'On the other hand, then it goes really fast with the development of mobile phones, so you can say that if they copy something that has already been developed, then they would still lag behind, because then we are working on something new' (interview with the line manager in BenQ Siemens Mobile). In contrast the development cycles in GN ReSound and to a great extent Novo Nordisk (where it takes app. 15 years to develop a product) are slower, whereby lead-time advantage is not as significant.

An effective way to deter piracy of key assets is to hold *complementary assets* at different R&D sites, which are difficult to imitate. In countries with weak IPR regimes, effective strategies to overcome hold-up, imitation, or piracy of key assets is to own or control key complementary assets, so even if imitation should occur, the total pirated value is limited (Anand and etovic 2004). We found that internal complementary asset within the international R&D organisation was utilized to a high extent in the case companies. Nevertheless, it did not seem as a conscious IP strategy on behalf of the companies. Since the Chinese R&D unit GN ReSound works on their own models, there is a lesser extent of cross border complementary assets involved.

Features of Chinese Innovation Systems Influencing Knowledge Exchange

Next, we return to the Chinese innovation system and examine features influencing international exchange of knowledge. We will discuss perceptions of the geographic distance; differences of time zone, language, and culture; the issues of 'saving face' and hierarchy; and perceptions of creativity and entrepreneurship of Chinese labour.

The *geographic distance* is perceived as holding the greatest challenges for the Novo Nordisk R&D unit. One of the most cited challenges from a Chinese perspective was the lack of synergy effects with the home-based R&D unit and the difficulty in getting an overview of the whole project on which they collaborate: 'Sometimes we make mistakes in our part of the project because we don't know about the new developments or change of goals' (interview with a Chinese scientist in Novo Nordisk). Since the Novo Nordisk R&D unit is focused on applied research and the scientists work closely on cross-border projects generating new knowledge, the physical distance can more easily become a challenge for the successful exchange of knowledge. In GN ReSound and BenQ Siemens Mobile this challenge did not appear prevalent as they work on their own models and specified components.

The *time zone difference* is not seen as a particular challenge since the Chinese employees will wait until the afternoon to call Denmark, where it is morning. For BenQ Siemens Mobile and to a lesser extent GN ReSound the time difference is seen as an advantage due to the fact that they can delegate problems to China. The following morning, Chinese colleagues will return the solution to Denmark. In this way the R&D units can engage in around the clock and year-round development.

The *language differences* are perceived to be a relatively great challenge, particularly for BenQ Siemens Mobile and GN ReSound. The lack of adequate English skills for some of the Chinese colleagues makes it difficult to exchange knowledge. In all of the case companies interviewees state that it is difficult to find employees with a high quality education and a good command of the English language. A number of the Chinese employees in all of the R&D units emphasize that they prefer to write English than to speak on the phone.

In general the *cultural distance* between the Danish and Chinese culture did not seem to create great challenges to the exchange of knowledge, also because the Chinese employees easily adapted to working with Danish colleagues. Differences in personalities seem to be a more profound challenge. 'I think that it is a very easy cultural interaction. I actually think that there are bigger problems within Europe' (interview with the Vice President of Microbiology in Novo Nordisk). Another cultural aspect that was observed was the internal cultural difference between the Chinese employees that have been studying and working in the USA and those who have not. It was noticed that the Chinese employees with extensive experience from USA also found it difficult to adapt back to the Chinese culture.

Challenges to an open and unfettered exchange of knowledge are the cultural issues of *saving face and a hierarchical mentality* in China. These challenges were found in all three case companies. Face saving in the Chinese culture is often perceived as a problem for innovation, because it implies complying with the preferences of a superior. This perception found support in the interviews in the case companies: 'It can actually decelerate innovation a bit that they are so authoritarian. There is a great loyalty and belief in what the grey haired is saying is probably true [...] In the Danish management culture everything is constantly challenged' (interview with the Vice President of Microbiology in Novo Nordisk).

A *lack of creative knowledge* was reported as a challenge. The Chinese educational system is based on a very rigid structure, which leaves less room for innovative thinking or creativity. For Novo Nordisk it has been a problem to find creative scientists to be part of the discovery department: 'It is difficult to find creative people. I see it as culture related. I don't think it is possible in one area to have a top-governed system where everything is controlled and then a freely thinking in another area'. As a consequence the Chinese R&D units tends to receive well-defined assignments. On the other hand the case companies emphasize the high technical skills and stringent manner of working as positive aspects that contribute to the work flow across borders. For example, in Novo Nordisk it is perceived as a good complement to the Danish less structured way of working. Accordingly, the cultural differences can constitute both a challenge and an advantage for the management of offshore R&D.

Conclusion

We have analysed the phenomenon of high-tech investments to China from two different angles. In the first part of the chapter we focused on the supply side of the Chinese ST&I system. China is in the process of reforming a national innovation system that still reflects weaknesses from the planned economy period. During this process China has made impressive gains in some key ST&I areas, such as increasing the percentage of high-tech exports, increasing R&D investments made by businesses, attracting foreign high-tech investments, improving the legal IPR environment, and revitalising the educational system.

Seen from the demand side of foreign firms investing in high-tech in China there has been an increase in more advanced FDI inflows that are not just focused on low-cost human resources but also are attracted to the Chinese market, skilled human resources, and scientific clusters. Through analysis of the Chinese R&D units of Novo Nordisk, GN ReSound and BenQ Siemens Mobile it was illustrated that the motives for offshoring R&D to China were varied, ranging from mainly cost-driven and market-driven motives in GN ReSound and BenQ Siemens Mobile, to policy-driven, technology-driven, and innovation-driven motives in Novo Nordisk. Furthermore, the strategies and organisation of the R&D units depend much on the type of R&D conducted.

We also investigated the management of offshore R&D to China. The results uncover that there are differences within the case companies depending on which type of R&D the unit conducts. Since GN ReSound and BenQ Siemens Mobile focus on development work that builds on existing knowledge platforms, and Novo Nordisk focuses on research where the work tasks are highly complex, the companies are faced with different challenges. Furthermore, BenQ Siemens Mobile has a global R&D network, in which we found that they do not experience the same extent of challenges, due to an increased incentive to exchange knowledge in order to make the global workflow function.

With regards to the knowledge sharing propensity of the Danish R&D unit, then we found the managerial challenges to be the 'China threat' and fear of losing work, lack of priority of the Danish colleagues, and diverse skills levels. One aspect that positively influenced the knowledge sharing propensity was the additional resources that the Chinese R&D unit brings for the R&D activities. The Chinese employees were highly motivated to receive transfers of technology and knowledge but absorptive capacity and lower level of experience were seen as a challenge to knowledge exchange.

In spite of the lax IPR regime in China the case companies have still offshored knowledge to China. Admittedly, all the case companies place importance on patents, however they serve as 'thickets' to exchange complementary knowledge or as proprietary assets for the global market. In addition to a patent strategy, all the companies employed secrecy as a mean to deter infringement risks. However, particularly for GN ReSound and Novo Nordisk, they were mindful about transferring core knowledge to China. Moreover, the lead-time advantage strategy was only noticed in BenQ Siemens Mobile, due to the extremely short development cycles. Finally, both BenQ Siemens Mobile and Novo Nordisk are, more or less consciously, employing a strategy based on complementary assets.

With respect to features of the Chinese innovation system influencing the knowledge exchange process, the geographic and cultural distance did present some challenges. For GN ReSound and BenQ Siemens Mobile, where the R&D units are focused entities, the geographic distance did not prove to be a barrier. Furthermore, they are able to take advantage and exploit time zone difference. For Novo Nordisk the geographic distance does constitute a challenge. The Chinese employees particularly found it difficult to get an overview of the projects and to obtain the synergy effects of being in a larger R&D organisation. In all of the R&D units the language and lower English skills in China was perceived as an obstacle. Concerning the cultural distance, it was emphasized that differences in personalities rather than culture is a greater challenge. Nevertheless, there are a number of Chinese cultural traits, which were believed to be a challenge to the knowledge exchange between the R&D units. These reflect issues of saving face, hierarchical mentality, and reported less creative mindset in the Chinese culture.

In conclusion, as the People's Republic of China is liberating its market and FDI flowing to the country at high speed, the ST&I system is also evolving. One of the parameters for developing a successful ST&I system has been to attract foreign high-tech investments to China. For firms, offshoring of R&D is a non-trivial and risky endeavour. Nevertheless, the Chinese R&D units included in this case study analysis have proven to be very successful and growing ventures.

Acknowledgement
This chapter also appears in: Govindan Parayil and Anthony D'Costa (eds.), *The New Asian Innovation Dynamics: China and India in Perspective*, 2008, Palgrave Macmillan. Reproduced with permission of Palgrave Macmillan.

References
Anand, B. and A. Galetovic 2004. 'Strategies That Work When Property Rights Don't.' in Gary Libecap (ed.), *Intellectual Property and Entrepreneurship*, Greenwich, Conn.: JAI Press.

Cohen, W. M., R. R. Nelson and J. P. Walsh 2000.,'Protecting Their Intellectual Assets: appropriability conditions and why U.S. manufacturing firms patent (or not).' *NBER Working Paper 7552*, National Bureau of Economic Research, Mass, Cambridge

Cohen, W. M. and D. A. Levinthal 1990. 'Absorptive Capacity: a new perspective on learning and innovation.' *Administrative Science Quarterly,* 35: 128-152.

Cummings, J. L. and B-S Teng 2003, 'Transferring R&D Knowledge: the key factors affecting knowledge transfer success.' *Journal of Engineering Technology Management,* vol. 20: 39-68.

Economist Intelligence Unit (EIU) 2005, *China, Country Profile 2005.*

Gammeltoft, P. 2006, 'Internationalisation of R&D: trends, drivers and managerial challenges.' *International Journal of Technology and Globalization,* 2: 177-199.

Gassmann, O. and Z. Han 2004, 'Motivations and Barriers to Foreign R&D Activities in China.' *R&D Management,* 34(4): 423-437.

Gu, S. and B-Å. Lundvall 2006, 'China's Innovation System and the Move Toward Harmonious Growth and Endogenous Innovation.' *Innovation: Management, Policy & Practice,* 8 (1-2).

Gupta, A. K. and V. Govindarajan 2000, Knowledge Flows Within Multinational Corporations.' *Strategic Management Journal,* 21: 473-496.

Haiyan, W. and Z. Yuan 2004, 'The Evolving Role of Universities in the Chinese National System of Innovation.' *National Research Center for S&T for Development, Ministry of S&T Peoples Republic of China.*

Huang, C., C. Amorim, M. Spinoglio, B. Gouveia, and A. Medina 2004, 'Organization, programme and structure: an analysis of the Chinese innovation policy framework.' *R&D Management,* 34 (4): 367-387.

InfoWorld 2005, 'New BenQ, Siemens mobile phone company opens' [online] Available from: http://www.infoworld.com/article/05/10/03/HNbenqsiemens_1.html, accessed 20 February 2007.

Kjersem, J. M. 2006, The Internationalisation of R&D – Offshoring Knowledge to China viewed through Case Studies of Novo Nordisk, GN ReSound and BenQ Mobile', Master Thesis, Copenhagen Business School.

Levin, R. C., A. K. Klevorick, R. R. Nelson, S. G. Winter 1987, 'Appropriating the Returns from Industrial Research and Development.' *Brookings Papers on Economic Activity,* 1987(3): pp. 783-831.

Lundvall, B-Å. (ed.) 1992, National Systems of Innovation; Towards a Theory of Innovation and Interactive Learning, London: Pinter.

Ministry of Science and Technology of the Peoples Republic of China, 2005 [online]. Available from http://www.most.gov.cn/eng/statistics/2005

OECD 2004, OECD Science, Technology and Industry Outlook 2004, Paris: OECD.

OECD 2005, *OECD Science, Technology and Industry Scoreboard 2005 – Towards a knowledge-based economy*, Paris: OECD.

OECD 2006, OECD Science, Technology and Industry Outlook 2006, Paris: OECD.

People Novo Nordisk 2004, Another first in China, 19 June.

Persuad, A., V. Kumar and U. Kumar 2002, *Managing Synergistic Innovations Through Corporate Global R&D*, Westport, Conn: Greenwood Press.

Schaaper, M. 2004, 'An Emerging Knowledge-Based Economy in China? Indicators from OECD Databases.' *STI Working Paper,* 2004/4

Share, quarterly investor update from Novo Nordisk 2005, Scientific satellites, May 2005.

Siemens Annual Report 2004 [online]. Available from: http://www.siemens.com

Simonin, B. 1999, 'Transfer of Marketing Know-How in International Strategic Alliances: An Empirical Investigation of the Role and Antecedents of Knowledge Ambiguity.' *Journal of International Business Studies,* 30 (3): 463-490.

Szulanski, G. 1996, 'Exploring Internal Stickiness: impediments to the transfer of best practices within the Firm.' *Strategic Management Journal,* 17: 27-43.

Teece, D. J. 1998, 'Capturing Value from Knowledge Assets: the new economy, markets for know-how and intangible assets.' *California Management Review,* 40 (3): 55-79.

Time Magazine 2005, Taiwan steps up, 25 June.

UNCTAD 2005, World Investment Report 2005: *Transnational Corporations and the Internationalization of R&D,* UNCTAD, New York & Geneva: UN.

UNESCO Institute for Statistics [online]. Available from: http://www.uis.unesco.org.

von Zedtwitz, M. 2004, 'Managing Foreign R&D Laboratories in China.' *R&D Management,* 34 (4): pp. 439-452.

von Zedtwitz, M. and O. Gassmann 2002, 'Market versus Technology Drive in R&D Internationalisation: four different patterns of managing research and development.' *Research Policy,* 31: 569-588.

Walsh, K. 2003, *Foreign High-Tech R&D in China,* The Henry L. Stimson Center.

Zander, U. and B. Kogut 1995, 'Knowledge and the speed of transfer and imitation of organizational capabilities; an empirical test.' *Organization Science,* 6 (1): 76-92.

CHAPTER FOUR

Subsidiary Influence and its Impact on Role Development: Three Cases from the Coatings Industry in China

Jens Gammelgaard

This paper examines foreign-owned subsidiaries in China and questions how far and for what reasons the subsidiaries are in a position to develop their role in the multinational corporation (MNC). The discussion of the topic, though, departs from former surveys, conducted in a West European context, which have revealed that some subsidiaries positively develop their role over time with regard to market, product, value-adding activities, along with strategic and operational autonomy associated to the subsidiary (Delany 1998; Dörrenbächer and Gammelgaard 2006; Egelhoff et al. 1998; Jarilo and Martinez, 1990; Pearce 1999). However, despite the fact that China plays a decisive role in today's world economy, surprisingly little attention has been paid to the development of subsidiaries in this part of the world. In general, writings about China, like Buckley and Meng (2006), have looked into effects of inward and outward Foreign Direct Investments (FDI) and, therefore, conceptually and empirically, surveys have been executed on the macro-economical level. This study investigates the effect of Western European FDI at a micro-economic level, and discusses effects of structural and managerial processes of the MNC in a Chinese context. These analyses will, in this chapter, depart from three case studies within the coatings industry. The empirical context includes two Danish companies (Hempel and Flügger), and the Swedish and Dutch conglomerate Akzo Nobel.

The empirical findings demonstrate the impact of subsidiary influence on subsidiary role development. First, changes in the organizational structure of the MNC, a process leading to the redefinition of roles across subsidiaries – and the increasing economical importance of China – show to be important. Second, the subsidiary managers' abilities to act in an institutional 'dual world' (i.e., being a West European affiliate located in China) when requesting more resources and mandates from headquarters' managers are decisive to role change.

The paper is organized as follows: first, a literature review provides a brief overview of White and Poynter's (1984), and Birkinshaw and Morrison's (1995) role taxonomies. Then, the theoretical constructs regarding subsidiary role development and subsidiary influence are presented. Thereafter, the research methodology is described, followed by a presentation of the empirical survey. Finally, the last section includes conclusion and discussions.

Literature Review
Subsidiary Role Descriptions

Immense variations exist in the scale and scope of subsidiary activity and mandates. Typically, subsidiaries operate within a narrowed set of the value-chain (Roth and Morrison 1992) as headquarters typically allocates different mandates and set of activities to its various subsidiaries. Some subsidiaries focus on manufacturing, others solely act as sales outlets. Furthermore, headquarters establishes unique, particular, and dyadic relationships to each of its subsidiaries. Next, subsidiaries differentiate within the MNC, as they need to organize their activities in order to meet local competitive pressures. As an outcome of these circumstances, Nohria and Ghoshal (1997) have characterized the MNC as a differentiated network: a concept which encapsulates both a decentralized structure and a variation of role in relation to the subsidiary.

To reflect this situation, different typologies have described the variety of roles a subsidiary might undertake. White and Poynter (1984) presented the following taxonomy, where subsidiaries on an aggregate level played the following five distinct subsidiary roles: a) miniature replicas, which produce and market some of the parent's product lines in the host country, b) marketing satellites, which market centrally manufactured products and services into the host market or trading area, c) rationalized manufacturers that produce a designated set of component parts leaving sales activities to other corporate units, d) product specialists, which are units that develop, produce, and market a limited product line for global markets, and finally, e) strategic independent units, which have the freedom and resources to develop lines of business for local, regional, or global markets. In this classification, White and Poynter use the market, product, and value-adding scope of the subsidiary as categorization variables to reflect the number of markets served by the affiliate, its responsibilities with its product lines, and which area in the value chain (Porter's (1985) description is a well-known example hereof) the subsidiary works (e.g., sales, purchase, etc.). Finally, White and Poynter included 'autonomy' in order to label the 'strategic independent units' defined as units possessing the freedom to develop and manufacture new products. Here, autonomy should be viewed as both decision-making freedom at the overall strategic level and at the daily operational level (O'Donnel 2000), the former typically is limited in the case of subsidiaries, and the degree to which strategic and operational decisions is an outcome of negotiations between headquarters and subsidiaries or whether decisions are made solely by one of these actors (Taggart and Hood 1999).

In a later survey, Birkinshaw and Morrison (1995) distinguished between three subsidiary roles: a) the local implementer, which adapts global products to the local market; b) the specialized contributor, which is a unit which possesses specialized expertise within narrowly defined areas – and thereby remain tightly connected to other corporate units; and c) the world mandate subsidiary, which has global or regional responsibility for a product line or an entire business. This categorization approaches the White and Poynter taxonomy, such as distinguishing between manufacturing and downstream activity as a selection criteria, but Birkinshaw and Morrison further emphasize strategic autonomy by claiming this to be low in the case of the local implementer, medium in the case of specialized contributor, and high in the case of world mandate subsidiaries. Furthermore, they added three criteria, namely: a) the pressures for local responsiveness, building on the Bartlett and Ghoshal (1989) framework, b) product dependency of the parent, and finally c) the degree of inter-affiliate purchases as measurements for the subsidiary role. In this paper, building on these two theoretical frameworks, the subsidiary role is defined as the scale and scope of value chain activities, and the mandates are associated with rights to strategic decision-making.

Subsidiary Role Development

Several surveys have analyzed the reasons for subsidiary role development, such as increased market opportunities – often as an outcome of improved host country economy, or the effect of supranational institutions like the EEC – that have proven to positively affect the position of subsidiaries in the corporation (Delany 1998; Dörrenbächer and Gammelgaard 2006; Egelhoff et al. 1998; Jarilo and Martinez 1990; Pearce 1999). One survey by Walsh et al., (2002) focused on 66 Chinese subsidiaries or equity joint ventures of North American and Asian MNCs. The survey results showed a general change from production unit-based to more market-oriented activities due to an improvement in the Chinese economy, which in turn caused both higher employment costs and at the same time led to an increase in the local demand for the subsidiary products and services. Another common reason for subsidiary development has been the entrepreneurial efforts – often manifested through R&D processes – within the subsidiary (Egelhoff et al. 1998; Hood et al. 1994; Pearce 1999; Taggart 1998a; 1998b). Here, Birkinshaw (1999) demonstrated how subsidiary initiative in terms of entrepreneurship, led to enhancement of credibility in relation to headquarters, second, headquarters' openness towards the subsidiary, third, the communication between the two, and finally, the development of distinct capabilities in terms of technical, market-based or process-based skills. Furthermore, two surveys (Birkinshaw and Hood 1997; Delany 1998) pointed out the effects managerial ambitions and lobbying activities have on subsidiary role development. Moreover, subsidiary role development depends on location factors (e.g., market opportunities offered by the host country) and the subsidiary's relative strength compared to other host country market prospects of other subsidiaries within the corporation (Benito et al. 2003; Egelhoff et al. 1998, Holm et al. 2003). In addition, Birkinshaw and Hood (2000) demonstrated how location in leading edge clusters affected subsidiary development. The neglected issue in these studies are, though, the impact of subsidiary influence in relation to role development, which will be point for the further investigation.

Subsidiary Influence
Another stream of literature describes the role of the subsidiary in relation to its influential position vis-à-vis the headquarters, often manifested in the subsidiary's ability to have an effect on headquarters strategic and operational decision making procedures (Dörrenbächer and Gammelgaard 2006). The departure for the conceptual discussion, which will depart from the behavioural description of organizations (e.g., Cyert and March (1963) seminal work), is that organizations do have to allocate scarce resources within a context where optimal allo-

cation criteria do not exist: hence power enters into all important decisions (Fligstein 1985). On this point Pfeffer (1981: 2) emphasized: 'power affects outcomes ranging from the allocation of budgets to organizational subunits, to succession of executive and administrative positions, to the design and redesign of formal organizational structures'. However, the use the wording of power is less relevant in the case of subsidiary, being part of a hierarchy, where headquarters exercises its authority. In French and Raven's (1959) classical description of power, this type of command, together with reward and coercive power, will typically be the sort of authority possessed by headquarters. Instead, subsidiaries have the opportunity – in relation to French and Raven's framework – to exert power either through being 'experts' (i.e., where the subsidiary possesses some special knowledge or expertise) leading to resource-dependency situations of the headquarters (Pfeffer and Salancik 1978; Forsgren et al. 2005) or through 'referent power' where the subsidiary's power in relation to headquarters is a function of how attracted headquarters is to the subsidiary, a situation where the subsidiary manager can utilize e.g., his or her lobbyist or charismatic skills (Dörrenbächer and Geppert 2006; Mudambi and Navarro 2004). Therefore, as Surlemont (1998) noted, it is of higher relevance to use the concept of 'influence' since the subsidiary can cause changes in headquarters' decisions by persuasion, initiation, advice, or manipulations.

Furthermore, a Chinese subsidiary of a e.g., West European MNC, can be viewed as caught between two worlds. In terms of institutionalization theory, the subsidiary will be subject to isomorphic pulls from the local environment and, in a wider context, it will not always come across legal controls, norms, values, and cognitive constraints (Scott 1995). As described by Zaheer and Mosakowski (1993), firms must learn how to operate in the local market in order to develop relationships with local counter partners. Connections between the subsidiary and its local counter partners refer to transactions tying organizations to each other: from contractual-based arrangements to personal relationships. Isomorphism refers to firms imitating or resembling other firms which face the same set of environmental conditions (such as cultural expectations in the society (DiMaggio and Powell 1983)). However, this creates a problem in relation to headquarters and the subsidiary's ability to attract resources and mandates. The subsidiary can be 'over-embedded' into the local context that can create a lock-in effect, which constrains the subsidiary's ability to utilize relationships, knowledge sources, and market opportunities outside the small community in which the subsidiary operates (Woolcock 1998). Simultaneously, the MNC has its own institutions with rules, norms, values, and cognitive pillars from which to act. At the same time as subsidiaries are forced to adapt to the local environment, they are subject to isomorphic pulls internally in the MNC where they also must adapt to rules, norms, and values, and share the social context with other MNC-units in order to build strong internal relationships. Subsidiaries, therefore, exist in a world of institutional duality (Kostova and Roth 2002), caught between the MNC institutions and the local institutions. However, subsidiaries can, then, gain influence being mediator between these two worlds, possessing the ability to make the needed translations of local specific knowledge and the ability to simultaneously follow the internal corporate norms and rules. This solve the conflict of institutional duality producing higher influence to such subsidiaries in comparison with other more locally embedded units – and at the end of the day, makes these subsidiaries more visible in the internal competition for headquarters' resources and mandates, which is a current status for many MNCs (Birkinshaw et al. 2005)

Subsidiary influence is, therefore, defined in this text as the *subsidiary's ability to have an effect on headquarters decisions* regarding its role in relation to value-added activities and strategic responsibility. Consequently, this chapter will investigate what factors make subsidiaries influential in relation to role development. The more narrowly-defined research question to be analyzed is;

Research Question: what makes foreign-owned Chinese subsidiaries in the coatings industry influential and how does it have an effect on headquarters decisions regarding subsidiary role development?

Methodology and Delimitation

Three cases-Akzo Nobel, Flügger, and Hempel – are based on semi-structured interviews with one manager in each of the respective companies. Interviews were conducted in the Danish headquarters of Flügger and Hempel, and in a Danish subsidiary of Akzo Nobel. Interviews lasted 60-90 minutes, and were subsequently transcribed. Further information was collected from annual reports, newspapers, and journal articles.

On Subsidiaries in China

Before investigating the specific insights of the coatings industry, China, being the field of investigation, has on a general level been analyzed in relation to the foreign-owned subsidiary. Here, Walsh et al's.

(2002) study on small- and medium-sized enterprises documented a shift from wholly-owned subsidiaries which served export markets to a subsidiary focus on the development of firm-specific capabilities (rather than solely concentrating on utilizing low cost labour advantages). Buckley and Meng (2006) found that inward FDI in the Chinese manufacturing industry was typically oriented toward the local market. Cheung and Leung (2007) reported that MNCs in the Chinese advertising industry typically followed the internationalization process stage model, although operational changes were client-driven rather than a result of reduced market certainty. Researchers like Hong et al. (2005) analyzed knowledge transfer issues; in this survey the authors investigated how Japanese manufacturing firms transferred organizational learning systems to Chinese subsidiaries. Wilkinson et al. (2005) studied the human resource barriers to the establishment of local partnership arrangements through a survey of 47 UK-owned subsidiaries in China. Lou (2003) examined the performance of 196 MNC subsidiaries in China, and proved how the parent firm's control flexibility, resource commitment, and focus on local responsiveness positively influenced performance. Sanyal and Guvenli (2000) also observed a relation between control and performance in their sample of American firms and their subsidiaries in China. Subsidiary performance was the focal point in another survey by Lou (1997). This study showed factors such as product quality, sales force marketing, industry selection and timing of entry and in general the interaction between business strategy and investment strategy as influential factors of subsidiary performance. A recent survey by Xu et al. (2006) showed that private foreign-owned firms performed better than the state-owned firms.

Only the survey by Walsh et al. (2002) directly investigated changes in subsidiary role, primarily as an outcome of improved host country economic conditions leading to increased wages. The other surveys indicate dense relationships between the subsidiary and the local environment, which theoretically lead to an unbalanced subsidiary position vis-à-vis the corporate-driven institutions. Indications of this situation is inward FDI focusing on the local market, and only in few cases on re-export, the client-driven impact on internationalization processes, and in general the relationship between a focus on local responsiveness and subsidiary performance.

The Coatings Industry

The coatings industry is the supplier of colours and decorative surfaces which surround us in almost every area of life. Nearly every commodity we use in our daily lives – including the houses we live in and the infrastructure we utilize – have been coated. Paints and coatings are primarily used to protect products from environmental effects and to improve their consumer appeal (McCann 2003). A report by Akzo Nobel (2005) provides insights of this industry. In this report coatings are categorized into a) architectural/decorative coatings (i.e., paints, lacquers, and varnishes that protect and decorate surfaces like walls, doors, window frames, etc.), b) industrial coatings, which include all consumer durable products and all types of industrial equipment, and finally, c) special-purpose coatings including subgroups like protective coatings (i.e., for steel and concrete structures, car refinishes, marine coatings, and aerospace).

The report reveals that in 2005 the global coatings market was worth US$ 85.7 billion which is analogous to 26.5 billion litres. Since 2001, the annual average growth rate has been 2.7 percent in constant value terms and 4.2 in terms of volume. The growth rates in constant value terms for Asia Pacific were 26.3 percent. Western Europe diminished by -3.5 percent. Eastern Europe had the highest growth rate of 42.8 percent. These substantial differences are caused by the shift from US and Western Europe's status as the primary centres of manufacturing to the current state of production off-shoring and outsourcing to Asia and Eastern Europe. In 2005, the USA was still the world's largest market (US$ 18.8 billion). China, however, approaches this value; with a growth rate from 2001 and 2005 totalling 92 percent, the Chinese market ended 2005 with a value of US$ 7.3 billion.

China has grown extensively in both the property sector and within industrial coatings (i.e., especially appliances, automotive, and electronic industries.) Wang (2006) reported that the Chinese coatings industry increased by 14 percent in 2004 (based on a report from China National Coatings Industry Association). Since China hosts the 2008 Olympic Games, further growth is estimated for the architectural sector, and it is, therefore, not surprising that Phillips (2007) clams that China is to be the 'spearhead' of the Asian Coatings market.

The Three Cases
Hempel
Hempel was founded in 1915 as a wholesale business of ready-mixed paints for the Danish maritime industry. Since its establishment, Hempel has been a supplier to the Maersk Shipping Company. Hempel began its export activities as early as 1920 (Bernhard 1988). Throughout the Nineteenth century, related businesses have been added to the

product portfolio, such as coatings for containers, bridges, and yachts, as well as protective and decorative paintings. In 2005, Hempel's turnover was DKK 980 million (71 million litres) and the company employed 400 staff members in Denmark. Hempel is present in 83 countries, represented by 20 factories, 47 sales offices, three R&D centres, and more then 130 stock points (i.e., whole-sales units in ports.)

China became a market for Hempel in the mid-1950s, primarily in order to supply to the Maersk Corporation. The market entrance took place through a sales agent; later the market was accessed through a subsidiary in Hong Kong. Local production advantages and market opportunities were the initial reasons for the direct investment. A licence agreement with Hai Hong Chemicals, a division of China Merchants Group (CMG) (a state-owned conglomerate), has over time transformed into a joint venture Hempel-Hai Hong (HHH) that includes three factories (Yantai, Kunshan, and Shekou), six sales offices and nine stock points. Synergy effects were the strategic motivation for the joined activities of the Hempel subsidiary and the CMG affiliate, since Hempel gained access to manufacturing facilities, and CMG accessed the high value brand of Hempel, though the CMG brand (Seagull) is still offered to the local market. CMG has for a long time being a sleeping partner, but has recently, due to the growth and success of HHH, taken a greater interest in the business, which has resulted in the replacement of some of the Danish managers. The CEO of HHH is Danish, but to cite the interview respondent:

It is important that the Danish Management remains loyal, keeps the contact to Denmark, pays attention to Hempels' interest, and simultaneously services a Chinese partner that takes more and more control in the company.

In 2004 HHH employed 750 persons in China. Hempel has, furthermore, a clear segmentation strategy, operating within the following product lines a) containers; b) bridges; 3) harbour installations (e.g., cranes); d) road markings; e) tanks for oil and gas; and f) pipe lines. The selection of segments depends on both local and global market opportunities, but with the Chinese market strengths within these segments, HHH becomes an important player in the Hempel Corporation. For example, HHH has been able to win several important contracts in a growing property market where Hempel supplies to the two largest real-estate contractors. Secondly, the company delivers paint to bridges, and HHH recently won the contract for what will be the world's longest cable-stayed bridge: the Sutong Bridge that connects the cities of Suzhou and Nantong. Finally, Hempel supplies coatings to containers, 95 percent of which are currently produced in China. The recent move of most of the world's container production from Europe to China has given HHH a lucrative position in the corporation. Finally, HHH's presence (i.e., three factories) in China enables HHH to deliver large quantities with short lead times, ensuring its competitive position in the container market.

HHH's market mandate is geographically focused on China. However, in cases where the Singaporean unit – a wholly-owned subsidiary paint producer for the subsidiaries in Korea and Taiwan – lacks capacity, the Chinese production capacity is utilized for this purpose. The Singaporean unit possesses this production mandate because of Hempel's full ownership, which directly minimizes the power of HHH (since it is a joint venture) and its ability to obtain mandates serving other markets outside China. Regarding autonomy, the distribution of production and market mandates is solely made by headquarters. Previously, the Chinese subsidiary possessed high operational autonomy, but this has decreased over the years, and is today more centralized. Product development issues are also primarily centralized, though subsidiaries are here consulted regarding this issue.

The joint venture has its strengths through its low cost production, but this is considered by management in Denmark not to be a situation of resource dependency. The establishment primarily gains its power through its current performance and the high likelihood of a significantly positive future performance. The size of the subsidiary, furthermore, produces negation strength, since the Chinese entity takes 1/3 of turnover, volume, and number of employees. HHH is, therefore, the biggest subsidiary entity in the Hempel and is for that reason relatively more influential than the other subsidiaries in the corporation. Also the downturn of ship and container production in Europe, and China's future importance for these markets, together with the prospect within building constructions, place HHH in a very influential position in the corporation.

Flügger
Flügger is a Danish company within the decorative sector. The Danish company was established in 1890 as a subsidiary of the German company J.D. Flügger. The Danish subsidiary was nationalized following Second World War and was spin-off from the German ownership. Later the German company closed down its production in 1973. In

2004/05 Flügger had a turnover of DKK 750 million and employed 548 persons. Today Flügger has nine subsidiaries: seven are located in the Nordic countries, one is located in Poland, and one is located in China (i.e., Flügger Coating (Shanghai) Co Ltd.) The business model of Flügger is to sell directly to both professional decorators as well as to customers via retail shops. One third of the sales outlets are wholly-owned and the remainder operates through franchise agreements. This retail shop structure is implemented in the Nordic countries, where the company's products are offered through 750 retail shops. However, in China, decorative coatings are sold directly to building contractors or professional decorators.

Flügger's internationalization process followed the track described through the Uppsala internationalization model (Johanson and Vahlne 1977), with incremental steps of geographical representation. Following the Oil Crises in 1973-74, the company saw the need to expand its activities and, therefore, Flügger established its first subsidiary in 1975 in Norway. Throughout the 1990s, the company made a series of acquisitions in Scandinavia and in Poland. The investment in China broke the logic of the incremental internationalization process, and rather fit into the description offered through the Born Global literature that surveys the reasons for companies leapfrogging the Uppsala development. One explanation given for this break in process is the international background and mindset of the founder/manager (Knight and Cavusgil 2005), which was relevant in this case, due to the background and interest in China of one of the company's CEO's. Initially, Flügger secured a license agreement with a governmental-owned, but highly autonomous producer of combat aircraft, in order to supply coatings to the plant buildings. Flügger decided not to produce locally but rather decided to transport the paint from Denmark due to low shipment costs. In fact, the respondent claimed that it was cheaper to ship a container by boat from Denmark to China, than to transport it between two Danish cities by truck!

The Chinese subsidiary was established in 2005 as a wholly-owned unit employing 20 people. In 2007 the subsidiary employed 35 people. The role of the subsidiary is to market the corporate products, including paint and wallpaper. Due to the demand in the Chinese market for Danish design, wallpaper gained a strong market position. Over time, Flügger's subsidiary has extended its geographical mandates, and today it re-exports products to other Asian markets. The second role of the subsidiary is to purchase related products such as paintbrushes for resale in the Nordic countries. In this case, China demonstrates its advantages due to its access to cheap raw materials and low labour costs.

Flügger plans to expand the role of its subsidiary by establishing a production plant as a greenfield investment, which is going to be controlled by the Chinese subsidiary. Reasons for this change include high Chinese tariffs on imported goods, long delivery times on paint shipped from Denmark, cheaper raw materials, and, according to the company, new European regulations demanding approval of all chemicals, which demands substantial resources in order to produce the needed documentation.

There have also been changes in the level of autonomy of Flügger's subsidiary. The subsidiary is managed and controlled by a Danish expatriate, whereas all mid-level managers are Chinese. Most employees have been job-rotated to the Danish headquarters. Beyond the financial control, the expatriate exercises social control in order to avoid issues like corruption and the use of child labour. Initially, the subsidiary was assigned a high degree of autonomy, as the interview respondent revealed:

Bureaucracy is a killer in the start-up phase.

When the subsidiary reached 30 employees, it became more controlled by headquarters. The subsidiary still possesses a high level of operational autonomy with respect to its purchasing activities – a typical example of a resource dependency situation as the result of local expertise and the subsidiary's direct link and relationships with local suppliers.

Flügger further plans to change its corporate structure from the functional-based form to the area-based multi-divisional form, which is a typical path of MNCs when entries into new geographical markets create further complexity and ambiguity, thus making the functional form inefficient to control and manage the company (Chandler 1962; Stopford and Wells 1972). This change will certainly impact the role of the Chinese subsidiary, becoming a divisional headquarters of the corporation. Today, functions like marketing, finance, and the like are exercised through the Danish headquarters but a change of structure will imply strategic and operational decision making power to the Chinese unit.

The decision to turn the Chinese unit into a divisional headquarters is directly linked to the current and future market opportunities, and the profit that the subsidiary already is able to produce. The purchasing expertise, the market strength, and the future economic prospects of China bring influence to this subsidiary.

Akzo Nobel
The Danish paint producing company Holmblad was established 1777. In 1912 it merged with a paint producer Sadolin (established in 1907) to form the Sadolin & Holmblad Corporation. In 1945, the company established its first subsidiary abroad: Sadolin Färgfabrik and in this period Export activities to the Far East began (Bernhard 1988). Following the Second World War, the company acquired firms in the Far East. In 1987, Sadolin & Holmblad was acquired by the Swedish MNC, Nobel, which in 1994 merged with the Dutch corporation Akzo – hereafter renamed Akzo Nobel. The former establishment of Sadolin & Holmblad – today named Akzo Nobel Decorative Coatings – belongs to the division of coatings, and produces and markets paints, varnishes, and wood care products.

In 2005, Akzo Nobel closed down production in Copenhagen, primarily due to environmental reasons, since the plant was located in the centre of Copenhagen, and would needed heavy investment in order to meet new environmental regulations. The turnover of DKK 91 million in 2005 was, therefore, half of the turnover from the previous year, though the company managed to increase its profits in this period with 16 percent. In 2005 the Copenhagen unit employed 75 people. Increased competition in the industry has created a need for further rationalizations, leading to divestment of other European factories, and a stronger focus on the Asian market, since headquarters viewed Asia as a future growth market. To provide examples, Akzo Nobel acquired the Ferro Powder Coatings activities in America and Asia to expand its global position in powder coatings, and expanded it commitment in affiliates in Korea and Vietnam. Further, the company commissioned a coil coatings facility in Suzhou, China, and finally it build two wood coatings sites in China, and invested in a non-stick coatings facility in Dongguan City (McCann 2003).

The 2006 revenues of Akzo Nobel were Euros 13,737 millions, and the MNC employed 61,900 people. Akzo Nobel operates with three divisions: Health Care, Chemicals, and Coatings. The latter produces 45 percent of revenues, which are distributed over four sub-divisions: Decorative (36 percent), Industrial coatings (31 percent), Car Refinishes (15 percent), and Marine & Protective Coatings (18 percent). In total, 11 percent of revenues are produced in Asia (compared with

Europe's 61 percent) and 17 percent of the staff is employed in Asia (compared with Europe's 51 percent).

Since the 1980's Akzo Nobel has been active in China. Originally, the firm exported its products through five representative offices. Today, the company has 20 establishments in China, which include both joint ventures and wholly-owned subsidiaries. In China, Akzo Nobel operates within the following businesses: Car Refinishes, Decorative Coatings, Industrial Finishes, Industrial Products, Marine and Protective Coatings, and Powder Coatings.

This paper focuses on the subsidiary Akzo Nobel Decorative Coatings, which is headquartered in Shanghai, and which also maintains offices in Beijing and Guangzhou. Before the establishment of this wholly-owned subsidiary in 1998, Akzo Nobel formed two joint ventures, which both failed. The main products offered by the subsidiary are interior and exterior decorative paints.

Initially, the subsidiary was assigned the mandate to market the corporation's products, whereas production was carried out by another subsidiary. Products are sold through small retail shops offering a high variety of national and international brands, though with high preferences for local brands. A goal to sell 5 million litres was set for the subsidiary in order to obtain a production mandate; this goal was reached in 2003.

Akzo Nobel aims to be one of the largest players in this market, which today is led by Nippon (with a market share of 11 percent) and ICI (with a market share of 6 percent). The remaining producers take less than 1 percent of the market respectively, and in total, the interview respondent estimated there are more than 8,000 plants in China.

Because of Akzo Nobel's growth strategy, the subsidiary has been able to obtain acquisition mandates from headquarters, in order to grow in production capacity, to obtain local brands, and to secure a geographically appropriate spread of plants in China. Geographical proximity is needed in the construction industry, where the final product order is often placed late in the construction process. As the interview respondent explained:

The contract is made with the architect or with the contractor, you negotiate throughout the planning period, and suddenly when the concrete is dried – then you have to deliver within a very short time period – so you have to be close by.

Akzo Nobel decorative coatings decided to acquire a small local producer (10 million litres) in South China, following a negotiation period of more than 2.5 years. In Northern China, Akzo Nobel has established a greenfield plant, and plans a future establishment in Central China.

Dense relationships to local partners are a key factor for success, in the citation above illustrated by the long negotiations with contractors throughout the construction period. This high degree of local responsiveness is, furthermore, relevant in relation to the subsidiary's R&D activities. Often, local adaptations of paint formulations are needed in order to meet specific customers' requests. Factors like building materials, weather conditions, product applications, and the degree of pollution can create specific product needs, making corporate formulations obsolete. The R&D department further controls the quality of raw materials and finished goods.

Akzo Nobel organizes its activities via the multi-divisional structure, and, according to the respondent, the complexity the company faces in terms of product diversity and cultures has initiated centralization processes, and decisions about which geographical markets subsidiaries should serve, and strategic decisions concerning Human Resource Management, Corporate Social Responsibility, and financial practices are solely made in headquarters. Operational decisions concerning sales are the only value-chain activity to be decentralized. Furthermore, headquarters' requests for documentation and throughout descriptions for projects approval have been increasing. Subsidiary-driven initiatives need careful descriptions of the project and budgets to be presented for a committee in the Swedish regional board, which often requires further clarifications and specifications in order to accept the application. The Swedish regional board will then present the application to the board in headquarters in Holland. One example here was the acquisition of the Chinese coatings factory. The subsidiary easily got the approval to search for acquisition targets, but the subsidiary manager – a Danish expatriate – had to negotiate the screening criteria with the board members in Sweden. He must continually write descriptions of market opportunities, technologies, environmental issues, taxes, legal affairs, and especially risk assessments.

What makes this subsidiary influential is first and foremost its location in China, and secondarily the fact it is managed by an expatriate. Today the media and the public pay attention to China, and naturally headquarters' managers also watch China closely – manifested in yearly or quarterly visits from the corporate headquarters. As in the other cases, geography brings influence, and for that reason alone the subsidiary is strong. It can more easily develop its role (e.g., gaining production mandates, building plants, making acquisitions) compared to other subsidiaries. As our interview respondent stated:

It's easier to be subsidiary manager in China than in Bulgaria.

However, subsidiary role development depends on the allocation of resources from headquarters. Akzo Nobel is organized as an 'internal market', where the subsidiaries compete for these resources. The expatriate manager plays a key role in this game, since he or she often has a competitive advantage – compared to local managers – in terms of ability to communicate and to formulate the detailed report requirements from the West European headquarters. Our Interview Respondent expressed it in this way:

An expatriate manager is a key actor that can match and translate local business opportunities into project descriptions that is approved by headquarters – here I see myself as a intermediary between two worlds.

Subsidiary development, especially for those subsidiaries that culture-wise are far away from headquarters, therefore, depends on expatriate managers with ambitions and cleverness to translate local market opportunities to projects of interest for headquarters managers. The interview respondents gave several examples of subsidiaries that were started up with local management: managers who lacked the communicative competences, were too embedded in the local context, and who preferred managerial principles that did not fit the internal corporate competitive forces. Our interview respondent viewed expatriates as 'outsiders' (beyond the management and control functions they served) who could change the underperforming subsidiary into a success, and who could pave the way for subsidiary development. Subsidiary power in Akzo Nobel, therefore, relates to a combination of local expertise: in this case knowledge of how to operate in Chinese context, but also to position the subsidiary in the corporate Western European context. As the interview respondent stated:

You have negotiation power when you can formulate and sell your message to the Board. You need to be embedded in the culture of writing of concrete executive summaries, to make budgets, etc., this is the way to convince. Secondly, performance counts. How-

ever, it is also important with the network – whom to make phone calls to. I can call informally the Business Unit CEO in Stockholm. I have known him for many years.

The lobbying effect and the strength of personal networks are emphasized here. At the end of the day, the development of Akzo Nobel Decorative Coatings depended on its ability to convince headquarters management to allocate the needed resources and mandates for that purpose. Convincing management was achieved through lobbying power, gained via its position in China, but also the manager's ability to minimize the cultural distance between Holland/Sweden and China.

Conclusions and Perspectives for Further Research
The size and the profitable prospects of China without doubt make Chinese subsidiaries influential. Foreign-owned entities of MNCs are likely to develop the subsidiary role, measured as changes in activity and autonomy. However, the performance aspect is certainly the mediator between market opportunity and role development. In the case of the coatings industry in China, the ability to win contracts is of utmost importance: i.e., contracts in real estate, bridges, ships, etc. This often creates resource dependency situation, since winning these contracts demand both local connections and cultural knowledge. China is the 'hot spot' these years, since much of the production of containers, ships, and furniture now takes place in China. This positions the Chinese subsidiary relatively stronger than other subsidiaries in the coatings industry. China is, though, under pressure from countries like Vietnam – also a low cost area – where companies can access cheap labour and raw materials for coatings production and related by-products.

Changes in organizational structures, lead to further decentralization of mandates and strategic responsibility, increasing the prospect of influence. One the one hand, implementation of multi-divisional structures extends the level of formalized control mechanisms. On the other hand, converting a subsidiary into a division, as in the Flügger case, absolutely expresses autonomy and decision-making power. In these cases where geography is the ordering principles for divisions (alternatively it could be product/industry), China is likely to host the divisional centre for the Asian market, given the country's size and relative importance in this region. This development, though, needs to be seen in the current level of autonomy, where all three cases showed increased centralization of decision making rights. The change in subsidiary role, further, is driven by rather strict criteria, like reaching a specific sales figure, in order to gain a production mandate. Reaching pre-specified milestones is apparently important for subsidiary role development.

Finally, micro-political issues in terms of negotiations between subsidiary and headquarters management is of uttermost importance. The personal relationships of the subsidiary manager and his or her negotiation skills advocate for subsidiary influence in cases of expatriate management. Apparently, expatriate management is better to manage institutional duality than local management. In the case of Akzo Nobel, seemingly this factor is of higher importance, than the presumed performance effects of local management and its ability to fulfil local responsiveness. This is an interesting outlook, as dense relationships, which apparently is a key factor for winning contracts, on the one is essential to gain influence via performance, though, on the other hand, the concept of 'over-embeddedness' (Woolcock 1998) can be an obstacle to role developments. This relationship is recommended to be the focus for future investigations of subsidiary role development.

References

Akzo Nobel: The Global Coatings Report 2006, http://platform.akzonobel.com/Akzo.Web.GDS/Asset.aspx?id=59cd1d55-4a1e-497c-9bdd-fd156e23a11c&noredirect=true [accessed 15 June 2007].

Bartlett, C. A. and S. Ghoshal 1989. *Managing Across Borders – The Transnational Solution.* London: Century Business.

Benito, G. et al. 2003. 'Environmental Issues on MNE Subsidiary Roles: Economic Integration and the Nordic Countries.' *Journal of International Business Studies* 34(5): 443-456.

Bernhard, B. 1988. *Sådan Skabtes Danmarks Store Virksomheder.* København: Erhvervsbladet.

Birkinshaw, J. 1999. 'The Determinants and Consequences of Subsidiary Initiative in Multinational Corporations.' *Entrepreneurship Theory and Practice* 24(1): 9-36.

Birkinshaw, J. and N. Hood 1997. 'An Empirical Study of Development Processes in Foreign-owned Subsidiaries in Canada and Scotland.' *Management International Review* 37(4): 339-364.

Birkinshaw, J. and N. Hood 2000. 'Characteristics of Foreign Subsidiaries in Industry Clusters.' *Journal of International Business Studies* 31(1): 141-154.

Birkinshaw, J. et al. 2005. 'Subsidiary Entrepreneurship, Internal and External Competitive Forces, and Subsidiary Performance.' *International Business Review* 14(2): 227-248.

Birkinshaw, J. and A. J. Morrison 1995. 'Configurations of Strategy and Structure in Subsidiaries of Multinational Corporations.' *Journal of International Business Studies* 26(4): 729-753.

Buckley, P. J. and C. Meng, 2006. 'The Strategy of Foreign-Invested Manufacturing Enterprises in China: Export-orientated and Market-orientated FDI Revisited'. P. J. Buckley (ed). *The Multinational Enterprise and the Globalization of Knowledge.* Houndsmills, Basingstoke: Palgrave Macmillan 2006: 283-308.

Chandler, A. 1962. *Strategy and Structure.* Cambridge MA: MIT Press.

Cheung, F. S. L. and W-F Leung 2007. 'International Expansion of Transnational Advertising Agencies in China: An Assessment of the Stages Theory Approach.' *International Business Review* 16(2): 251-268.

Cyert, R. M. and J. G. March 1963. *Behavioral Theory of the Firm.* Englewood Cliffs: Prentice-Hall.

Delany, E. 1998. 'Strategic Development of Multinational Subsidiaries in Ireland.' in Birkinshaw, J., and N. Hood (Eds.). *Multinational Corporate Evolution and Subsidiary Development.* Houndsmill, Basingstoke: Macmillan Press 1998: 239-267.

DiMaggio, P. J. and K. Powell 1983. 'The Iron Cage Revisited: Institutional Isomorphism and Collective Rationality in Organizational Fields.' *American Sociological Review* 13(2): 147-160.

Dörrenbächer, C. and J. Gammelgaard 2006. 'Subsidiary Role Development: The Effect of Micro-political Headquarters-subsidiary Negotiations on the Product, Market, and Value-added scope of Foreign-owned Subsidiaries.' *Journal of International Management* 12(3): 266-283.

Dörrenbächer, C. and M. Geppert 2006. 'Micro-politics and Conflicts in Multinational Corporations: Current Debates, Re-framing, and Contributions of this Special Issue.' *Journal of International Management* 12(3): 251-265

Egelhoff, W.G. et al. 1998. 'Using Technology as a Path to Subsidiary Development.' In Birkinshaw, J. and N. Hood (eds). *Multinational Corporate Evolution and Subsidiary Development.* Houndsmill, Basingstoke: Macmillan Press: 213-238

Fligstein, N. 1985. 'The Spread of the Multidivisional Form among Large Firms, 1919-1979.' *American Sociological Review* 50(June): 377-391.

Forsgren, M. et al. 2005. *Managing the Embedded Multinational: A Business Network View.* Chelterham: Edward Elgar.

French, J. R. P., Jr. and B. Raven 1959. 'The Bases of Social Power.' In Cartwright, D. (ed). *Studies in Social Power.* Ann Arbor: University of Michigan Press: 150-167.

Holm, U. et al. 2003. 'Subsidiary Impact on Host-country Economies – The Case of Foreign-owned Subsidiaries Attracting Investment into Sweden.' *Journal of Economic Geography* 3(4): 389-408.

Hong, J. F. L. et al. 2005. 'Transferring Organizational Learning Systems to Japanese subsidiaries in China.' *Journal of Management Studies* 43(5): 1027-1058.

Hood, N. et al. 1994. 'Strategic Evolution within Japanese Manufacturing Plants in Europe: UK Evidence.' *International Business Review* 3(2): 97-122.

Jarillo, J.C. and J. I. Martínez 1990. 'Different Roles for Subsidiaries: The Case of Multinational Corporations in Spain.' *Strategic Management Journal* 11(7): 501-513.

Johanson, J. and J. E. Vahlne 1977. 'The Internationalization Process of the Firm – A Model of Knowledge Development and Increasing Market Commitments.' *Journal of International Business Studies* 8(1): 23-32.

Knight, G. A. and S. T. Cavusgil 2003. A Taxonomy of Born-global Firms.' *Management International Review* 45(3): 15-35.

Kostova, T. and K. Roth 2002. 'Adoption of an Organizational Practice by Subsidiaries of Multinational Corporations: Institutional and Relational Effects.' *Academy of Management Journal* 45(1): 215-233.

Luo, Y. 1997. 'Performance Implications of International Strategy: An Empirical Study of Foreign-Invested Enterprises in China.' *Group and Organization Management* 22(1): 87-113.

Luo, Y. 2003. 'Market – seeking MNEs in an Emerging Market: How Parent-subsidiary Links Shape Overseas Success.' *Journal of International Business Studies* 34(3): 290-309.

McCann, C. 2003. *Global Paints & Coatings Industry Competitors.* Case published at the European Case Clearing House. Babson College.

Mudambi, R. and P. Navarra 2004. 'Divisional Power, Intra-firm Bargaining and Rent-seeking Behavior in Multidivisional Corporations.' *Economics Bulletin* 4(3): 1-10.

Nohria, N. and S. Ghoshal (1997), *The differentiated network – organizing multinational corporations for value creation.* Jossey-Bass Publishers, San Francisco.

O'Donnell, S. 2000. 'Managing Foreign Subsidiaries: Agents of Headquarters, or an Interdependent Network?' *Strategic Management Journal* 21(5), 525-548.

Pearce, R. 1999. 'The Evolution of Technology in Multinational Enterprises: The Role of Creative Subsidiaries'. *International Business Review* 8(2): 125-148.

Pfeffer, J. and G. R. Salancik 1978. *The External Controls of Organizations – A Resource Dependence Perspective.* New York: Harper & Row Publishers.

Pfeffer, J. 1981. *Power in Organizations.* Boston: Pitman.

Phillips, K. 2007. 'China to 'Spearhead' Powder Coatings Growth in Asia'. *Chemical Week* January 3/10: 32.

Porter, M.E. 1985. *Competitive Advantage: Creating and Sustaining Superior Performance.* New York: The Free Press.

Roth, K. and A. J. Morrison 1992. 'Implementing Global Strategy: Characteristics of Global Subsidiaries.' *Journal of International Business Studies* 23(4): 715-735.

Sanyal, R. N. and Guvenli, T. (2000). 'Introducing Modern Management Control Techniques in an Economy in Transition: The Experience of American Firms in China.' *The Mid-Atlantic Journal of Business* 36(4): 217-228.

Scott, R.W. 1995. *Institutions and Organizations.* Thousand Oaks: Sage.

Stopford, J. M. and L. T. Wells 1972. *Managing the Multinational Enterprise: Organization of the Firm and Ownership of Subsidiaries.* London: Longman.

Surlemont, B. 1998. 'A Typology of Centres within Multinational Corporations: An Empirical Investigation.' In Birkinshaw, J. and N. Hood (eds). *Multinational Corporate Evolution and Subsidiary Development.* Houndsmill, Basingstoke: Macmillan Press: 162-188

Taggart, J. H. 1998a. 'Identification and Development of Strategy at Subsidiary Level. In Birkinshaw, J. and N. Hood (eds). *Multinational Corporate Evolution and Subsidiary Development.* Houndsmill, Basingstoke: Macmillan Press: 23-49.

Taggart, J. H. 1998b. 'Strategy Shifts in MNC Subsidiaries.' *Strategic Management Journal* 19(7): 663-681.

Taggart, J. H. and N. Hood 1999. 'Determinants of Autonomy in Multinational Corporation Subsidiaries.' *European Management Journal* 17(2): 226-236.

Walsh, S. et al. 2002. 'The Evolution of Technology Management Practice in Developing Economies: Findings from Northern China.' *International Journal of Technology Management* 24(2/3): 311-329.

Wang, L. 2006. 'China Meets Consumer Demand.' *Asia Pacific Coatings Journal* 19(1): 42.

White, R.E. and T. A. Poynter 1984. 'Strategies for Foreign-owned Subsidiaries in Canada.' *Business Quarterly* 49(2): 59-69.

Wilkinson, B. et al. 2005. 'Human Resource Barriers to Partnership Sourcing in China.' *The International Journal of Human Resource Management* 16(10): 1886-1900.

Woolcock, M. 1998. 'Social Capital and Economic Development: Toward a Theoretical Synthesis and Policy Framework.' *Theory and Society* 27(2): 151-208.

Xu, D. et al. 2006. 'Performance of Domestic and Foreign-invested Enterprises in China.' *Journal of World Business* 41(3): 261-274.

Zaheer, S. and Mosakowski, E. 1997. 'The Dynamics of the Liability of Foreignness: A Global Study of Survival in Financial Services.' *Strategic Management Journal* 18(6): 439-464.

CHAPTER FIVE

Guanxi Capital as a Sustainable Competitive Advantage

Mette Bjørn and Verner Worm

Today, it seems that fathoming China is still difficult. The Chinese dragon has risen and the world is trying to come to terms with the phenomenon. Western firms are scrambling for competitiveness in stagnating home markets. Therefore, firms are expanding to markets further and further away from home: to markets that are radically different in every aspect. One such market that has experienced a tremendous influx of investment is China. Firms hope that China will secure long-term profitability and competitiveness. These firms have been forced to rethink their strategic approaches; as a result, scholars must rethink their strategies, as well. The focus of this chapter is to introduce the new endogenous concept of *guanxi* capital and analyses how it can be used to build sustainable competitive advantages for western companies. The chapter contributes to the contextualization of strategic management by focusing on *guanxi* capital.

Research Question:
What is *guanxi* capital?

What are the dynamics and constraints of *guanxi* capital in explaining sustainable competitive advantage of a western company's Chinese operation?

To focus on *guanxi*, we do not contend that *guanxi* is the only important parameter for attaining competitive advantage. For example, others researchers argue forcefully for "cost innovation" as another important strategic tool for firms in China (Zeng and Williamson 2007). We do assert, however, that *guanxi* is a significant – although within itself insufficient–precondition for attaining sustainable competitive advantage. We will also touch upon the potential pitfalls. In order to place *guanxi* in relation to western theories that come close to *guanxi* capital theory, we will begin by briefly exploring social capital theory. These theories are inadequate to solve the strategic challenges of the Western firms in China, however.

Methodologically, this chapter is to some extent empirically supported by a confidential case company which has experienced successful operations in China for more than 10 years; the manager of this company has applied a *guanxi*-based strategy.

Social Capital

The central proposition of social capital theory holds that networks of relationships constitute an omnipotent direction for human behaviour (Bourdieu 1986). As indicated by Lin (2001), the notion of social capital contains the following ingredients: Resources embedded in a social structure; accessibility to such social resources by individuals; and the use or mobilization of such social resources by individuals in purposive actions.

One of the most widely used definitions derives from Bourdieu (1986) who consider social capital is the sum of the actual as well as potential resources embedded within, available through, and derived from the network of relationships possessed by an individual or social unit. It comprises both the network and the assets that may be mobilised through a network of mutual acquaintance and recognition.

Thus, social capital is a public good that consists of aspects of social structure and facilitate actions of individuals within the structure (Coleman, 2005). Social capital consists of the sum of the *"relational capital"* several individuals jointly hold and is governed by norms of reciprocity, which are enforced by peer pressure and gain or loss in reputation.

Guanxi as a contextual form of social capital is a personal relational asset and the discussions proceed with the individual in mind. While the authors make claims about the correlation between *guanxi* as a personal asset and those that are collective, i.e. generalised trust promotes trust in personal relations, the objective is the benefits accrued to the individual.

Trust is a critical building block of *guanxi* and within the collectivistic Chinese society (Kumar and Worm 2003). Therefore a further discussion of the concept follows.

Trust

Trust in relation to social capital relates to coordinating current behaviour and enlarging the extent of future cooperative behaviour. Efficiency within complex systems of coordinated actions is only possible when actors interact effectively (McAllister 1995). Trust between actors is seen as a determining factor. Hence, trust is important when leveraging social capital. Trust is what enables collaboration. Fukyama (1995: 26) defines trust as *"the expectation that arises within a community of regular, honest and cooperative behaviour, based on commonly shared norms, on the part of other members of that community"*. Trust emerges and develops over time. Social capital depends on the stability and continuity of social structures (Nahapiet and Ghoshal 1998). Thus, relationship stability and durability are network features associated with high levels of trust and norms of cooperation. Nahapiet and Ghoshal (1998: 242) write: *"trust lubricates cooperation, and cooperation itself breeds trust"*. In a void of trust, neither the production nor mobilisation of social capital is possible.

The concept of trust has been separated into various components. One such separation lies in cognitive-based trust and affect-based trust (McAllister 1995). *Guanxi* usually has a larger component of emotional trust, a trust that is based on affectional feelings and emotional ties (Kumar and Worm 2003). It is defined as *"trust grounded in reciprociated inter-personal care and corncern (McAllister 1995: 24)"*. Cognitive trust relates to trust as a result of the trustee's perception of the other's integrity and capabilities to adhere to obligations. It is defined as *"trust grounded in individual beliefs about peer reliability and dependability"* (McAllister 1995: 25). Generalised and institutional trust resembles the trust concerned with social capital as a collective asset, that is, generally trusting individuals and institutions. The trust component of *guanxi* has more of a personal and a more polycontextual nature (Shapiro et al. 2007); the important point is that polycontextual, interpersonal trust and the relational dimension of social capital best capture the priciples behind *guanxi*. Interpersonal trust in this chapter represents *"The extent to which a person is confident in and willing to act on the basis of, the words, actions, and decisions of another"* (McAllister 1995:37), and will be a important element for defining *guanxi* capital.

The Neglects of Theories of Personal Networks

Social capital has become a much-discussed concept in Western management literature. Most results of social capital are positive; however negative consequences exist as well. Firms high in social capital may become inflexible through their relatively restricted access to diverse sources of ideas and information (Nahapiet and Ghoshal 1998). This is due to the density and frequency of interaction in these networks.

Moreover, the boundaries of social capital create opportunity cost. The ties within one network may forestall ties in other networks and current networks demand both time and money investments. Network relationships built over time become self-reinforcing and could lead to path dependency; firms can only access and develop resources allowed by network ties (Hitt, Lee and Yucel 2002) At the individual level, social ties can restrict individual freedoms and bar outsiders from gaining access to the same resources (Portes 1998). Individuals may also become restricted in their individual freedoms, because due to the level of social control (Fukuyama 1995).

Conversely, there is little acknowledgement on behaviour directed by feelings of sentiment and fondness, which is pivotal to *guanxi*. While feelings of affection are touched on in relation to family and church in Coleman's texts, they are rarely mentioned in a broader context. Similarly Burt's views actors as self-maximising entities operating in a competitive environment in search of information that will enable controlling the flow of that information piece and subsequently the action paths of others (Burt 1992).

Lastly and perhaps most importantly, the theory lacks consensus about how to measure social capital and how to separate cause and effect (Wu and Choi 2004).

The Nature of *Guanxi*

Network capitalism implies a system of reciprocity, trust and loyalty in a specific context. It is commitment and interdependence that creates value from the effective use of social capital, that is, relational capital (Hitt, Lee and Yucel 2002). This form of social capital is inherent in the personal network labelled *guanxi*. *Guanxi* is a cultural characteristic that has strong implications for interpersonal and interorganisational dynamics in Chinese society. As the word *guanxi* is an everyday word in the Chinese language, there is no consensus in the translation or definition of the term *guanxi* (Dunfee and Warren 2001). *Guanxi* is here defined as affectionate feelings with the implication of continued exchange of favour (Pye 1982). This is very different from an individualistic Western view, where affectionate feelings, such as friendship, prohibit rather than promote the exchange of favours. Contrary to this in collectivist China, characterized by an interdependent

Guanxi Capital as a Sustainable Competitive Advantage

self (Markus and Kitayama 1991) meaning that people define themselves in relation to others, friends have an obligation to help each other. *Guanxi* is cultivated extensively and governs attitudes towards long-term social and personal relationships. A Chinese saying states, *"Who you know (i.e. personal connections) is more important than what you know"* (Yeung and Tung 1996: 55). The practice of *guanxi* stems from Confucianism and collectivism, which is manifested in the importance of networks of interpersonal relations within the in-group. The characteristic of collectivist societies is a clear distinction between in-groups: such as the family (jiaren) and others (wairen). Collectivist societies like China tend to have low social trust (Fukuyama 1995). You care about your family – friends at the expense of strangers. People in poor societies cannot care about everybody. As some scholars perceive *guanxi* as the opposite of profit-oriented business (Jakobsen 2007) a more detailed description of the concept is presented below.

Figure 5:1 Dyadic & Concentric Guanxi

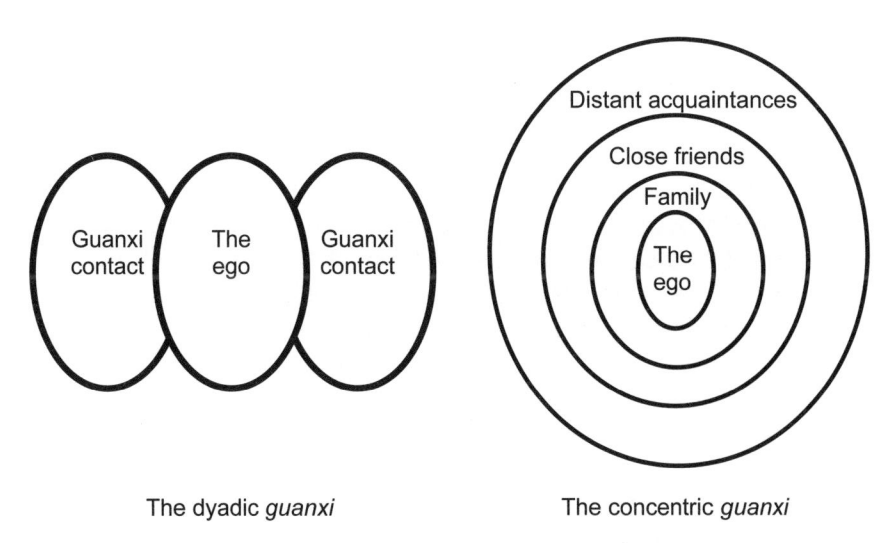

The dyadic *guanxi*   The concentric *guanxi*

Guanxi means "gate/pass" or "to connect" and reflects deliberate fibres woven into every aspect of Chinese society (Yeung and Tung 1996). Guanxi operates "in concentric circles with close family members at the core and with distant relatives, classmates, friends and acquaintances arranged at the periphery according to the distance of relationship and trust" (Park and Luo 2001: 460). When a situation arises which is outside the realm of the individual, guanxi relations are called upon for reaching desired outcome. Chinese society places great importance on face and guanxi emphasises the enjoyment of prestige without the loss of face. Face is a form of social currency and status, which is determined by one's social status and material wealth (Park and Luo 2001). It is chief to maintain a high level of face in order to cultivate and expand one's guanxi and status. The dyadic guanxi shows the linkages between the individual and guanxi contacts, the concentric circle shows the strengths of such contacts (Figure 5:1).

The principles that capture the nature of a *guanxi* network are:

Reciprocity: Reciprocal human obligations (Renqing) (Worm 1997) related to *guanxi* is an embedded resource representing an informal social obligation to another member as a result of calling upon a *guanxi* relationship. If one disregards this reciprocal human obligation, one hurts one's own and related parties' face and jeopardises the *guanxi* network (Park and Luo 2001). Renqing, face, and *guanxi* are consequently entangled and inseparable. In practice at least today there is an 'economic of *guanxi*' meaning that you cannot draw indefinitely on a relationship without contributing something in return. In a mutual relationship both parties must contribute something.

Transferability: Guanxi is transferable through a common connection, i.e. an intermediary. This means that unacquainted actors will only commence a business relation with each other, if introduced and recommended by a common connection (Luo 2000). It is clear that affection can be indirect as a basis for *guanxi* cultivation through an intermediary. In the holistic Chinese worldview 'my friend is your friend'.

Intangibility: Guanxi is an intangible resource embedded in a personal network. *Guanxi* is implicit in terms of code of conduct and specificity of interaction. *Guanxi* builds an unspoken expectation of unlimited exchange of favours (Luo 2000). Furthermore, *guanxi* is contextual, acts of *guanxi* are contingent on the situation and thus makes implementation an art rather than science.

Utilitarianism: Guanxi or affectionate personal relations in China is ultimately based on favours. *Guanxi* relations that violate the principles of *guanxi* are eventually discarded (Yeung and Tung 1996).

Long-term orientation: Guanxi is developed and reinforced through continuous long-term interaction and is often passed through generations. Westerners usually see networks efforts as isolated occurrences with immediate returns as the focal point (Luo 2000).

Personal: Guanxi has no group connotation; *guanxi* is a personal asset glued to the holder and is therefore largely different from inter-organisational networking in the West (Michailova and Worm 2003). The concept of inter-organisational *guanxi*, Guanxi Hu, where an organisation or governmental department is included in an individual's *guanxi* implies that individual becomes quite indispensable to the firm. The fact that *guanxi* is personal is often a surprise to western companies because an employee might promote a competitor's product at the expense of his employer's product because he has stronger *guanxi* with the competitor (Vanhonacker 2004).

Instrumental and Affective *Guanxi*
While there is discussion amongst scholars about how *guanxi* functions, there is debate about the purpose of *guanxi*. Some *guanxi* considered to have only instrumental or rent-seeking purposes (Su and Littlefield 2001), in Chinese called "*jiaoyi guanxi*" (utilitarian *guanxi*), contributes to corrupting the Chinese society, while real *guanxi* are expressive with favour-seeking obligations ("*renqing guanxi*") which is in accordance with Chinese cultural norms (Zhang and Zhang 2006). As China develops an increasingly efficient legal framework and infrastructure, and as some of the structural conditions for a relation-based society disappear, *guanxi* could become less important. This is especially true for *guanxi* that mainly relates to overcoming inefficiencies. *Guanxi* with this purpose has been criticised ever since the Communists came to power in 1949 (Guthrie 1998).

If *guanxi* is an integrative part of Chinese norms, *guanxi* will persist regardless of the marketplace as it is then culturally embedded (Yang 2002). The authors' view is that while *guanxi* naturally is contingent on the marketplace, i.e. the purposes for *guanxi* shifts with the marketplace, the emotional attachments associated with *guanxi* implies that *guanxi* remains even under an efficient marketplace. The cultural heritage with strong and often blood-based *guanxi* will remain; Hong Kong, Taiwan, and Japan are examples of *guanxi*/personal relations that survive in modern, rule-of-law societies. Each *guanxi* will have a distinctive weighting of personal and instrumental purposes, but most relations will aim at developing trust and face in order to cultivate relations that solve problems over the *long term*, which implies a cultivation of expressive *guanxi* (Luo 2000). The increasingly modern and open environment in China is likely to bring more emphasis on material values with more demanding and assertive *guanxi* partners (Vanhonacker 2004). The *guanxi* concept is also likely to mature, becoming less visible and more sophisticated with more emphasis on business outcomes than on politics and the acquisition of consumer goods. Nonetheless, *guanxi* relationships, with their unique code of ethics, will in a foreseeable future be an ingredient of every day life in China.

Can *Guanxi* be a Sustainable Competitive Advantage?

As *guanxi* is culturally embedded,- not merely a means to overcome inefficiencies – firms are continuously faced with *guanxi*-related challenges and opportunities, which mean that investigating these is an integral part of revealing sources of competitive advantage.

The focus on western theories of the firm such as the resource-based view (RBV) is on the individual firm; by specifying a resource-profile an optimal product-mix profile can be developed (Wernerfeldt 1984). Further, an optimal product-mix is the one that best fits external threats and opportunities. This is both true of industry- and macro-level changes. Western firms increasingly expand to settings that are radically different from that of the West. In the Western setting firms are already familiar with the environment, and thus these requirements must be an implicit part of their strategy.

China is undergoing rapid change, but certain traits such as the cultural values are rather static. These traits run through the entire setting and thus represent a critical requirement for business success. Western firms without *guanxi* therefore suffer a competitive *disadvantage*. Yet, *guanxi* by no means guarantees sustained competitive advantage. It depends on the nature of that *guanxi* and how well it fits with given situations, and the firm's idiosyncratic need for *guanxi* (Luo, 2000). The question is whether and when *guanxi* can be a basis for a sustainable competitive advantage. The conditions that such an advantage rests on – value, rarity, substitutability, and imitability – need comparison with the components of *guanxi*. *Guanxi* needs to fulfil the conditions for a sustained competitive advantage, in order to become more than an important asset and shift into the circle of strategic assets, as indicated in Figure 5:2.

Figure 5:2 Guanxi as a Strategic Component within the RBV

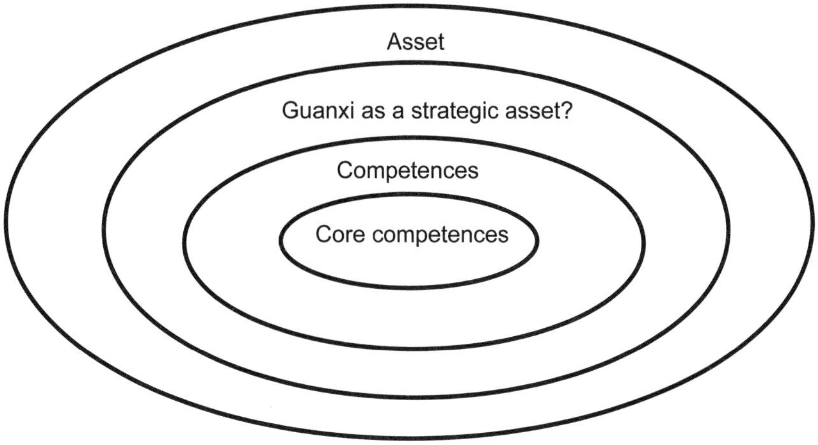

[Figure: Concentric ovals labeled from outermost to innermost: Asset; Guanxi as a strategic asset?; Competences; Core competences]

Source: *Inspired by Bogner, Thomas and McGee 1999*

Value

Guanxi is an intangible resource. Intangible resources are some of the most strategically important to the firm. *Guanxi* as a means to secure favours is a resource as the "receipt" for favours is possessed/controlled by the firm. While resources are the basic unit of analysis, the authors put forward that it is the capabilities these resources instigate which are the source of competitive advantage, i.e. what a firm can achieve when possessing *guanxi*. The higher the value of the capabilities, the higher the value of the *guanxi*. Hence, it is important the employee has the capability to understand and manage the *guanxi* in order to strengthen, maintain, and expand the *guanxi* and its associated capabilities; – valuable *guanxi* needs organisational underpinning. The value and capabilities *guanxi* may engender are exemplified in Figure 5:3. *Guanxi* is indispensable in Chinese society. While the authors have clarified why *guanxi* is a valuable resource and can, at least, lead to competitive parity, *guanxi* must also be rare and difficult to substitute and imitate to generate sustained competitive advantage (Barney 1991).

Rarity

Rare resources are those that are controlled or possessed by no other or very few firms; i.e. resource endowment is heterogeneous which prevents competitive erosion. Although *guanxi* connections are not rare per se, each web of connections is unique and organisationally-embedded. Even if two firms posses similar connections, relations vary in terms of firmness, reciprocity, sustainability, and favourability. Thus the network structure is rare. In general, valuable and rare resources can induce a temporary competitive advantage. They create ground for first mover advantages (Barney 1991). Inimitability and non-substitutability must be fulfilled for *guanxi* to create a sustained competitive advantage.

Figure 5:3 Business Benefits of Guanxi

Reducing	Increasing	Prompting
Transaction costs	Institutional support	First mover advantages
Operational uncertainty	Economic return	Expansion of network
Information costs	Business effectiveness	Access to top people
Contextual hazards	Firm legitimacy	Sales growth
Competitive threats	Strategic capabilities	Competitive opportunities

Imitability

A valuable and rare *guanxi* network might provoke attempts of imitation, but due to the uniqueness of a network, *guanxi* is subject to time compression. Firms that have an old *guanxi* network have an edge over those with newer networks, as network membership enlarges both current and future modes of choice (Gulati et al. 2000). Further, the notion of assets mass efficiency and accumulative assets advocate that *guanxi* breeds *guanxi*; a favourable stock of *guanxi* secures new and accumulating flows of *guanxi* (Diercikx, Cool and Barney 1989). The casual ambiguity, path dependency and invisible ties additionally shields competitive erosion. Moreover, *guanxi* capacity in itself can be a resource position barrier as maintenance skills such as time, money and effort plays an important role in the continuous closeness of the network (Luo 2000). Furthermore tie modality ensures cooperative behaviour amongst members through norms, obligations, and sanctions; firms outside the network cannot imitate derived benefits without such cooperative behaviour (Gulati et al. 2000). The strength of the *guanxi* may therefore shield competitive erosion of that network's benefit, when competitors attempt overlapping network partners.

Substitutability

Ex-post limits to competition preserves resource heterogeneity, by means of hindering imitability and substitutability. It is not sufficient to control a resource that is inimitable, if another bundle of resources can be used for the same strategy, thus there must not exist such an equivalent or the option of doing without.

The Chinese business milieu shows that in a network capitalism society, *"Whom you know is more important than what you know"*. Short-term *guanxi*, which is primarily utilitarian and acts as a means to overcome institutional shortcomings, is likely to decrease. Nonetheless, long-term *guanxi* relations will still be critical to individual lives and business growth (Luo 2000). Therefore the strategic consideration lies not in whether a firm can do without but rather if there is an equivalent that will do instead, such as a superior product or cost-effectiveness.

Guanxi is such a ubiquitous part of Chinese way of life with very meticulous norms and prescriptive behaviour, that there is no substitute feature that is so integral to the entire environment. No company can go far unless it has an extensive *guanxi* network in such a setting (Luo 2000).

Even though a complete imitation is not possible, there is the possibility that another firm's unique *guanxi* can act as a substitute and create the same capabilities. However, as long as resource heterogeneity is partially preserved, firms can still enjoy sustained competitive advantage. The authors argue that it is a matter of luck if firms succeed in developing substituting *guanxi*, and thus it is implausible that many firms will.

Sustainability

Even though the four conditions for a competitive advantage may be fulfilled, such a *guanxi* advantage may not be sustainable. As *guanxi* is tied to the employee participating in that network, mobility barriers will cease to exist if that individual leaves the firm. Luo (2000) suggests that in order to reduce mobility and increase sustainability, firms should convert personal *guanxi* into inter-organizational *guanxi*, so as to bind organisations rather than individuals together. Importance is placed on top managers to get involved in *guanxi* taking place at lower levels. Social activities and financial support from the firm achieves this. A network analysis at the firm level may reveal both current and advantageous networks; such an analysis should include monitoring, redirecting and reinvesting in *guanxi* relations in order to sustain current capabilities (Luo 2000).

Guanxi as a From of Social Capital

The question is how *guanxi* relates to social capital as a relational asset. The interesting point is how these embedded resources are produced, sustained, and mobilised. The RBV mainly looks at the sources of sustained competitive advantages, whereas social capital looks at how such sources are produced and mobilised. On the surface, social capital and *guanxi* are analogous concepts. Firstly, *guanxi* is most approximate to Bourdieu's notion of social capital. Social capital and *guanxi* are private assets that only serve the holder of such connections, thus personal networks produce social capital (Bourdieu 1986). Both *guanxi* and social capital involve social relations. The outcome of having such relations is instrumental, and is actually/potentially productive. *Guanxi* is defined as an instrumental social relationship and social capital is described as playing a functional and positive role in outcome (Huang 2001). Social capital increases the capacity for action and facilitates various ends for a member and/or for a group (Bian 2001). The productive outcome of social capital lies in the conversion into other forms of capital; *guanxi* is clearly also accumulated to convert into instrumental favours (Gold, Guthrie and Wank 2002).

Furthermore, the functioning of social capital and *guanxi* are reinforced by norms and reciprocity. Norms define actions considered acceptable or unacceptable in a particular culture. Interpersonal trust and norms enhance co-operative actions (Coleman 1990). The norm of reciprocity and trust is also an essential component of *guanxi*. The relational dimension of social capital that pays attention to affective feelings also has many similarities with *guanxi*.

Finally, the usage of intermediaries - an important component of *guanxi*- is equivalent to structural holes. These weak ties instigate access to various other *guanxi* networks.

Disparties with Social Capital Theory

Nevertheless, *guanxi* has traits that set it a part from a generalised notion of social capital (Gold, Guthrie and Wank 2002). Social capital is regarded as both the attributes of individuals and organisations while *guanxi* concerns interpersonal relationships which are relatively complicated to transfer into an organisational attribute (Huang 2001). Academics have different views on how the intended outcome of social capital or *guanxi* is produced. Some maintain that social capital, as a public property, is an unintentional by-product of other social activities, such as participation in a sports clubs, etc. (Putnam 1993). Similar to *guanxi*, social capital is the product of investment by individuals who aim at establishing or reproducing such social relations. The investment implies expenditure of time and energy, which in turn means direct or indirect expenditure of economic capital (Bourdieu 1986). The deliberate system of gifts and favours is much more than just social embeddedness and connections (Yang 1994). *Guanxi* has specific rites, rules, and rituals and is therefore more implicit and culturally specific than classic social capital Gold, Guthrie and Wank 2002. In addition, social capital and *guanxi* do not share the same understanding of trust and effect. Interpersonal and special trust, both of which refer to trust based on experiences refer to trust from *guanxi*. Generalised institutional trust is close to trust in social capital, when it is viewed as a collective asset. An affection element is involved in *guanxi* exchange. However affection is not really addressed by classic theorists of social capital (Huang 2001). Finally, *guanxi* is a product of an understanding of the individual as interdependent while social capital builds on western theories of the self as independent. This combination of instrumentality and sentiment is very distinct from social capital theorists who view social capital as purely a self-maximisation endeavour.

Guanxi Capital

A distinct definition of *guanxi*, as a China-specific form of social capital, will be helpful for empirical research. We call this *guanxi* capital and define it as:

> *Guanxi* capital is the collection of actual and potential resources and capabilities accrued by the individual that are embedded in a network of *guanxi* members. *Guanxi* capital is upheld by interpersonal trust, affection, reciprocity, norms of interdependence, long-term orientation, and face.

Thus, these resources and capabilities are accrued, tied, and mobilised by the individual and the structure is sustained by means of interpersonal trust, durability, reciprocity, norms, and face. These components of *guanxi* capital capture the nature of *guanxi*, whereas the RBV captures the strategic relevance of such relationships. The RBV mainly looks at the sources of sustained competitive advantages, whereas theories of personal networks look at how such sources are produced and mobilized.

Is *Guanxi* a Sustainable Competitive Advantage?

Guanxi is affectionate interpersonal linkages with the implication of continued exchange of favours (Luo 2000). Our respondent stated that, *"guanxi is best described in English by network, but it reaches much deeper than what we in the West usually call network, as it involves the possibility of use of indirect relations. Also, it involves building friendships and following the rules with the anticipation of favourable treatment by your network".*

To be a source of sustained competitive advantage a resource must be rare, valuable, and isolated from imitation and substitution (Barney 1991). The RBV focuses on internal factors, resources, capabilities and competencies, which are more important in acquiring and sustaining a competitive advantage than the organization's position in relation to its competitive environment. These internal factors are drawn upon to explain intra-industry performance discrepancies. With the intention of evaluating to what extent the intangible resource *guanxi* and its adjacent capabilities is a source of sustained competitive advantage for our case company; the authors turn to the four conditions upon which sustainability rests.

Value

For *guanxi* to confer a competitive advantage, it must be valuable to the firm. A company uses *guanxi* at every organisational level. At rare times, it is the only advantage needed; typically it needs combining with complementary assets to create valuable capabilities. The capabilities include access to information about competitors, increasing sales, shortcutting bureaucracy, encouraging opinion leaders, and consequently increasing profit levels. Calling upon a *guanxi* contact is very speedy and efficient; *guanxi* enhances problem solutions. Figure 5:4 presents the business values of *guanxi*. *Guanxi* is *"an easier road to the pier with the anticipation of favourable treatment by your contacts – In a commercial world, all is ultimately about increasing profits"* (Respondent). Without *guanxi*, penetrating the Chinese market would be an uphill battle, as authorities treat those actors unfavourably and everyday operations become time consuming. This validates the postulation that Chinese treat contact accordingly to closeness, contacts are divided into in-side and out-side groupings. The distribution and registration of many products is under tight state control, which means that *guanxi* relations with authorities can aid in easing and shortcutting such procedures.

The company seems to have had clear advantages in developing *guanxi*; firstly, they have had little interference from HQ and therefore had the discretion to adapt to the Chinese culture, which is what sets the bases for understanding *guanxi*. They have a clear understanding of the etiquettes of Chinese society, about who to contact and why and how to go about it. Secondly, the mix of being an international firm and their adaptation to Chinese culture implies that a company utilises *guanxi* differently from their Chinese and international counterparts. Another advantage point may stem from the deliberate usage of intermediaries. By way of dyadic relationships, a company extends their *guanxi* to indirect relations and thereby increases the variety and quality of receipts for favours. The authors thus infer that using intermediaries increases the quantity and possibly the quality of the associated capabilities that *guanxi* prompts. This is in line with Tung and Worm (2001) who found that when controlling for economic growth, firms that did not use go-betweeners only "kept up" with the national growth rate. Therefore, employees have the capabilities to manage and administer *guanxi*, thereby extracting latent valuable benefits.

The authors have clarified why *guanxi* is a valuable resource for a company, but *guanxi* must also be rare and difficult to substitute and imitate to generate a sustained competitive advantage.

Rarity

The first cornerstone of competitive advantage is resource heterogeneity; firms differ in their resource endowment. Ex-ante limits to competition ensure that firms differ in their perception when trading in factor markets. The contention is that the appropriateness of a web of dyadic relationships "*guanxi-wang*" will differ amongst firms, as strategic factors markets are imperfectly competitive.

Our respondent claims, two firms can seem to have similar connections, if they have the same or overlapping contacts in their respective *guanxi* network. Thus, similar network structure can exist amongst several firms. However, the strength of the network structure can be considered rare. The extracted benefits, that is, derived capabilities will always differ. This is due to differences in the strength of those connections, how far the connections will exert themselves, which is a function of friendliness, trustworthiness, and previous *guanxi* record. "*Even though, someone from a different firm has the same contact as me, it is not the same relationship. I guess you could compare it to friendships, they are all different."* Even though firms may have the same *guanxi* web with equal level of strength, the RBV claims that as long as resource heterogeneity is partially preserved, firms holding such resources will still be able to uphold their strategic relevance.

In sum, our respondent's *guanxi* web is a rare resource, which can induce a competitive advantage and eventually lad to a sustained competitive advantage if the additional conditions are fulfilled; inimitability and non-substitutability.

Figure 5:4 Business Values of Guanxi

Shortcutting bureaucracy
Shortcutting registration procedures
Efficiently speeding up solution findings
Information advantages
Encouraging opinion leaders
Increasing sales & profit levels
Increasing trust and co-operative behaviour amongst stakeholders to a company
Expanding access to actors in the market
Obtaining advantageous taxation schemes

Imitabilty

A valuable and rare *guanxi* network might provoke attempts of imitation; successful attempts would make derived sustained competitive advantages short-lived. The RBV states that resource heterogeneity is feasible due to the existence of ex-post limits to competition; two such critical isolating mechanisms are inimitability and non-substitutability. The authors claim that the strength of *guanxi* ensures rarity and that the social complexity ensures inimitability. The causal ambiguity lies in invisible ties; our respondent cannot *"map the guanxi of others and vice versa"*. Everyone is the centre of his own *guanxi* network (Fei 1992).

Guanxi is a covert activity that is not discussed with others. Our respondent states that *guanxi* is not something that is talked about. Cultural norms and face denotes that *guanxi* is kept under the surface according to our respondent. Even if visibly displayed, human behaviour is complicated to uncover and replicate.

Further, our respondent claims that when entering China, building *guanxi* relations was chief. This implies time compression factors, that is, first mover advantages in the sense that *guanxi* breeds *guanxi*. Also, the dynamic capabilities and alliance management capabilities associated with *guanxi* is evident here; a favourable stock of *guanxi* enhances the flows of *guanxi*, those that are quick to establish stocks of *guanxi* will also be those that achieve the best quality flows of *guanxi* later on.

Substitutability

Ex-post limits to competition preserve resource heterogeneity by means of inimitability and non-substitutability. It is not sufficient to control a resource that is inimitable if another bundle of resources can be used for the same strategy. Thus an equivalent or the option of doing without must not exist such.

There is no substitute for *guanxi*; it is an integral part of Chinese life which is culturally deeply embedded. Our respondent maintains that nothing can substitute *guanxi* – *"No one can do without guanxi in China"*. The intuitive question is then whether a higher quality product can render *guanxi* superfluous. However, even a higher quality product relative to competitors cannot replace the capabilities an effective *guanxi* network instigates. The reason is that *the* most important capability associated with our respondent's *guanxi* is shortcutting bureaucracy and registration difficulties. Therefore, the importance *"is not the product, but the time to reach the market"*; first mover advantages, time compression factors, and brand building are chief. Obviously holding both a higher quality product and an effective *guanxi* is the optimal competitive situation. That is, complementarities between various assets instigate the most strategic capabilities and core competencies. Nevertheless, in the industry, the legislative footwork necessary to launch a product is both very time-consuming and can make or break the product. When authorities have remarks concerning the registration, a *guanxi* member can prompt instant knowledge of such complications and the problem can be solved immediately rather than after several months. In general, the entire legislative apparatus can be mobilized if the firm has the right connections.

Sustainability

Sustainability of strategic relevance rests on ex-post limits to competition and imperfect mobility. In earlier chapters, two distinct and seemingly contrasting concepts were introduced; mobility barriers as a means of sustainability of competitive advantages, and *guanxi* have no group connotation. As a consequence, if an employee with rare, valuable, non-substitutable, and inimitable *guanxi* leaves a company, a company loses the employee's *guanxi* and the associated competitive advantages. Scholars advocate that managers should attempt to tie personal *guanxi* to the firm, so as to make *guanxi* firm-specific rather than person-specific. This is in line with our respondent's treatment of *guanxi*. Firstly, it is *"important that everyone meets everyone"*, in order to increase the number of employees that are connected to a valuable *guanxi* contact. Thus, our respondent uses himself or employees as intermediaries in order to introduce various contacts. The functioning of such "meet and greet" activities is naturally very dependent on strong and attentive leadership and organisational support. Therefore, our respondent ensures that he and other managers take the time to undertake such socialising conducts. It is the company that organises such events in order to make the firm visible and central to the invited *guanxi* contacts. This is consistent with theories suggesting that in order to reduce mobility barriers and increase sustainability, personal *guanxi* should be converted into inter-organisational *guanxi* (Tsang 1998).

Secondly, our respondent holds that *"guanxi is more than a business network"*. Guanxi is *"like a stove with a small flame that is turned up and down as needed"*. Our respondent keeps in touch with former employees, in case he needs their assistance at a later stage. Maintaining good relationships and *"keeping the door open"* is fundamental, as hostility can have negative spillover effects. Former employees are natural gatekeepers to their current and future *guanxi* connections, and negative endorsements are counter productive for *guanxi* cultivation.

Even though *guanxi* is vulnerable to sustainability, measurements can be and are taken to avert the loss of mobility barriers, which in turn increases the likelihood of *sustained* competitive advantages.

guanxi capital can become a strategic country factor when such relations are key determinants of economic rent in a particular geographic area: in this case China. For *guanxi* capital to become a strategic country factor, it needs to be valuable, rare, inimitable, difficult to substitute, sustainable, be complementary with other assets, and be accumulative in nature.

Structural Holes
Structural hole theory highlights the importance of weak ties in creating favors; an actor bridging a structural hole to a non-redundant actor

can gain valuable and pristine insights and thus earns a greater return that when interacting with strong ties (Burt 1992). In relation to *guanxi*, the role of an intermediary acts as such a bridge. *Guanxi* partners with infrequent interaction and few mutual acquaintances belong to different *guanxi* networks and thus they bridge a structural hole when meeting. Further, the utilitarian purposes for *guanxi* capital are evident in this theory; actors are self-maximising individuals who compete and leverage opportunities for information arbitrage.

Our respondent used the metaphor of a spider web; he sits in the middle of this ego-centred network and pulls strings to match needs with solutions. He can either pull strings to current actors in his web or jump to other webs via current actors. The reason for jumping webs lies in current actors not having the necessary tools for meeting a given need. *"I might need contact to such diverse actors as a high-ranking tax official, an acknowledged doctor, a marketing specialist, or an event-planner for the next office party."* Hence, when bridging structural holes via intermediaries, the non-redundancy and instrumental value is the key yardstick.

However, our respondent claims that it is not the frequency of interaction that solely decides the strategic relevance of strong and weak ties. Other factors such as affectionate feelings and strategic fit between demand and supply of favours are also important in deciding the economic value of any given contact. Having said that, it is evident that contacts associated with the highest value of information and favours come from the pool of weak contacts. *"The strongest contact I have, I see less than once a year. We do not go out every weekend and socialise with drinks and golf, but when we meet I receive utmost valuable information, he is very valuable to me and to the company"*. Also our respondent asserted, *"Personal relations are a part of guanxi but it encompasses much more"*. The utilitarian ends are not to be underestimated, and the authors maintain that *guanxi* capital, strong ties, bridging structural holes, and instrumental intentions are intertwined. These concepts are related in complex ways to the mobilisation of *guanxi* capital and hence to the source of sustained competitive advantage. Figure 5:5 outlines the central points derived from the case study in relation to *guanxi* capital.

In sum, it was found that these relations and their associated capability of mobilising a receipt for favour exchange have a detectable effect on a company's sustained competitive advantage in China. Consequently, producing and mobilising Guanxi capital is an important aspect of conducting business in China.

Figure 5:5 Central Points in Relation to Guanxi Capital

Social capital	Actual and potential resources embedded within, available through, and derived from the network of relationships possessed by an individual or social unit	*Guanxi* has traits of social capital as a relational asset held and accrued to the individual
Guanxi capital	The actual and potential resources & capabilities accrued to the individual, embedded in a network of *guanxi* members, which is upheld by interpersonal trust, reciprocity, norms, long-term orientation, and face	Our respondent's *guanxi* capital are person-specific relations, concerns the mobilisation of resources available only through his network, upheld by the cultural specifications underlying *guanxi*
Guanxi capital production	The production of *guanxi* capital involves cultural investment strategies	Our respondent uses tools such as hosting banquets and "go-betweeners" for producing *guanxi* capital with existing and new relations
Expressive *guanxi* capital	Expressive ties are a prerequisite for cultivating and mobilising *guanxi* capital	Our respondent stresses the importance of loyalty to affections not favours. Leveraging strategic relevance must refrain from perceiving *guanxi* as a rent-extracting activity
Affect-based trust	Trust grounded in reciprociated inter-personal care and corncern	Trust is based on feelings of affection, *"you cannot have guanxi without caring feelings"*
Structural holes	Structural holes separate clusters of strong tie networks	A respondent is a spider central in its own web and can jump to outskirts of other webs
Instrumental *guanxi* capital	Instrumental *guanxi* is concerned with quality of favours rendered and information arbitrage	*"Guanxi is ultimately about increasing profits"*. Relations are only initiated if they can aid in competitive advantage
Non-redundant contacts	Weak ties provide the largest rent, as they allow for bridging structural holes	Our respondent's most valuable contact is a weak contact, the utilitarian ends are the focal point as they create rents
Unbeneficial *guanxi*	*guanxi* may prove unbeneficial as it restricts individual freedom and is associated with opportunity costs	Unconscious path dependency has lead to our respondent never ending a relationship. There are signs of corruptive behaviour

Overall, this chapter brings the conclusion that Guanxi *can* explain sources of sustained competitive advantage for in China, when examined from a RBV. Nevertheless, the RBV may only give a useful explanation when supplemented by a country level analysis that both identifies and explains country specific factors and their production and mobilisation, such as Guanxi capital.

Recent Development
China appears more and more corrupt. Its position on Transparency International Index has been decreasing over recent years. In 2006 China's position has declined to the level of India (2006 Transparency International Corruption Perceptions Index). In a recent ground breaking essay about China's demoralization, Luo discusses the possible intertwinement of guanxi and corruption and flatly states that the book he wrote in 2000 would not be appropriate in 2007 (Luo 2007). Luo argues that when relational norms are eroded, guanxi can bring out further opportunism and instrumentality. As stated above, guanxi is intimately related to face and "renqing" (affectionate human obligations). If the interconnectedness between face, Guanxi, and Renqing is eroded in a collectivist society with low social trust, the favour exchange becomes power exchange and favour-seeking behaviour becomes rent-seeking behaviour.

The increasing existence of corruption has huge implications for the dynamics of guanxi as it becomes increasingly difficult-or maybe even impossible-to distinguish between guanxi and corruption despite the fact that guanxi by nature is almost the opposite of corruption as corruption is not exclusive. "If I can bribe you so can everybody else".

From a western perspective there is no trust aspect in corruption, whereas trust building is the time consuming part of establishing guanxi. In China, on the other hand, it has been argued that you cannot pay a big bribe without guanxi (Langeberg 2007). If there is not a certain element of acquaintance most cadres would not dare to take bribes. Even this seems to have evaporated in many areas in China during recent years. A Danish company set up a wholly foreign-owned subsidiary a few years ago in Shanghai and the tax authorities asked whether the company preferred to pay six percent or 33 percent tax. The last figure is the official tax rate in China for foreign companies. When the general manager for obvious reasons opted for six percent the local tax authorities agreed. The case is that with six percent tax the local tax authorities in Shanghai can keep the whole amount, whereas if the company paid 33 percent the local tax authorities would have to send 30 percent to the central government in Beijing.

This intertwinement of guanxi and corruption is a long-term process that can be anticipated to be highest in Guanxi with "wairen" (outside the family circle), which comprises Western firms. The reason is that although family-based relations are also somewhat influenced according to one of the author's observations, these relations are founded in the deeper layer of culture,-called values or basic assumptions,-and therefore are more difficult to change.

Assuming that the above development is correct, what are the implications for Western companies trying to create sustainable competitive advantages in China? It goes without saying that these companies should be prepared to meet destructive opportunism in their interaction with Chinese counterparts. Legitimate business will face increasing pressure to engage in corrupt activities, which may be part of the reason that Western companies increasingly establish wholly-owned subsidiaries in China, where they can diminish the number of corrupted relationships (Vanhonacker 2004)

In addition, some Western companies are reducing Guanxi to "fee-for-service" by overemphasizing gift-giving and wining and dining. In this way these Western companies are enhancing the demoralisation and erosion of Chinese values, albeit often unconsciously.

Despite these caveats, the authors do not advocate entering or operating in China without building guanxi. It is probably impossible as it will be perceived by the Chinese stakeholders as unfriendly. But it does make the strategic options more complex, because while the norms in China are eroding, the question of ethical business is becoming stronger in Western societies. These developments require cautious and deliberate actions from Western companies operating in China.

It takes a certain cultural understanding and intelligence to be able to build proper Guanxi. An example of how this is done has been described by our case company respondent. As suggested it is important for Western companies to learn more about the deeper layers of Chinese culture in order to be able to deal with the intricacies of appropriate Guanxi building and maintenance. The Chinese culture is substantially different from western analytical tradition. The Chinese mindset is built on a holistic (yin-yang) approach that sees everything as interconnected (Lynton and Thøgersen 2006). If the companies do not adapt they may in the worst case, bring both themselves and the Chinese counterpart in a bad position. They will not attain a sustainable competitive advantage, but contrary expose themselves to criticism from both Western and Chinese stakeholders.

References

Barney, J. 1991. Firm resources and sustained competitive advantage. *Journal of Management,* 17(1): 99-120.

Baron, S., J. Field, and T. Schuller 2000. *Social capital – critical perspectives*, Oxford: Oxford University Press.

Bian, Y. 2001, Guanxi Capital and Social Eating in Chinese Cities: Theoretical models and Empirical Analyses, in Lin, N., K. Cook and R. Burt 2001. *Social capital – theory and research.* New York: Aldine de Gruyter.

Bogner, W., H. Thomas and J. Mcgee 1999. Competence and Competitive Advantage: Towards a dynamic model. *British Journal of Management,* 10(4): 275-290.

Bourdieu, P. 1986. The forms of capital, in J. Richardson (ed.) *Handbook of Theory and Research for the Sociology of Education.* New York: Greenwood Press.

Burt, R. 1992. *Structural Holes – the Social Structure of Competition.* Cambridge: Harvard University Press.

Chen, C., Y. Chen and K. Xin 2004. Guanxi Practices and Trust in Management: A Procedural Justice Perspective. *Organization science,* 15(2):200-209.

Coleman, J. 2005. A Rational Choice Perspective on Economic Sociology in The Handbook of Economic Sociology. New Jersey: University Presses of California, Columbia and Princeton,

Dierickx, I., K. Cool, and B.J. Barney 1989. Asset stock Accumulation and Sustainability of Competitiveness. Management Science 35(12): 1504-1511.

Dunfee, T. and D. Warren 2001. Is Guanxi ethical? A Normative Analysis of Doing Business in China. *Journal of Business Ethics* 32(3): 191-204.

Fei, X.T. 1992. *From the soil: The Foundations of Chinese society.* Berkeley, University of California Press.

Field, J. 2003. *Social Capital, Key Ideas.* New York: Routledge.

Fukuyama, F. 1995. *Trust – the social virtues and the creation of prosperity.* London: Hamish Hamilton.

Gold, T., Guthrie, D. and D. Wank 2002. *Social Connections in China -institutions, Culture, and the Changing Nature of Guanxi.* Structural Analysis in the Social Sciences. No. 21. Cambridge, UK: Cambridge University Press.

Grant, M. R. 1991. The resource – Based Theory of Competitive Advantage: Implication for Strategic Formulation. *California Management Review* 33(3):114–135.

Gulati, R., N. Nohria, and A. Zaheer 2000. Strategic Networks. *Strategic Management Journal,* 21(3): 203–15.

Guthrie, D. 1998. The Declining Significance of Guanxi in China's Economic Transition. *China Quarterly,* 154: 254-282.

Hitt, M.A., H. Lee and E. Yucel 2002. The importance of social capital to the management of multinational enterprises: Relational networks among Asian and Western firms. *Asia Pacific Journal of Management 19 (2,3)*:353-72.

Huang, Q., 2001. Social Capital in the West and China, http://esnie.u-paris10.fr/pdf/st_2003/14_mmuworkingpaper.pdf (only accessible via the Internet) last accessed 3/1/2006).

Jakobsen, M. 2006. Doing Business the Chinese Way? On Manadonese Chinese Entrepreneurship in North Sulawesi. *The Copenhagen Journal of Asian Studies* 24:72-104.

Kumar, R. and V. Worm 2003. Social Capital and the Dynamics of Business Negotiations between the Northern Europeans and the Chinese. *International Marketing Review,* 20(3):236-62.

Langenberg, E. 2007 *Guanxi and Business Strategy*. Heidelberg: Physia-Verlag.

Lin, N. 2001. *Social capital – A theory of Social Structure and Action.* Cambridge UK: Cambridge University Press.

Luo, Y. 2000. *Guanxi and Business*. Asia-Pacific Business Series – vol. 1, Singapore: World Scientific Publishing Co. Pte. Ltd.

Luo, Y. 2007. The Changing Chinese Culture and Business behaviour: The Perspective of Intertwinement Between Guanxi and Corruption. Forthcoming in *International Business Review.*

Lynton, N. and K. Thøgersen 2006. How China Transform an Executive's Mind. *Organizational Dynamics* 35(2): 170-181.

Markus, H and S. Kitayama 1991 Culture and the Self." Implications for Cognition, Emotion, and Motivation. *Psychological Review*. 98(2): 224-253.

McAllister, D. 1995. Affect- and cognition-based trust as foundations for interpersonal cooperation in organizations. *Academy of Management Journal,* 38(1): 24-59.

Michailova, S. and V. Worm 2003. Personal networking in Russia and China: blat and guanxi. *European Management Journal,* 21(4): 509-520.

Nahapiet, J. and S. Ghoshal 1998. Social capital, intellectual capital, and the organizational advantage. *The Academy of Management Review,* 23(2): 242-66.

Park, S. and Y. Luo 2001. Guanxi and Organizational Dynamics: Organizational Networking in Chinese Firms. *Strategic Management Journal,* 22(5):455-477.

Putman, D.R., R. Leonardi, and R. Nanetti 1993. *Making Democracy Work – Civic Traditions in Modern Italy.* Princeton: Princeton University Press.

Pye, L. 1982. *Chinese Commercial Negotiating Style.* Cambridge MA: Oelgeschlager. Gunn and Hain.

Shapiro, D., M. Von Glinow and Z. Xiao 2007. Towards Polycontextually Sensitive Research Methods. *Management and organisation Review* 3(1): 129-153.

Su, C. and J. Littlefield 2001. Entering Guanxi: A Business Ethical Dilemma in mainland China? *Journal of Business Ethics* 33(4): 199-210.

The 2006 Transparency International Corruption Perceptions Index. (2007) http://www.infoplease.com/ipa/A0781359.html Accessed July 17, 2007.

Tsang, E. 1998. Can Guanxi be a Source of Sustained Competitive Advantage for doing Business in China? *Academy of Management Executive,* 12(2): 64-73.

Tung, R. and V. Worm 2001. Network capitalism: the role of human resources in penetrating the China market. *International Journal of Human Resource Management,* 12(4):517-534.

Yang, M. 2002. The resilience of *Guanxi* and its new deployments: a Critique of some new G*uanxi* Scholarship. *The China Quarterly,* 170(1): 459-476.

Yeung, I and R. Tung 1996. Achieving business success in Confucian societies: the importance of guanxi (connections). *Organizational dynamics,* 25(2):54-65.

Vanhonacker, W. 2004. When Good Guanxi turns Bad. *Harvard Business Review,* 82(4): 18-19.

Wu W. and W. L. Choi 2004. Transaction Cost, Social Capital and Firms' Synergy Creation in Chinese Business Networks: An Integrative Approach. *Asia Pacific Journal of Management,* 21(3): 225-43.

Wernerfelt, B. 1984. A Resource-based View of the Firm. *Strategic Management Journal,* 5(2):171-180.

Worm, V. 1997. *Vikings and Mandarins.* Copenhagen: Copenhagen Business School Press.

Zeng, M. and P. Williamson 2007. *Dragons at your Door – How Chinese Cost innovation is disrupting Global Competition.* Boston: Harvard Business School Press.

Zhang, Y. and Z. Zhang, Z. 2006. Guanxi and Organizational Dynamics in China: A Link between Individual and Organizational Levels. *Journal of Business Ethics* 67(4): 375-392.

CHAPTER SIX

Micro-Evidence on Investment Patterns and Motivations of Chinese Multinationals

Bersant Hobdari, Marina Papanastassiou and Evis Sinani

Over the last two decades China has made significant progress in attracting and promoting foreign direct investment (FDI). By year 1992, China was one of the largest receivers of inward FDI and was experiencing growing outward FDI (UNCTAD 2005). One of the striking features of Chinese outward FDI (OFDI) is that differently that from the other emerging economies is not limited to neighboring countries but spans significantly to industrialized countries (Wang 2002). The search for more advanced technologies and better management practices help explain this pattern (Deng 2007).

The "gradualist" approach of economic development with little political changes that China follows has resulted in two main types of enterprises: the state owned enterprises (SOEs), owned by the central government, and township village enterprises (TVEs), owned by village governments and/or private firms. Since SOEs are under tight government control, they are sometimes more favored (Deng 2007). By introducing regulations to improve their competitiveness and supporting investments in R&D, the Chinese government has played an important role in motivating Chinese enterprises invest abroad. The unique "gradualist" approach to development accompanied by a strong government support indeed has promoted high levels of outward FDI.

In this chapter we explore the investment pattern of Chinese multinationals using a sample of 603 subsidiaries of 125 Chinese MNCs, especially focusing on the regional and industrial distribution. Before that we briefly review the implications of the literature on outward FDI in general and Chinese outward FDI in particular. Our analysis shows that Chinese multinationals display a strong home bias in their investment strategies. Further, Chinese outward FDI displays strong regional and industrial bias, pointing to industry and location being two important determinants of the pattern of outward FDI.

Literature Review

The understanding and study of Chinese multinationals falls in the wider analysis of MNCs coming from developing countries. Early work by Lall (1983) and Wells (1983) aimed at providing the theoretical foundations of the understanding of MNCs that come from countries that are usually recipients of FDI. Since then, an extensive empirical literature has investigated inward FDI in developing countries with emphasis on Latin American and South East Asia (for recent research on these issues see, for instance, Lauridsen 2004; Galan and Gonzalez-Benito 2006; Treviño and Mixon 2004). Similarly, empirical work exists on OFDI that concentrates on domestic MNCs coming from mainly South East Asian countries (Kim and Mah 2006).

Since the early 1990s China has attracted the attention of scholars as the host country of MNCs (Buckley et al. 2007; Cassidy and Andreosso-O'Callaghan 2006; Wei and Liu 2006; Xing 2006). At the same time Chinese firms have increasingly engaged in overseas activities. However, the emergence of Chinese multinationals and their OFDI are still not a very well explored topic. Among the first attempts to explain the phenomenon of Chinese MNCs is that of Young at al. (1996) who provide some initial empirical evidence on the internationalization process of Chinese multinationals. Their investigation relied on a case study of five state-owned Chinese MNCs involved in manufacturing. Their findings showed that the companies under investigation not only had a strong regional presence in Asia, but also they had a quite strong presence outside Asia and in particular in the North American market. Their choice of entry mode into new markets included all possible modes ranging from greenfield investment to joint ventures and it was closely related to the characteristics of the host market as well as the underlying motivation to invest abroad. The authors showed that knowledge and market seeking were among the most important investment motives for Chinese MNCs.

Earlier work by Li (1993) discussed the nature of Chinese investment in Canada. In particular, he shows that Chinese investment in Canada in the late 1980s and early 1990s was the outcome of economic reforms in China and the emergence of business like and professional Chinese entrepreneurship. Later research on Chinese MNCs by Ding (2000) discusses the relationship between internationalization and what he calls *informal privatization*. In his paper he demonstrates how publicly owned Chinese companies invested abroad and how through this process public funds were re-baptized as private creating serious issues of corporate governance. Nevertheless, Ding's study confirms the earlier work of Young et al. (1996) with regard to the geographical pattern as well as the motivation of Chinese MNCs. Similar are the findings of Frost and Ho (2005) whose main concern though is the impact of the increasing volume of Chinese OFDI on corporate social practices and thus the export of possibly poor management and labor practices.

Finally, Hong and Sun (2006) discuss investment strategies of Chinese MNCs. In their findings they acknowledge the strong domestic presence of Chinese MNCs through joint ventures with foreign investors. This finding is also confirmed by Liu and Li (2002) in their case study of the Haier Group. Hong and Sun (2006) underline the emerging drive of resource seeking and emphasize the technology seeking nature of Chinese outward FDI, which has been the major strategic motivation behind the successful story of the Haier Group (Liu and Li 2002).

Patterns and Rationale of Chinese Direct Investment

In this section we would first explore the trends and patterns of Chinese MNCs investments and then argue on the motivations behind Chinese firms expansion strategies. To this end we use a sample of 603 subsidiaries of 125 Chinese firms. The data are obtained from the summer 2006 edition of Corporate Affiliation Directory. The directory includes parent companies and their subsidiaries, no matter where the subsidiaries are located. Parent companies included have revenues in excess of US$10 million and/or employment in excess of 300 employees. The average number of subsidiaries of included parent firms is about 5 per parent. Nevertheless, it would be misleading to conclude that all firms are engaged in investments to the same degree. The number of subsidiaries per parent firm differs markedly, ranging from 1 to 60. Further, 34 percent of all subsidiaries belong to only 5 firms, namely China National Chemicals Import & Export Corporation, China Minmetals Corporation, CITIC Group, Gold Peak Industries (Holdings) Limited and Bank of China, while 42 percent of firms have only one subsidiary.

Table 6:1 Industrial Distribution of Investment by Chinese Firms

Industry	Number of Chinese Firms
Resources and Construction	59
Food Production, Textile and Apparel	19
Wood, Paper Products, Chemicals and Pharmaceuticals	36
Other Manufacturing	62
Electronics, Transport Equipment and Instruments	67
Total Manufacturing	184
Services	162
Trade	89
Finance and Real Estate	109
Total	603

Table 6:2 Regional Distribution of Investment by Chinese Firms

Region	Number of Firms
Africa	2
Asia – Pacific	451
Europe	63
Middle East	1
North America	83
South America	3
Total	603

The international business literature identifies, by and large, four different motivations to invest abroad: to gain resources, efficiency, markets and strategic assets, in the form of technology or knowledge. (Dunning 1993). These underlying motivations have implications for the distribution of subsidiaries across industries and regions. Table 6:1 and Table 6:2, as well as illustration in Figure 6:1 and Figure 6:2, show this distribution across nine aggregated industries defined at 4-digit level and six geographical regions. First, it is clear from Table 6:1 that most of Chinese subsidiaries are concentrated in financial and real estate (18 percent) and other services (27 percent), with trade (15 percent) being the next popular industry. From the rest of industries investments seem to go to other manufacturing (10 percent) and electronics, transport and instruments (11 percent) and oil and gas (9 percent). Turning to Table 6:2 we see that distribution of investments instead of being globally distributed has a strong geographical dimension, with almost 75 percent of projects going to firms' home region, i.e., Asia-Pacific, with North America being a second distant popular destination with almost 14 percent and Europe following with about 10 percent.

Micro-Evidence on Investment Patterns and Motivations

Combining the industrial and regional distribution of subsidiaries in Table 6:3 we observe that within Asia-Pacific finance and real estate investment account for about 23 percent, other services for 25 percent, other manufacturing and electronics for 9 percent and oil and gas for 10 percent. In comparison the respective share of investment in these industries in North America and Europe are the following: finance and real estate about 5 percent and 6 percent, other services for 30 percent and 37 percent, manufacturing 11 percent and 17 percent, electronics for 8 percent and 11 percent and oil and gas about 4 percent and 6 percent. Curiously the share of investments going to these industries as a total of overall investments in the respective region is larger in Europe than in North America, with the latter dominating Europe in the share of trade investment: 33 percent versus 17 percent.

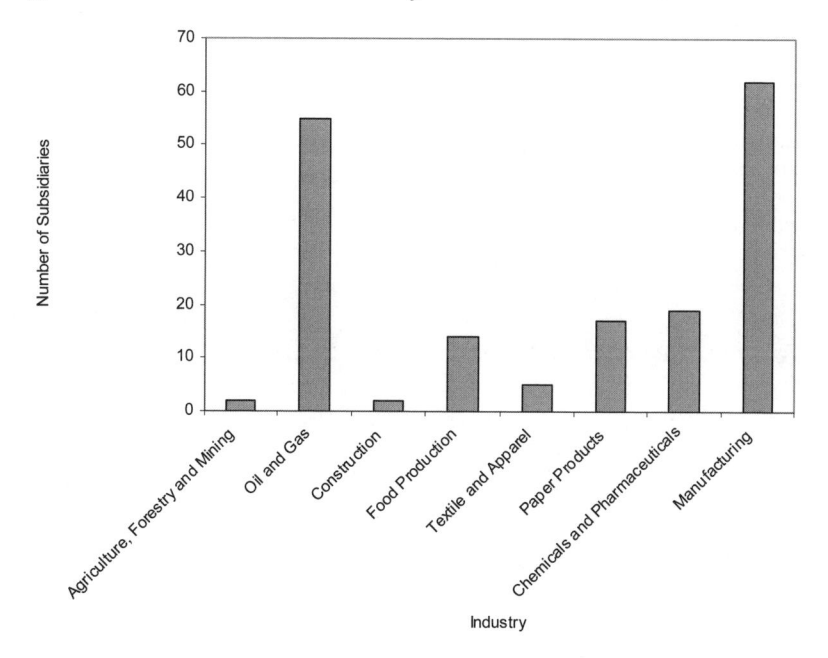

Figure 6:1 Industrial Distribution of Chinese Subsidiaries

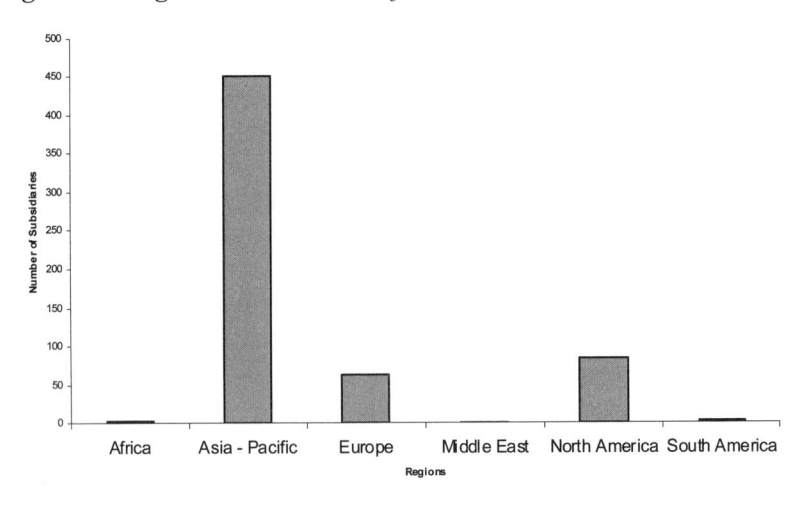

Table 6:3 Industrial and Regional Distribution of Investment by Chinese Firms

Industry	Regions					
	Africa	Asia	Europe	Middle East	North America	South America
Agriculture, Forestry and Mining	0	2	0	0	0	0
Oil and Gas	1	46	4	1	3	0
Construction	0	2	0	0	0	0
Food Production	0	14	0	0	0	0
Textile and Apparel	0	1	1	0	3	0
Paper Products	0	13	1	0	3	0
Chemicals and Pharmaceuticals	0	19	0	0	0	0
Manufacturing	0	41	11	0	9	1
Electronics	0	41	7	0	7	0
Automobile and Transport Equipment	0	6	0	0	1	0
Instruments	0	2	2	0	1	0
Services	0	114	23	0	25	0
Trade	1	48	11	0	27	2
Finance and Real Estate	0	102	3	0	4	0

Figure 6:2 Regional Distribution of Chinese Outward FDI

Table 6:4 Geographical Distribution of Investment by Chinese Firms

Host Country	Number of Firms
Australia	11
Austria	1
Belgium	1
Brazil	3
Canada	8
China	234
China (Hong Kong)	155
China (Macau)	3
Cyprus	1
Denmark	1
Finland	1
France	3
Germany	18
India	1
Indonesia	2
Italy	4
Japan	8
Korea (South)	3
Malaysia	5
Netherlands	5
New Zealand	2
Norway	2
Philippines	1
Russia	1
Singapore	15
South Africa	2
Spain	2
Sweden	5
Switzerland	2
Taiwan	9
Thailand	1
USA	76
UAE	1
United Kingdom	16
Total	603

In fully determining the importance of Asia-Pacific as a destination region of Chinese investments one needs to separate the effect of investments within China itself, i.e. home investment, from those in the rest of the region. Table 6:4 gives the distribution of subsidiaries according to host country. Several points are worth noting. First, there are 34 different countries in which Chinese firms have established subsidiaries. Second, about 39 percent of investment projects are undertaken within China. As already discussed, this pattern is not surprising and actually is consistent with findings of Wong and Chan (2003) and Hong and Sun (2006) who find that internationalization strategies of

145

Chinese firms involve initially the establishment of joint ventures with Western companies within China before embarking on overseas investment. The reasons behind this strategy seem to be the acquisition of advanced production methods, technology, knowledge, expertise and managerial skills, which are essential to building competitive advantage and to succeed overseas. At the same time, we should not ignore that the large size of the Chinese market encourages Chinese MNCs to expand into China and compete for a share of this dynamic and growing market with foreign owned subsidiaries. Third, even accounting for this Asia-Pacific remains the most important destination for Chinese investments with about 36 percent of total number of investment projects. If, however, Chinese investments in Hong Kong are also classified as mostly home than foreign then the importance of Asia-Pacific drops substantially, attracting only about 11 percent of investment projects, making it the second most important region after North America. Fourth, focusing on the number of subsidiaries established abroad, the USA is the most important destination of Chinese investment attracting about 36 percent of investment projects, followed by Germany (8 percent), Singapore (7 percent) and Australia (6 percent). These data are in line with previous studies that report the value of outward Chinese FDI as opposed to the number of investment projects. For instance, (Deng 2004) emphasizes that by the end of 2001 Chinese outward FDI is strongly concentrated in a small number of destinations. Further, UNCTAD (2005) reports that, for the period 1997-2002, about 62 percent of China's FDI outflows went to four top destinations, that is Hong Kong, USA, Canada and Australia. Finally, our data also provide support to the conjecture that Chinese firms invest more in higher income and industrial countries due to their superior investment environment, high technology and advanced management methods.

Table 6:5 Size Distribution of Investment by Chinese Firms

Sales	Number of Firms
Up to 100 million dollars	186
100 – 500 million dollars	183
500 million – 1 billion dollars	33
1 – 1.5 billion dollars	5
More than 1.5 billion dollars	40
Total	447

Table 6:6 Size and Regional Distribution of Investment by Chinese Firms

Sales	Regions					
	Africa	Asia-Pacific	Europe	Middle East	North America	South America
Up to 100 million dollars	1	105	40	1	38	1
100 – 500 million dollars	0	150	8	0	25	0
0,5 – 1 billion dollars	0	30	0	0	3	0
1 – 1,5 billion dollars	0	4	1	0	0	0
More than 1,5 billion dollars	0	33	1	0	6	0
Total	0	322	50	1	72	1

Analyzing the scale of investment would have required data on investment spending. In their absence we use sales data as a proxy for the size of investment projects. For the purposes of this analysis we have classified subsidiaries into five groups according to sales revenue they generate as follows: those generating up to 100 million dollars in sales, those generating between 100 and 500 million dollars, those generating between 500 million and 1 billion dollars, those generating between 1 and 1.5 billion dollars and those generating more than 1.5 billion dollars. In constructing these groups we do not posses data on the exact level of sales. Rather we have data on the interval where sales fall. In constructing the groups we have balanced the need to keep their number manageable and not to pool together firms of substantially different size. The distribution of firms across these five groups is given in Table 6:5. Due to missing sales data there are only 447 observations. Most of investment projects are of a relatively small size, with 41 percent of projects generating sales of up to 100 million dollars and another 41 percent generating sales of up to 500 million dollars. This result is again in line with those of Deng (2004) who finds that the average size of an investment in most countries is relatively small. The pattern does not seem to alter when looking at size distribution across regions represented in Table 6:6. In all major regions, i.e., Asia-Pacific, North America and Europe, dominant investment projects are relatively small. Of note is the fact that big projects, those generating more than 1.5 billion in sales, are predominantly carried out in Asia-Pacific and, except for one investment located in Singapore, are all located in China or Hong Kong.

Table 6:7 Distribution of Firms by Legal From

Type	Number of Firms
Affiliate	9
Branch	18
Group Insurer	34
Joint Venture	53
Subsidiary	475
Unit	3
Other	11
Total	603

So far we have used the term subsidiary to refer to all firms in our sample. Yet, the term might be a misnomer as the establishment of subsidiaries might not be the most preferred form of investment by Chinese firms. This requires a review of legal forms of establishment, reported in Table 6:7. The table reveals that in our sample subsidiaries are indeed the most preferred form of establishment as they constitute 78 percent of all investment projects. Joint ventures are the second most important mode with 8 percent of investment projects, with the rest of establishment forms accounting for the remaining 14 percent. Even accounting for the large number of subsidiaries within China, the share of subsidiaries in overall investment projects is still dominant. This finding contradicts that of Deng (2004) who finds that by the end of 2001 joint ventures with local firms were the most preferred form of investment for Chinese firms.

Table 6:8 Distribution of Firms by Equity Shares and Legal Form

Firm Type	Ownership Share (in percentage)		
	Less than 50	50 – 99	100
Affiliate	1	1	0
Branch	0	0	10
Group Insurer	0	4	16
Joint Venture	3	4	7
Subsidiary	3	24	169
Unit	0	1	1
Other	1	0	5
Total	8	34	208

A final issue related to forms of establishment is the degree of involvement of parent firms in terms of equity shares. Information of the degree of ownership from the parent firm could be extracted for 250 of the sample firms (about 42 percent of the sample) and in Table 6:8 we report the distribution of firms by equity shares and form of establishment. In light of the previous finding on the preference of subsidiary establishment it is not surprising to find that wholly owned subsidiaries constitute the bulk of the sample, with 67 percent. Only in three subsidiaries the parent firm had less than 50 percent equity involvement. Overall, only in 3.2 percent of cases the equity involvement is less than 50 percent. The average equity share over the whole sample is 93 percent, with the lowest value being 20 percent. This finding coincides with that of previous studies, which have found parent involvement in terms of average equity shares to be high and increasing over time. For instance, MOFTEC (1997) reports that this share was 46 percent in 1995 and increased to 48.5 percent in 1997.

As already mentioned, the industrial distribution of investment projects could be used to understand parent firm's underlying motivation for investing. Often, however, firms invest having multiple motivations. Alternatively, motivations change, subject to evolution of firms, their strategies and the environment they operate over time. The results of Table 6:1 could, at least, be indicative of the underlying investment motivations of the firms in our sample. One common rationale of establishing subsidiaries abroad is to acquire stable supply of resources for use in own production operations. Given that China is a country with relatively low per capita availability of resources, it could be conjectured that resource-seeking motives would constitute an integral part of firms' investment strategies. Buckley et al. (2007) stress that this strategy would lead to Chinese firms investing in resource rich countries such as Australia and Canada. Further, Dunning (2001) argues that resource-seeking investment could also take the form of specific assets embedded in developed country firms, which become target of joint agreements and/or takeovers. Overall, the search for resources implies that one would expect to observe a large number of investment projects in natural resource industries such as agriculture, fishing and mining and oil and gas. Overall, only 10 percent of investment projects in our sample belong to these industries suggesting that, although present, this motive is not the one driving the pattern of outward investment. This is especially true as 60 percent of these investments are carried out within China and only 40 percent abroad.

Another motive often cited for OFDI is efficiency-seeking, which reflects the efforts of a multinational group to organize its international and domestic operations in a more rational way, thus in a way where a more productive use of resources is applied. Thus, efficiency seeking reflects restructuring of the value chain. Such strategies would require firms to invest abroad as part of a global production and marketing strategy. In the case of Chinese MNCs efficiency-seeking may be related with the search of a productive and knowledgeable labour force. It could also be related with host country markets that exhibit more friendly business environment such as less bureaucracy. At the same time efficiency seeking can be related with the search of new, improved technology in order to upgrade existing production processes. The latter though also reflects a strategic-asset seeking motivation. Dunning (1998) emphasizes this motive to be geared less towards exploiting ownership specific advantages and more towards protecting and augmenting that advantage. Luo and Tung (2007) argue that multinationals from emerging economies, which would include Chinese ones, use outward investments as a springboard strategy in acquiring strategic assets in order to overcome several handicaps such as latecomer disadvantage, domestic institutional constraints or rapid changes to technological and production development. Such strategies would, in general, require firms to invest abroad as part of a global production and marketing strategy. This will allow firms to accumulate knowledge and skills, which could be eventually turned into strengths. Whether this is the case or not would require a more in-depth investigation of investment strategies than simply looking at the industrial distribution. Overall though we expect this motive to be present in Chinese firm strategies in light of Chinese government encouragement, through its 1999 "Go Global" strategy, to firms to invest abroad in order to increase their international presence, sharpen their competitive edge and expand their technological trajectory. Thus, one would expect to find Chinese investment in developed countries to be concentrated in industries characterized by the use of advanced technology and know-how such as electronics, chemicals and pharmaceuticals, instruments, automobiles and manufacturing. In our sample 25 percent of the observations fall into these industries suggesting both efficiency-seeking and strategic asset motives associated with access to a sophisticated business environment, expertise as well as improved technology.

The FDI literature refers to market seeking as another motivator for FDI. This is driven by the limits of domestic demand and/or barriers to foreign market entry in the form of either price of quantity restrictions. This would imply that investments in industries that exhibit certain trade barriers or market saturation such as textile and apparel, footwear, food products, paper products, simple manufacturing production would fall into this group. Another driver of market seeking strategies is to service large Chinese communities in various countries, especially in Asia-Pacific and North America. This would imply investments in finance and real estate and service industries to be driven by market seeking objectives, making these objectives the most important in firm strategies. A variation to a market seeking strategy is a diversification-seeking strategy. This variant of market seeking, often adopted with the encouragement of the state, is driven by the desire to become a multinational through international diversification. At the same time we could argue that diversification-seeking strategies also incorporate elements of strategic asset-seeking behaviour in the sense that Chinese MNCs seek to acquire new knowledge and expertise in areas where they are obviously lacking such proficiency. It is mainly firms that held monopoly over China's foreign trade in the past that have followed this route towards becoming a multinational. Examples of such firms in our sample are China National Chemicals Import & Export Corporation, China Petrochemical Corporation and Bank of China. Thus, depending on the type of manufacturing investment our sample suggests that this category of motivation constitutes in between 20-30 percent of all investment projects.

Conclusions

Using a sample of 603 subsidiaries of 125 Chinese MNCs, we have explored the regional and industrial pattern of Chinese MNCs' investment patterns and motivations. There are some important facts that emerge from our analysis. First, most of Chinese investment is directed in non-productive industries, with finance and real estate and services being the most attractive ones. Second, by far the majority of investment projects are carried out in the home region of Asia-Pacific. Yet, within this region most of investment projects are carried our within China itself and Hong Kong, giving so Chinese firms' investment strategies a strong home bias. If this bias is corrected for, North America becomes the region that attracts most of Chinese OFDI. Third, OFDI is highly concentrated geographically and the average investment project is relatively small. Fourth, establishment of subsidiaries is the most preferred way of carrying out investment as opposed to joint ventures and other legal forms. With regards to the motivations we introduced a variant to market seeking, i.e. diversification seeking, and argued that there is no such a clear cut distinction among certain motives such as efficiency seeking and strategic asset seeking. Nevertheless our findings suggest that, market-seeking motives seem to drive most of OFDI strategies.

References

Buckley, P.B, J. C. Clegg and C. W. Wang 2007. 'Is the relationship between inward FDI and spillover effects linear? An empirical examination of the case of China.' *Journal of International Business Studies* 38(3): 447-459.

Cassidy, J.F. and B. Andreosso-O'Callaghan 2006. 'Spatial determinants of Japanese FDI in China.' *Japan and the World Economy* 18(4): 512-527.

Ding, X.L. 2000. 'Informal privatization through internationalization: The rise of nomenclature capitalism in China's Offshore Businesses'. *British Journal of Political Science* 30(1): 121-146.

Deng, P. 2007. 'Investing for strategic resources and its rationale: The case of outward FDI from Chinese companies.' *Business Horizons* 50: 71-81.

Deng, P. 2004. 'Outward investment by Chinese MNCs: Motivations and Implications.' *Business Horizons* 47(3): 8-16.

Dunning, J. 1993. *Multinational Enterprises and the Global Economy*. New York: Addison Wesley.

Dunning, J.H. 1998. 'Location and the multinational enterprise: A neglected factor?' *Journal of International Business Studies* 29(1): 45-86.

Dunning, J.H. 2001. 'The Eclectic Paradigm of International Production: Past, Present and Future.' *International Journal of the Economics of Business* 8(2): 173-190.

Frost, S. and M. Ho 2005. 'Going out: The growth of Chinese FDI in Southeast Asia and its implications for Corporate Social Responsibility.' *Corporate Social Responsibility and Environmental Management* 12: 157-167.

Galan, J.I. and J. Gonzalez-Benito 2006. 'Distinctive determinant factors of Spanish foreign direct investment in Latin America.' *Journal of World Business* 41(2): 171-189.

Hong, E. and L. Sun 2006. 'Dynamics of internationalization and outward investment: Chinese corporations' strategies.' *The China Quarterly* 12:610-634.

Kim, E.M. and J. S. Mah 2006. 'Patterns of South Korea's Foreign Direct Investment Flows into China.' *Asian Survey* 46(6): 881-897.

Lall, S. (eds) 1983. *The New Multinationals*. Chichester: John Wiley.

Lauridsen, L. 2004. 'Foreign Direct Investment, Linkage Formation and Supplier Development in Thailand during the 1990s: The Role of State Governance.' *The European Journal of Development Research*, 16(3): 561-586.

Li, P. 1993. 'Chinese investment and business in Canada: Ethnic entrepreneurship reconsidered.' *Pacific Affairs* 66(2): 213-243.

Liu, H. and K. Li 2002. 'Strategic implications of emerging Chinese multinationals: The Haier case study.' *European Management Journal* 20(6): 699-706.

Luo, Y. and R. L. Tung 2007. 'International Expansion of Emerging Market Enterprises: A Springboard Perspective.' *Journal of International Business Studies* 38(1): 481-498.

MOFTEC (Ministry of Foreign Trade and Economic Cooperation) 1997. *Almanac of China's Foreign Economic Relations and Trade.* Beijing.

Trevino, L.J and F. G. Mixon 2004. 'Strategic factors affecting foreign direct investment decisions by multi-national enterprises in Latin America.' *Journal of World Business* 39(3): 233-243.

UNCTAD (United Nations Conference on Trade and Development) 2005. *World Investment Report, 2003-2005.* New York, UNCTAD.

Wang, M.Y. 2002. 'The motivations behind China's government-initiated industrial investment overseas.' *Pacific Affairs* 75(2): 187-206.

Wells, L.T. 1983. *Third World Multinationals*, Cambridge, MA: MIT Press.

Wei, X.L. and X. L. Liu 2006. 'Productivity spillovers from R&D, exports and FDI in China's Manufacturing Sector.' *Journal of International Business Studies* 37(4): 544-557.

Wong, J. and S. Chan 2003. 'China's Outward Direct Investment: Expanding Worldwide.' *China: An International Journal* 1(2): 273-301.

Xing, Y. 2006. 'Why is China so attractive for FDI? The role of exchange rates.' *China Economic Review* 17(2): 198-209.

Young, S., C. H. Huang and M. McDermott 1996. 'Internationalization and competitive catch-up processes: Case study evidence on Chinese multinational enterprises.' *Management International Review* 36(4): 295-314.

CHAPTER SEVEN

Ethnic Chinese Entrepreneurship in Southeast Asia: Measuring the Economic Impact of Mainland China

Michael Jacobsen

Assessing Mainland China's economic performance from a Southeast Asian perspective

According to observers, it is critical for the Southeast Asian economies to understand China's economic development and to figure out how to counter a potentially devastating predatory competition from that country. The main background for such a statement is based on the fact that a consequence of the emergence of China as the world's largest recipient of foreign direct investment (FDI) has also meant a diversion of substantial amounts of FDI flows that would otherwise have gone to Southeast Asia. For example, from 1988 to 2000, five Southeast Asian countries – Singapore, Malaysia, Thailand, the Philippines, and Indonesia – have experienced declining inward FDI. Furthermore, the relative shares of FDI in the GDPs of all five Southeast Asian countries between 1988 and 2000 have decreased quite significantly: a reflection of both the rapid GDP growth of some countries (Singapore + 2.2 %) and a dramatic net decline in inward FDI in others (- 0.7 % for Indonesia). China, on the other hand, has experienced an increasing share of FDI ranging from 1 % from 1988 to 1990 to 1.3 % from 1998 to 2000 (Yeung 2006: 6).

Furthermore, roughly 75 % of China's cumulative inbound FDI has come from Asian economies. Almost 80 % of all FDI into Asia in 2001 went to China. Previously China was first and foremost competing with Malaysia, Thailand, the Philippines, and Indonesia since they have been mostly dependent on foreign investment and technology, but now, however, global capital flows into China, thus restraining the Southeast Asian countries from moving up the value chain. This means that Asian economies with the technical capabilities to stay ahead of China will benefit from China's economic growth whereas those that rely on foreign technology will find their positions threatened by China (Wanandi 2002: 231, Bolt 2000: 111).

Arguably, the economies that will benefit the most from China are those that have the capabilities to penetrate the growing Chinese market, develop complementary relations with the Chinese economy, attract investment from China, and create development partnerships with China. Mari Pangesty adds that given greater openness, growth in Chinese domestic demand coupled with growth of its labour-intensive exports, which are still dependent on raw material and intermediate inputs, certain imports from Southeast Asian countries are likely to increase. The products that will benefit these countries are oil, gas, wood, rubber, agriculture-based products, together with manufactured products such as electrical machinery and the like. Indonesia is a case in point due to its huge quantity of natural resources. Basically, it is up to the Southeast Asian countries to ensure regional competitiveness when supplying these products to China. (Pangesty 2002: 85).

Actually, the rising economic might of China when combined with Japan and Korea- threatens to turn Southeast Asia with the exception of Singapore into an economic sideshow. Jusuf Wanandi stresses that it will be wise for Southeast Asia to commit China to a regional web of rules and institutions so as to be able to contain and partly control the economic might of China (Wanandi 2002: 232-33). Mari Pangesty also stresses the importance of creating regional networks based on free trade agreements such as the Association of Southeast Asian Nations (ASEAN) Free Trade Area (AFTA), ASEAN+China and the ASEAN+China, Japan and South Korea combined with bilateral trade relations between China and each of the ten ASEAN countries.

However, it is imperative to prevent the development of rigid bilateral centre-periphery like structures between East and Southeast Asia with all the patron-client relationships that this might entail. The means to contain or rather to create – manageable cooperative economic relationships with China – and, to a lesser extent, East Asia in general – seen from a Southeast Asian perspective – is thus through regional cooperation where free-trade agreements are the means and equality in partnership is the goal. Compared to regionalism in the Americas and the enlargement of Europe, however, East and Southeast

Asia are still searching for their own institutional identity (Pangesty 2002: 81).

China's rise to economic superpower status does not, however, only mean doom and gloom for the Southeast Asian economies. Becoming a big economy also brings about a growing domestic demand for imported goods and thus expands a home market. For example, according to Bloomberg News 12 January 2004 the Asia-Pacific region exported 44 % to China in the first 10 months of 2004. That is equivalent to about US$219.7 billion. Malaysia alone sent 16.2 % of its foreign shipments to China in the first half of 2003: five times as much as in 2000. Because of an annual growth rate of about 8.5 % in 2003, 9.3 % in 2005, and as forecasted by BBC Business News in December 2005 with a further 9.4 % in 2006, and 9.5 % in 2007, China is the fastest-growing economy among the 10 largest economies in the world. China is also a new source of income for the developing economies in Asia.

The downside of this speedy growth, which attracts a huge amount of FDI, however is that it may reduce the prospects for growth in such countries as South Korea, Singapore, Malaysia, and Thailand, according to the Bloomberg News agencies (Yeung 2006: 7-8). The combination of low inputs of FDI and a China-oriented export economy carry the potential threat for at least some of the Southeast Asian economies that it makes them even more dependent on China's ability to drive export-led recoveries, thus creating the background for the before-mentioned highly problematic centre-periphery structure. As Mari Pangesty puts it, however, this potentially negative development is more or less outweighed by the acknowledgment that a growing China is like a rising tide, as it lifts all boats in its vicinity.

It is against this background of a fluid and potentially volatile economic landscape in East and Southeast Asia that this paper focuses on one particular ethnic group that has become a centrepiece in the discussion of whether a rising Chinese economy is a benevolent or predatory force: we are refer to the ethnic Chinese in Southeast Asia (Bolt 2000). Despite the coherent ethnic and cultural nature generally ascribed to this particular group, this article argues that, in actual fact, this group is divided into many fractions. The group is divided economically, politically, and culturally due to issues of national loyalties combined with a host of different economic and cultural preferences on behalf of the countries in which the ethnic Chinese reside. This differentiation among the ethnic Chinese in Southeast Asia, it is argued, is a reflection of multi-dimensional impacts such as colonialism, different types of social and political entrenchments in the different communities, and nations of residence. This again makes the ethnic

Chinese, conceived of as regional-wide minority groups, vulnerable towards the effect of a rising Chinese economy and especially the impact it has on the individual Southeast Asian national economies – thus boomeranging back more or less negatively on their respective ethnic Chinese minorities. To further zoom in on the ethnic Chinese, this paper concentrates on those who live in Indonesia and Malaysia. Finally, the paper does not concentrate on Chinese controlled MNCs or conglomerates, but rather Chinese SMEs, as it is mostly those types of companies that are torn between national political loyalties and local constraints in terms of doing business in their respective local communities.

Southeast Asian Ethnic Chinese and the Impact of Mainland Chinese Capital

The impact of the ethnic Chinese in Southeast Asia has been documented since the 14th century. It was, however, not until the beginning of the 18th and 19th centuries that migrants and sojourners from especially the southern part of Mainland China, Fujian, Guangdong, Hainan, and Guangxi provinces began in earnest to settle down in Southeast Asia: in particular in today's Malaysia and Indonesia. Here some worked as indentured labours in the European-owned rubber plantations and tin mines, while others settled down as traders. These migrants used already-existing Chinese networks based on transplanted conceptions of professional guilds, which were organised like secret societies around religious orientation, language, dialect, or ancestral affiliations to certain geographical locations in China. The common denominators for these guilds were basically group identification; principles of *guanxi* (reciprocal relationships) and *xinyong* (trust), just to mention the most important (Jacobsen 2005).

Guanxi affiliations, in particular seem to have survived the test of time. For example, several observers have argued that *guanxi* affiliations within a Chinese network were – and still are – a type of *modus operandi* for doing business within the ethnic Chinese business community (Luo (2000), Yang (1994), Weidenbaum and Hughes (1996), Kotkin (1992)). The all-encompassing nature attributed to *guanxi*-affiliated networks is also prevalent in discourses on the Chinese diaspora – that is – the generic name for overseas Chinese networking practices (McKeown 2001, Bolt 2000 and Gipouloux 2000). For Kotkin (1992), the Chinese diaspora is characterised by an enduring sense of group identification and global linkages. For Callahan (2002), the comparative advantage of the diaspora's Confucian reading of capitalism is that cultural ties lower the transaction costs of doing business in

China and Southeast Asia, since the legal system in this region is not fully developed and implemented.

These perceptions of capitalism in a Chinese environment – within this context, a Southeast Asian Chinese milieu – seems to portray the ethnic Chinese as having constructed a kind of fifth-column, non-grounded, transnational flow of ethnicised capital that mainly thrived within closely-knitted circles, maintained by age-old Chinese kinship, language, or even philosophical affiliations. However, one cannot help feeling that such perceptions have an Orientalist feel attached to them (Yao 2002, Dirlik 1996, Ong and Nonini 1997). When looking critically at the literature on the relationship between contemporary Chinese business enterprises and *guanxi*-affiliated networks in East and Southeast Asia, both an absence of a profound influence of the latter on the former together with a lack of cohesiveness within the Chinese diaspora per se are revealed. Wong (1998), Gomez and Hsiao (2001) and Jacobsen (2006, 2007) have difficulty finding evidence for a dominance of chain-related *guanxi*-affiliated business deals within the diaspora which are based on ethnic affinities or shared identities.

On the contrary, profit-driven motives seem to prevail – be it with intra or inter-ethnic business relations thus also linking up with domestic, non-Chinese, business communities in the country of residence. This in- and out-flow of the Chinese diaspora, governed partly by personal strategies and partly by contextual circumstances, is a practice that Riggs (2001) has defined as a process of diasporisation and de-diasporisation, when switching from mono-ethnic to multi-ethnic spatial relations, be they local, national, or international. Cribb (2000) and Gomez and Hsiao (2004) furthermore, contest the thesis that the institutions, norms, and practices of the ethnic Chinese are the main reason for the growth of their enterprises. They question whether Chinese entrepreneurs have depended primarily on business networks based on shared identities to develop their corporate base.

This argument is further spelled out by Qiu Liben (2000), who writes that if one examines contemporary Southeast Asian Chinese networks in an historical context, it can be seen they were not products of the economic and cultural expansion of China, but rather they were the product of a global capitalist expansion. She continues:

The Chinese networks themselves have changed with the needs of time; they developed from the networks of bangs [organisations based on guanxi like connections, MJ] to the networks of the overseas Chinese and then to the open and multi-cultural net-

works shared by citizens of various countries. This has enabled them to play an important role in the sustained economic development of Southeast Asia and in integration of the region' (Qiu 2000: 203).

This confirms Arif Dirlik's (1996) proposition that *guanxi* business practice is an ethnicisation of universal capitalist practices and not a specific Chinese economy which parallels global capitalism. Returning to the discussion of cohesiveness generally attributed to the Chinese diaspora, this paper subscribes to the idea that a diaspora constitutes a decentred, multi-levelled, fractious, generally ethnically-affiliated, ideational network that allows people to move in and out of a given diaspora depending on their current social and political situation (Ang 2001 and Riggs 2001). The adherence to a perceived pertinent diaspora thus depends on relative social, economic, and political contextual givens. An understanding of a given diaspora does not, therefore, depend on systemic network approach, that is, theoretical constructs hovering above empirical and geographical constraints as indicated by Ong and Nonini's notions of 'ungrounded empires' (1997). On the contrary, it is crucial to undertake contextually based analyses of *de facto* socio-political events that delineate the positioning of a Chinese individual within a pertinent diaspora. With such an approach it is imperative to focus on those social, political, and economic forces that have the capability of generating changes in the societal embedment of the ethnic Chinese.

On the Relationship between Chinese Entrepreneurs and the Impact of Mainland Chinese Capital

This leads us to forward the main question in this paper. Having disentangled Chinese network practices and having stressed how important it is to focus on those social, political, and economic factors that have the capability of generating changes in the societal embedment of the ethnic Chinese, this prompts us to ask how the ethnic Chinese have reacted towards the growing Mainland Chinese economy? Arguably, by focusing on ethnic Chinese SMEs and stressing the importance of analysing them in relation to their societal embedment, the importance of the Mainland Chinese economy is secondary to those entrepreneurs. They have to primarily secure their freedom of manoeuvre in their communities of residence, a freedom that is guided just as much by political and cultural engineered strategies as by cynical economic calculations or emotional or ideological attachments towards 'the old country'.

This argument becomes so much more important as the rising Chinese economy influences, positively or negatively on the economic performance of the various countries in the Southeast Asian region. This, again, influences the domestic attitude towards the ethnic Chinese in their respective communities of residence (Bolt 2000: 119-25, Yeung 2006: 14). Arguably, the ethnic Chinese in Southeast Asia do not unilaterally embrace or cheer the expanding Chinese economy, as it has a profound influence on their freedom of manoeuvre in their communities of residence. Instead, we see a careful balance of how to achieve the better of the two worlds: increased potentials for expanding one's business without jeopardising the relationship to a domestic non-Chinese social and political environment.

Two case studies of ethnic Chinese SME business communities follow: one in Manado, the provincial capital of North Sulawesi, Indonesia, and one in Johor Baru, in the State of Johor, southern Malaysia. The paper focuses in particular on how they relate to their respective communities of residence and whether the current economic developments in Mainland China have any influence on their current economic performance.

Two Southeast Asian Case Studies
Manado in North Sulawesi Province, Eastern Indonesia

Two things stand out when studying the Manadonese Chinese Business community. The first is a high emphasis of assimilating into the Minahasa community (is the main ethnic group in North Sulawesi Province) – a preferred societal positioning that is underlined by referring to oneself as a *peranakan*. Stressing assimilation instead of integration and categorising oneself as *peranakan* is similar to stressing both a diachronic and synchronic sense of belonging. To be a *peranakan* emphasises having roots in the local community and being assimilated refers to an abolition of ethnic differences. At face value these two main aspects of being Manadonese Chinese could be one of the factors that explain why there have not been any violent clashes between ethnic Chinese and the Minahasa before, during and after the fall of the New Order regime.

The second thing about the Manadonese Chinese is that they do not stand out as a distinct ethnic group among the Minahasa. On the contrary, even the Minahasa stress the almost total assimilation of the Chinese into local communities. It seems as this can to a certain degree, be attributed to the fact that the mechanisms for establishing oneself as a distinct group do not influence the current inner functioning of the Manadonese Chinese conceived of as an ethnic group. For example, *guanxi* affiliations do not play an important role within the ethnic Chinese business community, even though they can still be identified as a social signifier amongst the Manadonese Chinese. As such, this study subscribes to Gomez and Hsiao's critique of *guanxi* practices in a modern economy. As previously stressed, it is the profit motive that plays the greatest role for the Chinese entrepreneurs when conducting business, not ethnic factors or cultural preferences, a fact that also applies to Manadonese Chinese entrepreneurs. Because of this, I take Dirlik's point that *guanxi* is more about a rhetorically dictated ethnification of capitalist practices: not a practical one. *Kongsi* (clan) practices and *guanxi* affiliations are thus only invoked if they can lead towards higher or more stable profit margins. In this sense, to continue stressing *guanxi* as a dominant aspect of Chinese business practices – at least in Manado – can be categorised as a kind of cultural chauvinism within a specific business environment.

An interesting consequence of the non-dominant position of *guanxi* in the Manadonese Chinese business community is that, because it is so weak, it actually undermines the functioning and effectiveness of *kongsi* organised businesses. Arguably, *guanxi* affiliations can be conceived of as reinforcing the inner workings of *kongsi* organised businesses, as both strive towards reinforcing relations between the Chinese partners and thus they indirectly promote a distinct Chinese-ness in terms of business practices. However, as it is now, *guanxi* only constitutes but one of several business strategies when establishing *kongsi*-based companies. This de-linked relationship between *guanxi* and *kongsi* thus reinforces processes of assimilation and downplays the development of a distinct ethnic (Chinese) identity. Such a development is reinforced by yet another factor, namely religious affiliations like as Christianity. Christianity is the dominant religion in North Sulawesi and is generally seen as a facilitator between non-Buddhist Chinese and Christian Minahasans. Since the Christian Chinese by far outnumbers the Buddhist Chinese, processes of assimilation are further reinforced.

However, taking processes of assimilation to their ultimate limits leads one toward the assumption that ethnically distinctive features become hybridised to such an extent that the original ethnic identities involved are gradually dissolved and a new common cultural denominator arises. Such a perspective can only be an illusion. Assimilation processes are always based on asymmetrical relationships. In the case of the Manadonese Chinese and the Minahasa, the latter is the dominant part and it would be difficult to imagine that they would give an inch of their perception of ethnic supremacy in relation to the ethnic Chinese. As such, assimilation processes are about stipulated power relations that are manifested in social integration and more or less peaceful co-existence. Ethnic distinctions remain, despite these processes, but they descend towards a lower level of social practice. They only resurface during ceremonial occasions, which are societally detached and socially accepted by the dominant 'other'.

A somewhat unexpected consequence of these processes is that the Manadonese Chinese becomes de-linked from the Chinese diaspora. By far the greatest numbers of informants have detached themselves from their ancestral root in either Fujian or Guangdong Province. Mainland China is currently being conceived of as either a potentially promising target for doing transnational business or as an interesting tourist destination. The 'home' part of the Chinese diaspora has thus been separated from the otherwise classical triangular perception of diasporic constellations, namely the 'home-host-migrant' construct. This points toward the fact that diasporas are multi-dimensional entities that are contextually defined. Even though the Manadonese Chinese have currently cut off the 'home' part of the Chinese diaspora, the linkages are still there, but dormant. This means that when not activated, diasporic links descend into a deeper layer within people's minds and remain there until various social and political events reboot them into existence.

Thus, it is possible to suggest that a diaspora is a latent structure: that is, it is not a permanently established ethnic oriented national or international router for migrant and sojourners. A diaspora only comes alive locally when certain social, political, or economic events highlight or squeeze a certain ethnic group: for example, the Chinese, as has been the case several times in Indonesia. This confirms Riggs's (2001) notion of diasporasation and de-diasporasation as people utilise a given diaspora when need be. In between it does not exist in their minds. For now, North Sulawesi provides them with a social and political safe haven, and the Minahasa accepts them in their midst as they constitute an important economic factor in the province. So, for the time being the Manadonese Chinese are highly localised; that is, they are 'assimilated' and thus de-linked from the Chinese diaspora. How long these positive inter-ethnic relationships will last depends on a whole range of things. Economic performance (locally as well as nationally), religious harmony, and amicable and non-competitive interethnic relationships are just a few areas of potential contention. When and why a shift in these relationships might occur – thereby giving rise to a potential re-linking of the Manadonese Chinese to the Chinese diaspora – can only be determined through empirical studies and through not theoretical predictions (Jacobsen 2006).

Johor Baru in the State of Johor, Southern Malaysia
Contrary to the Manadonese Chinese entrepreneurs in North Sulawesi, there is a clear perception among the ethnic Chinese SME entrepreneurs in Johor Baru (JB) of being different from other ethnic groups in this part of Malaysia and of being treated accordingly by their community of residence. The blame for this state of affairs is laid on the official *bumiputra* ('sons of the soil') policy that promotes affirmative action of the Malay population at the expense of the Indian and, in particular, the ethnic Chinese populations. A consequence of this policy, according to ethnic Chinese spokespersons, is that the Malaysian people get most public benefits in terms of education, jobs and financial support from the government (both at state and federal level). For example, in terms of education, this leads to the fact that most Chinese students attend the many private school and higher education institutions to be found throughout Malaysia or they go abroad for their education. There are quite a few Chinese students in JB, but many prefer to cross the Johor Strait in order to get or to continue their education in Singapore. The negative consequence of this is that many graduates do not return to JB to apply their new skills to work, but they choose instead to settle down and marry in Singapore.

The relationship between ethnic Chinese and the *bumiputra* are not governed by policies of assimilation, but rather by a policy of a peaceful co-existence based on a public framework of mutual interdependency. In a sense, this relationship is perhaps more honest towards the reality, as it is not "dressed up" in a rhetoric of assimilation as in North Sulawesi. This proves our previous stands on the relationship between integration and assimilation in that the latter is but a "cover up" for an asymmetrical power relationship between the two groups. In JB this power relationship is not covered up; it is in public! Because of this officially sanctioned practice of positive discrimination ethnic, Chinese identity contrasts sharply to that of Malay identity. It is spelled out in specific Chinese cultural and religious associations and trade organisations such as the Chinese Chamber of Commerce and Industry, amongst other professional or non-professional organisations which are mainly serve ethnic Chinese interests. A somewhat negative consequence of this segmentation is that the ethnic Chinese feel superior towards the Malay and Indian communities in terms of economic performance. Pragmatically, they recognise that the Malays, in particular, have the political power to impose their aspirations and ambitions on the Chinese, thus forcing them to support – or at least accept – a *status quo* as defined by the Malays.

An example of these ethnic Chinese organisations is the clan-based language groups. There are a variety of ethnic Chinese languages spoken in JB, which is in contrast to the situation in Manado in North Sulawesi, where Hokkian dominates with about 85 % in relation to Cantonese and Mandarin speaking Chinese. In JB, there are Teochius, Hokkians, Hainans, Hakka, and Cantonese-speaking Chinese in almost equal proportions. Representatives from these language groups intermix but are nonetheless divided into clans that provide each other with help when doing business amongst themselves, with *bumiputra* entrepreneurs, and when linking up to business contacts in Mainland China. In fact, all five language groups have formed their own associations. They are primarily social associations and are not specifically oriented towards economic or political ends. Basically, these associations are interest groups. This means they can exert pressure on politicians and parties by giving advice about the needs and demands of the ethnic Chinese community. These associations maintain strong ties to Mainland China and see it as their main priority to uphold the ties to the "old country" in terms of culture and language. Especially within the area of language are they very active, as many of the younger Chinese have problems speaking the various Chinese dialects or even Mandarin for that matter.

As mentioned, the different clans are not exclusive in the sense that they isolate themselves. On the contrary, they intermarry and initiate joint business ventures. There are, however, rather strained relations towards the b*umiputra* business community and towards the local and federal governments of the close relationship between the three. The b*umiputra* business community is explicitly supported by the state and federal governments thus leaving the ethnic Chinese and the Indian business communities more and less outside the realm of influence. Despite these constraints there are business-related joint ventures between the ethnic Chinese and *bumiputra*. This is necessary if ethnic Chinese entrepreneurs are interested in securing government contracts for major projects. If the Chinese companies succeed in gaining government contracts, they must have at least one Malay representative in the company's board of directors, in accordance to the law. Such arrangements are similar to an *Ali-baba* business relationship, that is, a joint Indonesian-Chinese business venture arrangements in Indonesia.

The Cantonese association is in JB the oldest of the five 'clans'. Founded around 1880 it has been active ever since. The Hokkien association is the youngest. The three other associations were founded in between the Cantonese and Hokkien ones. For many, especially older ethnic Chinese entrepreneurs in JB, *guanxi* affiliations are important for governing interaction within and between firms. This goes even more in relation to the work done within and between the language associations. Interestingly, the *guanxi*-governed associations do not automatically invite new migrants from Mainland China to settle down in JB even though they have quite close connections to Mainland China. A new migrant who originates from, for example, Guangdong, would not necessarily contact the Cantonese association before leaving Mainland China. Generally, migration occurs on a personal initiative without the help of the association. The association only becomes important when the new migrants have settled down in JB. At that point, the migrant is invited to utilise the various networks that the Cantonese association had.

Guanxi practices are still important though, not only within these associations, but also within the business community: a fact that is reinforced by a general perception of exclusion and social marginalisation. There are, however, different attitudes towards *guanxi* practices within the ethnic Chinese business community. It is in particular among the older generation of entrepreneurs that *guanxi* affiliations are regarded very important, especially when initiating new business ventures. The initial meeting between new business partners, for example, is arranged along *guanxi* lines. That is, it is pre-organised by an intermediary that both parties trust.

This way of initiating and conducting business is not so prevalent among the younger generation of entrepreneurs. For them, Chinese entrepreneurs do not exist in a vacuum, as some of the older entrepreneurs seem to think. They must take into account the changing modes of doing business with the outside world: not only in relation to the Malaysian economy but also to the global economy, forcefully represented by Singapore just across the Johor Strait. Many young entrepreneurs regard a *guanxi*-dominated economy as a hindrance towards economic flexibility and a free flow of capital. Both of these economic premises are necessary when addressing the occasionally volatile fluctuations within the global economy. As a consequence, business practices within the ethnic Chinese business environment in JB is under consideration, as stiff competition combined with a "brain drain" of the best young entrepreneurs towards Singapore is on the rise thus threatening the overall economic environment and performance in Johor Baru.

Interestingly, it is thus Singapore – and not Mainland China – that poses the greatest threat towards the economy in JB. Mainland China is perceived as an opportunity – not a threat or a must – that can be exploited if the possibility for going there presents itself. This is because most of JB's SME enterprises (both Chinese and non-Chinese) are multi-directional in their search for new markets, for example, towards the domestic market, towards the important Singaporean market or towards other East and Southeast Asian markets (Wee, Jacobsen, Wong 2006).

The China Factor and the Constraints of the Local

One of the main purposes of this paper has been to assess the importance of Southeast Asian countries social and political attitudes towards the ethnic Chinese entrepreneurs and whether they have any influence on how the latter relate to Mainland China. The main focus has been on Chinese SMEs, since they are much more societally grounded – and thus vulnerable – in relation to the social and political whims of their respective communities of residence than the ethnic Chinese controlled MNCs and major conglomerates. The latter two are in a much stronger position to weather awkward shifts emanating from the political establishment in their respective communities than the SMEs, as they are capable of moving their production lines and capital assets to other locations outside their Southeast Asian location necessary. Furthermore, conglomerates and MNCs are also more prone to follow the mainstream of international capital flows in order to maximise their output. In these cases *guanxi* and *xinyong* together with other culture-specific Chinese modes of doing business have little influence, as the rate of profitability within global capitalism carry much more weight (Gomez et al. 2004).

From a general perspective, Southeast Asian Chinese SMEs are more or less forced to comply with the rules of doing business in their resident communities. That applies in particular when dealing with non-Chinese entrepreneurs. When conducting business on an intra-ethnic basis (e.g. with other ethnic Chinese entrepreneurs), *guanxi* and other culture-specific Chinese modes of business practice have a much greater leeway. This does not mean, however, that intra-ethnic business practices are exclusively conducted along culturally-defined modes. On the contrary, as shown in the Manado case, the culturally-informed business practices constitute but one set of practices out of other business practices when designing various intra- and inter-ethnic business strategies.

The differences between SMEs and the large Chinese controlled MNCs and conglomerates furthermore entail different attitudes towards the economic possibilities in Mainland China. As stipulated in the beginning of this paper, the economies that will benefit most from China are those that can penetrate the growing Chinese market, develop complementary relations with the Chinese economy, attract investment from China, and develop partnerships with Mainland Chinese entrepreneurs. MNCs and conglomerates are more capable of taking advantage of the opportunities offered by an expanding Mainland Chinese market, since they can penetrate it by offering superior management expertise, technological know-how and have access to large amounts of capital and production assets – things that are in great demand by Mainland Chinese entrepreneurs and governmental development schemes. Furthermore, if MNCs prefer to remain in Southeast Asia but still wish to enter the Mainland Chinese market, they also have an advantage compared to the SMEs, since they are capable of conforming and changing their production base locally so as to be able to meet the needs of Mainland Chinese investors. In this capacity, Mainland China is major attraction seen from the perspective of MNCs and conglomerates.

These possibilities do not apply to SMEs, as they are more or less dependent on local conditions such as *bumiputra* policies in Malaysia, *Ali-baba* relationships, combined with negative stigmatisation in Indonesia. In order words, SMEs they are more grounded and dependent on contextual constraints. This also means that the question of integration and assimilation in relation to the host community becomes much more important. It is actually decisive for whether ones SME should orient itself towards Mainland China or the host community. In reality, there is not much choice. The local always prevails over the international, as it is the former which provides the individual ethnic Chinese entrepreneur and his company with a framework which to thrive and die: a framework that is not only constrained in terms of business opportunities, but also in terms of ethnicity and negotiated identities. On this basis, the market in Mainland China remains a distant and problematic potential.

References

Ang, I. 2001, On Not Speaking Chinese. Living Between Asia and the West, London: Routledge.

Bolt, P.J. 2000, China and Southeast Asia's ethnic Chinese: state and diaspora in contemporary Asia, Westport: Praeger.

Callahan, W.A. 2002, *Diaspora, cosmopolitanism and nationalism: overseas Chinese and neo-nationalism in China and Thailand*, Hong Kong: City University of Hong Kong, Southeast Asia Research Centre, Working Paper Series no. 35, November.

Cribb, R. 2000, 'Political Structures and Chinese Business Connections in the Malay World: A Historical Perspective', in Chan Kwok Bun (ed.) *Chinese Business Networks. State, Economy and Culture.* Singapore: Prentice Hall, pp. 176-92.

Dirlik, A. 1996, 'Critical reflections on "Chinese Capitalism" as a paradigm', in R. Ampalavanar Brown (ed.), *Chinese business enterprise*, Vol. I, London: Routledge, pp. 17–38.

Gipouloux, F. 2000, 'Network and Guanxi: Towards an Informal Integration through Common Business Prectices in Greater China', in Chan Kwok Bun (ed.) *Chinese Business Networks. State, Economy and Culture.* Singapore: Prentice Hall, pp. 57-70.

Gomez, E.T. 1999, *Chinese Business in Malaysia. Accumulation, Ascendance, Accommodation.* Surrey: Curzon Press.

Gomez, E.T. and Hsiao, Hsin-Huang 2000, *Chinese business in Southeast Asia: contesting cultural explanations, researching entrepreneurship*, Richmond: Curzon Press.

Gomez, E.T. and Benton, G. 2004, 'Introduction: De-essentialising Capitalism: Chinese Enterprise, Transnationalism and Identity', in Edmund Terence Gomez and Hsin-Huang Michael Hsiao (eds), *Chinese Enterprise, Transnationalism and Identity.* London: Routledge/Curzon, pp. 1-19.

Jacobsen, M. 2005, 'Islam and Processes of Minorisation among Ethnic Chinese in Indonesia: Oscillating between Faith and Political Economic Expediency', in *Asian Ethnicity,* Vol. 6, No. 2. June pp. 71-87.

Jacobsen, M. 2006, 'Doing Business the Chinese Way? On Manadonese Chinese Entrepreneurship in North Sulawesi' in *Copenhagen Journal of Asian Studies.* No. 24.

Jacobsen, M. 2007, 'Re-Conceptualising Notions of Chinese-ness in a Southeast Asian Context. From Diasporic Networking to Grounded Cosmopolitanism', in *East Asia. An International Quarterly.* Special Issue. Vol. 24, No. 2. Summer.

Kotkin, J. 1992, *Tribes: how race, religion, and identity determine success in the New Global Economy*, New York: Random House.

Luo, Y. 2000, *Guanxi and business*, Singapore: World Scientific.

McKeown, A. 2001, *Chinese migrant networks and cultural change: Peru, Chicago, Hawaii, 1900-1936*, Chicago: The University of Chicago Press.

Ong, A. and Nonini, D.M. 1997, *Ungrounded Empires. The Cultural Politics of Modern Chinese Transnationalism.* New York: Routledge.

Pangestu, M. 2002, 'China and Southeast Asian Regional Trade Co-operation: Trends and Perspectives'. International Conference Paper on East Asian Cooperation: Progress and Future Agenda. Hosted by the Institute of Asia-Pacific Studies (IAPS), CASS. Center for APEC and East Asia Cooperation (CAEAC), CASS. 22-23 August. Beijing.

Qiu, L. 2000, 'The Chinese Networks in Southeast Asia: Past, Present and Future', in Chan Kwok Bun (ed.) *Chinese Business Networks. State, Economy and Culture.* Singapore: Prentice Hall, pp. 193-206.

Riggs, F.W. 2001, *Glocalization, Diaspora and Area Studies*, pp. 1–4, <http://www2.hawaii.edu/~fredr/glocal.htm>

Wanandi, J. 2002, 'The rise of China: A Challenge for East Asia'. *The Indonesian Quarterly.* Vol. XXX, No. 3, Third Quarter, pp. 224-33.

Wee, V., Jacobsen, M., Wong, T.C. 2006, 'Positioning Strategies on Southeast Asian Chinese Entrepreneurs'. Journal of Contemporary Asia. Vol. 36. No. 3.

Weidenbaum, M.L. and Hughes, S. 1996, *The bamboo network. How expatriate Chinese entrepreneurs are creating a new economic superpower in Asia*, London: The Free Press.

Wong, J. 1998, *Southeast Asian Ethnic Chinese Investing in China*, East Asian Institute, Singagpore: National University of Singapore, Working Paper No. 15.

Yang, M. 1994, *Gifts, favours, and banquets: the art of social relationships in China*, Ithaca: Cornell University Press.

Yao, S. 2002, Confucian Capitalism. Discourse, Practise and the Myth of Chinese Enterprise, New York: Routledge/Curzon Press.

Yeung, H.W.C. 2006, 'Change and Continuity in Southeast Asian Ethnic Chinese Business'. *Asia Pacific Journal of Management.* Vol. 23. Issue 3, pp. 229-54.

CHAPTER EIGHT

The Danish Seduction of the China Outbound Tourism Market: New Issues for Tourism Research

Can-Seng Ooi

Never before has a country with 1.3 billion people become a source of tourists. China is still a developing country but its sheer size and fast-paced economic development have resulted in a huge affluent population that has the ability to travel overseas for leisure. The growing Chinese outbound tourism market has generated excitement, leading to grand visions and strategies for various tourism destinations. For instance, thanks to Chinese tourists, Macau has overtaken Las Vegas as the biggest gambling destination in the world; although the American city is unlikely to regain that crown, it hopes to improve its fortunes if it can attract massive numbers of Chinese (*Seattle Post-Intelligencer*, 3 June 2007). The Ritz-Carlton Hotel wants the brand-conscious Chinese to recognize it as a premier global hotel chain; it is opening six hotels in China (out of 19 worldwide) in the next few years to heighten its brand presence in the Middle Kingdom (*Seattle Post-Intelligencer*, 3 June 2007). In wanting to attract more tourists to Australia, Pan and Laws (2002) argue that it is necessary to make use of Chinese *guanxi* (connection); Australian inbound tour operators could improve their services by linking up with Chinese travel agencies. And in Seattle, they imagine the Chinese are like the Japanese, the city is repeating a successful campaign in Japan for the Chinese – "Living Cool, Loving Nature" (*Seattle Post-Intelligencer*, 3 June 2007). In most instances, destinations around the globe are anticipating a flood of Chinese tourists to their shores in the near future (Cai, Lehto and O'Leary 2001; Pan and Laws 2002; Ryan and Mo 2002; Yu, Weiler and Ham 2002; Zhang and Heung 2002).

But in order for Chinese citizens to travel overseas, they must seek official permission. In the last decade, more and more destinations have been given Approved Destination Status (ADS) by the Chinese government. An ADS country is a pre-approved destination where Chinese citizens can travel in organized groups for leisure. Most EU member states, including Denmark, attained their ADS in September 2004. The increasing number of ADS countries shows that the Chinese government is slowly allowing the outflow of foreign exchange via outbound tourism. The Chinese government is also pleased that its citizens are warmly welcomed around the world, indicating the growing global respect China has today.

Tourism, like in other international businesses, is entwined in economics, politics, culture, and social life. This chapter will not only discuss some issues related to the economic and social impact of China outbound tourism market in Denmark but will also propose some rethinking of theories in relation to tourism studies. But first, I would like to accentuate four intrinsic elements of the international tourism industry that characterize the encounters of business, culture and politics.

One, the destination or the host country sells itself as a playground – its spaces, culture, amenities and facilities are to be shared with foreign guests. Like foreign investments, tourism offers economic benefits: revenue, employment, infrastructure development, skill transfer and so forth. In the case of visiting tourists, many aspects of the society's social and cultural life are also put up for consumption – the host society is not promoted as an environment for production but as a product for consumption. Notwithstanding, in many cases, foreign companies may invest and establish branded attractions, such as Disney theme parks, Hilton hotels and Gucci shops, in tourist destinations. Host countries vie for them, so as to enhance their location attractiveness. But in the business of tourism, *the host society is essentially promoted as a site for consumption, not production.*

Two, foreign tourists have special needs – they visit a place for a short period of time, they lack local knowledge and most of them are there to enjoy themselves (Ooi 2002). As a result, tourists must be nurtured during their visits and provided for in the most mundane manner; they must be provided information on local facilities, they must be taught how to be sensitive to local customs, and they must be shown how to move around and where to feed themselves. Like local residents, tourists need access to information, the right to gaining assistance, and in case of emergencies, they must know how to be protected. In other words, a destination has to provide the resources to *help and serve tourists and protect their rights and interests.*

Three, as related to the above points, tourism authorities that want to attract more tourists must also deal with issues related to the commodification of local life (Cohen 2002; MacCannell 1976). The intertwined relationships between tourists and host country are manifested in all aspects of social life, including at the cultural, economic and political levels. While one may argue that investing in the local tourism industry is also investing in local society, local residents may lament that resources for the industry should be directed towards local needs and not towards tourists. Foreigner-local relationships are potentially tenuous. In mass tourism, the large number of curious and insensitive tourists in local society may draw angry responses from residents. Investing in the tourist market means *having to placate and convince local residents about the worthiness of the tourism investment* – the off-sets from resources used and daily inconveniences caused must be less than the economic and social benefits from mass tourism.

Four, as in wanting to attract foreign investors, a country wanting to attract tourists must market, brand and sell itself. Local identities are constructed and re-invented – elements are selected while others are marginalised (Ooi 2004a; 2004b). Seductive brand images and stories may entice potential tourists but they may alienate local residents. In some host countries, such as Singapore and China, the vision of a vibrant and exciting destination has become a blue-print for social engineering the local population. *Resources used in attracting tourists may offer opportunities to direct social and cultural change in desired tourism-oriented directions.*

As a result of these intrinsic characteristics, the relationship between guest and host is a central issue in tourism studies. Problems arising from mass tourism, such as traffic and parking, pollution, "wear and tear" of heritage sites and price inflation are likely to annoy and even infuriate the local population (van der Borg, Costa and Gotti 1996). Aspects of the host society may also be commodified and touristified; mass trinketization, for instance, debases local handicrafts (Cohen 1988). To many local residents, foreigners do not appreciate the host in its complexity and diversity. While foreigners enjoy themselves, locals work to serve the tourists. This is a common concern in tourism; the guests are conspicuous in their presence, not only in their odd behaviour but also in their supposedly higher spending power. As a result, Mathews (1975) argues that tourism is sometimes seen as "whorism". Based on the direction of the flow of tourists, tourism is often seen as an industry that maintains the domination of developed tourist-supplying countries over developing tourist-receiving countries (Morgan and Pritchard 1998; Ooi, Kristensen and Pedersen 2004; Selwyn 1996; Silver 1993).

On the other hand, there are economic benefits from tourism. The social impact of tourism is not necessarily negative. For example, tourists bring diversity and life to street markets, they prompt the conservation of local heritage sites and they garner resources for physical and cultural development (i.e. concerts, theme parks, landscaping, illumination of monuments); improvements which also benefit locals. Researchers advocate a balanced and sensitive approach to the management of tourism's impact (Chang 1997; Jenkins 1997; Newby 1994; Teo and Yeoh 1997). In using Gidden's "Third Way", Burns (2004) paints a bipolar view of tourism planning in bringing different interested parties together. The first – the leftist development first" – view focuses "on sustainable human development goals as defined by local people and local knowledge. The key question driving development is 'What can tourism give us without harming us?'" (Burns 2004: 26). The second – "the rightist tourism first" – view aims to "maximize market spread through familiarity of the product. An undifferentiated homogenized product depends on a core with a focus on tourism goals set by outside planners and the international tourism industry" (Burns 2004: 26). In an attempt to bring different interests together, the Third Way conceptually bridges the two poles. These are streams of tourism impact studies. They emphasise the influence of tourists on the host society. There is, however, no study on how tourists are managed and socialised, although tourists must learn new ways to do things and to blend into the host society during their relatively short visits.

This chapter suggests that the China outbound tourism market offers avenues for researchers to re-evaluate some aspects of tourism studies. With the advent of the China outbound tourism market, the view that tourism is an industry that encourages the domination of developing tourist-receiving countries by developed tourist-supplying countries must be reconfigured. Similarly, tourism studies have focused only on the impact on the host society, ignoring how tourists themselves are socialised and managed in the global tourism industry.

Forecasting the China-Outbound Tourist Market

The Chinese started travelling overseas in the early 1980s, at the start of the post-Mao economic reform (Zhang 2006). China outbound tourism growth has been growing phenomenally. According to official statistics, in the period between 1995 and 2005, the number of Chinese travelling outside China increased from 4.5 million to 31 million; outbound travel expenditure climbed from US$3.7 billion to US$21.8 billion (Zhang 2006). The vice chairman of the China Tourism Association, Wu Wenxue, boasted that the Chinese made 34.5 million departures abroad in 2006 and that Chinese travellers are changing the tourism pattern in the Asia-Pacific region and in the world (*People's Daily*, 15 June 2007). According to the World Tourism Organization (2003), China will provide 100 million outbound travellers by the year 2020 and would be the fourth largest source of outbound travel in the world.

At the moment, the number of organised groups of Chinese travelling for leisure remains relatively small compared to the number of Chinese who travel for business (Zhang 2006). 90% of all outbound travels by the Chinese are within Asia; neighbouring Hong Kong and Macau make up 70% of the total (Zhang 2006). And in terms of outbound tourist expenditures, the massive bulk are spent by business tourists; their trips are supported by the government, by companies and by other organisations. These business tourists do not necessarily reflect the spending power of the for-leisure Chinese tourists. The China tourism outbound per capita expenditure was only US$15 in 2004: one-sixth of the world's average (Zhang 2006). This number alerts us to the less-than-rosy reality of the Chinese outbound tourism market. On the other hand, this number alludes to the potential in the China tourism outbound market as the Chinese economy charges ahead.

Europe – a long haul and high status destination to the Chinese – attracts more affluent tourists. Travelling to Asian countries is still the first choice for the Chinese. But Europe has become popular. 1.9 million Chinese visited Europe in 2006, and the UK saw a more than 20% increase in Chinese tourists over the previous year (*People's Daily*, 15 June 2007; *People's Daily*, 3 October 2004). Denmark is not the first European destination of choice for the Chinese but the Danes want a bigger slice of the growing cake as the China tourism outbound market expands. Excitement about the impending arrival of Chinese tourists was fervent in 2004, when Denmark and most other EU countries attained their ADS. During that year, Wonderful Copenhagen (WoCo) – the Danish capital city's tourism promotion agency – organized a conference to increase awareness of the potential of the Chinese outbound tourism market in Denmark. At that conference, the Danish General Manager of Global Refund – an international company facilitating tax-free refunds in numerous countries – presented a positive picture of the Chinese driving the tourism industry forward (Møller 2004). Based on their tax refund data, Global Refund observed that despite the relatively high cost in Europe, the Chinese still bought many things in the continent, including perfumes, shoes, leather goods, clothing and souvenirs. In France, the Chinese spent 4300 DKK each on luxury products in 2004; 3825 DKK in Italy and 1619 DKK in Denmark. In their statistics, each trip to Europe cost the Chinese about US$5500 and US$2000 was spent in Europe. And between 2003 and 2004, the number of Chinese tax free refunds increased by 80% in Denmark. These numbers show that Denmark was already benefiting from the influx of Chinese tourists before the country had its ADS.

To drum up more enthusiasm in the industry during the conference, WoCo presented a survey of more than 400 Chinese tourists in Denmark in 2004. The survey found that the Chinese tourist spent an average of 900 DKK a day in Denmark, excluding accommodation expenses (Wonderful Copenhagen 2004a). The Chinese chose to visit Denmark mainly because of recommendations from family and friends (37%) and because of advertisements in newspapers and magazines. Most of them visited various tourist attractions in the country (e.g. Tivoli, the Little Mermaid) and they shopped. The Chinese tourists had a good impression of Copenhagen. For instance, the Chinese found Copenhagen clean and environment-oriented, safe and secure, culturally rich, romantic and charming, trendy and modern, and informal and relaxed. They also found the hotels, restaurants and shops of high international standards. The Danes were perceived as friendly and helpful, Danish cultural heritage was exciting and Copenhagen was considered to be an easy city to get around. Essentially, Copenhagen fulfilled their expectations (Wonderful Copenhagen 2004b). Armed with optimism, WoCo predicts in the best case scenario that by 2020, more than half a million Chinese will visit Denmark. In the worst case scenario, WoCo predicts that about a quarter of a million Chinese will visit (Wonderful Copenhagen 2004a). These estimates by far exceed the 60 000 Chinese tourists who visited Denmark in 2004.

In 2005, Denmark celebrated the 200th birthday of Hans Christian Andersen. A big campaign to promote Denmark was launched in China. Symposia, operas, exhibitions and competitions were organised to generate awareness of Denmark via the famous author Andersen, with whom Chinese pupils are already familiar since they read his fairy tales in school.

Contextual Constraints on the China Outbound Market

While the statistics are generally promising, the forecasts may still be too forward-looking. There are many challenges in the China outbound tourism market. One, the Chinese may be getting richer but they have limited time resources for leisure travel. Workers in China are given three week-long national holiday periods built around the following occasions: Chinese New Year (January/February), Labour Day (1 May) and National Day (1 October). Traditionally, the Chinese New Year is for family reunions and thus the Chinese do not normally use this time for overseas travel. The Chinese authorities have suggested that workers should be given flexibility in taking their holiday leave, instead of having their days off dictated by these holiday periods. Until this practice becomes widespread, longer trips overseas will be difficult to arrange.

Two, China is still a developing country. While there is a class of affluent Chinese, the large majority finds it too expensive to take a holiday overseas. Global Refund estimated the potential China outbound tourism market to be only 3% (60 million) of the population (Møller 2004). According to the World Tourism Organization (2003), 100 million Chinese will travel overseas annually by 2020. These numbers are still large in absolute terms, but they are relatively small compared to the population of China. The large majority of Chinese cannot afford to travel overseas.

Three, while the number of ADS countries increases, the Chinese still face visa application problems, an issue to be elaborated on later. Many destinations fear that human trafficking gangs are making use of travel agencies to illegally move Chinese out of the country. Foreign governments must sort out the genuine tourists from the potential illegal immigrants, a process which results in lengthy and difficult visa applications. Thus, the ADS is only one of many administrative obstacles removed from the outbound Chinese traveller.

Four, while many people around the world speak Mandarin, most do not. The majority of the Chinese population has very little or no command of the global tourism *lingua franca*: English. Furthermore, many Chinese tourists are relatively inexperienced travellers. Many complaints made about the Chinese boil down to their lack of travel experience (*The Straits Times*, 31 July 2005). Thus, the Chinese outbound tourist is relatively nervous because s/he would inevitably feel insecure in the unfamiliar environment and would have difficulties communicating with the locals.

Danish Responses to Chinese Outbound Tourism Market

As mentioned earlier, Denmark has already benefited from the increase in Chinese tourists even before it attained its ADS. Because of the expectations of even more Chinese tourists, Denmark already prepares itself to welcome the Chinese. Regardless, rolling out the red carpet is a complex affair; there are concerns about how to manage the new China outbound tourism market. These concerns include the threat of illegal immigration, the fear of unscrupulous travel agents and the discouragement of ugly tourist behaviour. Some of these issues will be discussed in the next section.

Re-re-Packing Denmark

In a study conducted by WoCo, Chinese tourists like Copenhagen but had some reservations (Wonderful Copenhagen 2004b):

1. Chinese tourists are impressed by the historical architecture of the city but do not find the European heritage to be as rich and exciting as other European cities, such as Rome, Paris or London.
2. They find their experiences have been hindered by language. There are few signs marked in Chinese.
3. Hans Christian Andersen is a significant figure to them but they could not experience him or his fairy tales in Copenhagen
4. There are few perceived opportunities for the Chinese tourists to buy souvenirs.

In response to feedback, a new Hans Christian Andersen museum has opened at the Copenhagen town hall square. There are also plans to incorporate Chinese signage at appropriate places around the city. While there are a number of souvenir shops where tourists can buy cheaper products, businesses are trying to generate another class of souvenirs that Chinese tourists could appreciate since minimalistic Danish design and the high cost of goods do not necessarily appeal to the Chinese.

Since 2000, the Danish tourism authorities have tried to move away from the historical and romantic images of Denmark as reflected through their earlier marketing campaigns (Ooi 2004b). The current branding campaign accentuates and re-packages Denmark as a modern, chic and cool country, in contrast to popular traditional tourism images associated with the nation. Images of the statue of the Little Mermaid, Hans Christian Andersen, castles, churches and fairy tales will be sidelined, while images of modern buildings, Danish design and relaxing Danes enjoying themselves will be accentuated. The campaign wants to draw out positive emotions from audiences. The branding campaign is thus meant to change the world's perception of Denmark as essentially historical and classical to Denmark as basically contemporary and trendy.

In China, VisitDenmark – the Danish national tourism promotion agency – cooperates with other Scandinavian countries to promote the region, which is framed as "Uptown Europe: New Scandinavia". The Danes still promote their new trendy and funkier image in "Uptown Europe" (Wu 2005). But, as mentioned earlier, in 2005 Denmark celebrated H.C. Andersen's 200th birthday; the poet and fairy tale writer was used to enhance the country's image around the world. China received much attention in the celebrations because H.C. Andersen is a popular icon in China and the authorities want to draw the Chinese to Andersen's country. To the Chinese, H.C. Andersen is the quintessential icon of Denmark; Chinese pupils are familiar with the writer. They have read his fairy tales in school. It is thus considered wise to tap into the preconceived ideas of the Chinese and build an awareness of and affinity for Denmark. But as one tourism official lamented, celebrating H.C. Andersen and his fairy tales is not consistent with the attempt to brand Denmark as a cool, modern and trendy country. Andersen's works may be updated in the marketing events but the writer remains a centuries-old icon. While this strategy makes marketing sense, it also shows the tension between tapping into "dated" preconceptions that have strong commercial value and cultivating a new desired destination identity. Not all tourism officials were pleased with the tampering of the new destination brand identity. The branding of Denmark repackages the country, and with accentuation of H.C. Andersen, the country has been re-re-packaged.

Preconceived Ideas and Demand on Denmark
As alluded to earlier, tourists' preconceptions affect their experiences. Tourists seek out and affirm their preconceptions during their travels (McLean and Cooke 2003; Prentice 2004; Prentice and Andersen 2000). Often, 'authentic' cultural products are also created and staged for tourists. These products range from 'Voodoo' shows in Haiti (Goldberg 1983), the sale of Jewish 'religious' objects (such as skull cap and candles) in Israel (Shenhav-Keller 1995), to visiting an 'origi-

nal' Manggarai village in Indonesia (Allerton 2003). Many exotic images freeze the host society in the past and ignore the development that society has achieved. These images and reifications feed into the caricaturized tourist imagination. Researchers such as Echtner and Prasad (2003) and Silver (1993) have suggested that Third World representations in tourism foster a particular ideological position which place developing countries in an inferior position. These places are perceived to be backward, the people are perceived to be eager to serve and the destination is considered to be "just" a cultural playground.

Such arguments are being challenged now because China as a developing country is placing similar demands on developed countries like Denmark. The example of how H.C. Andersen is used to re-brand Denmark for the Chinese market is a case in mind. Another example is that the Chinese (along with many other people in the world) perceive Denmark to be country with many beautiful blonde people. Denmark is also seen as an open and tolerant society: the sense of sex, drugs and rock 'n' roll. A travel operator who brought in Chinese tourists found a persistent problem with this image; her male customers always want to visit the infamous strip clubs in Copenhagen but are always disappointed. Many Chinese male tourists want to see tall, beautiful, blonde girls performing in clubs but instead, they mostly see girls from Asian countries. The tourists complain about this mismatch in expectations to the travel agent. Many Danes do not support the sex trade. Many Danes also find it offensive that the monthly tourist guide *Copenhagen This Week* offers a massive advertising section on escort, massage and strip club services. Politicians have withdrawn their support for the monthly publication, but the advertisements provide valuable revenue for the publisher. Those who are against the advertisements – including the tourism authorities – do not want to continue propagating sleazy images of the city. To others, the sex trade is part and parcel of the city and the country. As the Chinese case shows, Chinese tourists actively seek out these services for which they perceive Denmark to be infamous. Foreign and local interests may differ and paying tourists can beef up demands on products and services that many locals do not want.

Tourism and Human Trafficking

Political debates in a country may also affect tourism. The development of the tourism industry requires cooperation amongst various agencies. Tourism authorities, local government, land control authorities, cultural management agencies and others need to cooperate to develop the industry. How different agencies and political institutions within a country coordinate themselves to plan, develop and promote the place affect the manner of support for the tourism industry (Elliot 1983; Leheny 1995; Ooi 2004b; Pearce 1997; Richter 1985; Wanhill 1987). But each of these agencies has its own interests and agendas. Consequently, the tourism policy in a destination may not be consistent.

For example, since 2001, the right-wing Danish People's Party is a supporting partner party for the minority Danish government. As a result, immigration policies have been toughened and laws related to foreigners living in Denmark have been changed. Some policy changes include the shift in legislation governing permanent residency. Previously, foreign spouses of Danes could apply for permanent residency after three years of marriage/residence in Denmark. It has now been extended to seven years of marriage/residence. Immigration laws also require a foreigner to be at least 24 years of age before s/he can marry a Dane in Denmark. There is also concern with illegal immigrants disguised as tourists to enter the country; these people are most likely to come from developing countries; since China is a developing country, this is a concern.

While China offers a massive outbound tourism market, many Chinese citizens could not afford to leave the country for the pursuit of pleasure. On the other hand, there are many who want to leave China to seek a better future. The Chinese government acknowledges the problem of illegal immigration and is trying to crack down on travel agencies that are fronts for human traffickers (*People's Daily*, 7 September 2004; *People's Daily*, 1 October 2004). To show the scale of the problem, for example in 2005, there were at least 50 000 Chinese tourists who did not leave Malaysia (*The Straits Times*, 22 November 2005). There was also an increase in the number of illegal Chinese migrants found working in Malaysia, including in criminal activities. The Malaysian authorities claim that many have left for a third country after procurement of fake passports in Malaysia.

Because of the possibility of using tourism as a guise for human trafficking, many countries including Denmark, have been cautious in welcoming the Chinese. Although many European countries have ADS, the immigration formalities remain tedious. The strict processes to acquire EU visas cross several official levels. If there were members of tour groups who did not leave the country, the inbound travel agencies who brought in those tourists will be penalised. This policy is practised in Denmark. As a result, many Chinese outbound travel agencies collect a 50 000 Yuan deposit (35 000 DKK) from each tourist. This is an additional burden for Chinese tourists (*People's Daily*, 3 October 2004). Welcoming genuine Chinese tourists and at the same time, stopping overstayers is a problem faced by many countries. So, at the time of writing this chapter, the Danish embassy in Beijing had yet to issue any tourist visa for a Chinese person under the ADS scheme; visas have been issued for technical, educational and business visits. The Danish immigration authorities have also penalised inbound tour agencies that have brought in Chinese tourists who have disappeared in Denmark. One travel agent quit the business because two of her Chinese tourists disappeared during a technical visit; the investigations were lengthy, and she was not allowed to bring in more Chinese visitors until the investigations were complete. Thus, this tour operator was forced to close the business.

On the other hand, many Chinese apply for entry into Europe through the Finnish embassy. Finnair and Finland have not only promoted themselves aggressively in China, the Finnish authorities have also made it relatively easy for the Chinese to get visas. So, many Chinese tourists visiting Denmark travel via Helsinki as part of their grand Nordic tour.

Helping and Protecting Tourists
There is a general belief that tourists should visit a destination to enjoy and appreciate local cultures. They should also accept the local way of life. Such a view tends to ignore the fact that tourists are rather anxious when they travel. They do not have the local knowledge and thus, they feel alien to the destination. They are vulnerable and gullible in the foreign place. Tourists worry about being cheated by shopkeepers, they fear for their safety and they are anxious about finding reliable help. Their rights to information, their personal safety and their access fair treatment must be protected in the host society (Ooi 2005).

There are travel agents that cheat and are unprofessional (*People's Daily*, 1 October 2004; *People's Daily*, 7 September 2004). It was reported that guides are forced to cut costs and lower service quality levels, resulting in sight-seeing activities being removed from and shopping programmes added to itineraries, so that agents can earn commissions from tourist purchases in overpriced outlets. In Denmark, a number of tour agencies use unlicensed guides for Chinese tourists; many Chinese students function as drivers and guides. These agencies can get into trouble for cheating the tourists. Many tourists do not seem to know that they are being short changed.

Chinese tourists do complain, however. For example, a shop keeper in Singapore experienced shouting and a big row because a group of Chinese tourists changed their minds on a diamond pendant they purchased; they wanted a cash refund but the shop could only offer exchanges for other items (*The Straits Times*, 31 September 2005). A tourist explained that in her country, persons become aggressive when they feel "snubbed"; these tourists may perceive that the sales staff think the tourists are not worthy of their services, reflecting how Shanghai sales staff treat customers from poorer provinces (*The Straits Times*, 7 September 2005). A fundamental concern about such behaviour is that the Chinese tourists are unaware of how they may direct their grievances in the foreign place.

Some complaints of mistreatment can reach a national level. For instance, in a rather embarrassing incident in Malaysia, a video clip of a Chinese tourist being stripped and searched by immigration officers surfaced. The video clip caused a furore in China and Malaysia (*The Straits Times*, 29 November 2005; *The Straits Times*, 17 December 2005). The Malaysian deputy security minister defended his country, saying that if foreigners think Malaysia is cruel, then they should not visit the country (*The Straits Times*, 30 November 2005). This ministerial outburst reflects a prevalent view that many Chinese female tourists enter Malaysia to work illegally, especially in vice. The prime minister however immediately chastised the minister and apologized to the Chinese government (*The Straits Times*, 1 December 2005). Eventually, after an investigation, the woman turned out to be a local non-Chinese citizen. The bad publicity resulted in a sharp drop of tourists visiting Malaysia.

The status of tourists in a destination is more than a commercial one. While they are there to enjoy the local host society, they also have special needs. The host society has the responsibility to protect and help them. Some destinations do. For example, in Singapore, Members of Parliament and the Cabinet minister often champion tourist interests (Ooi 2005). In other countries, such as Thailand, there is a "tourist police force" which tourists can call upon for help. Shopowners and taxi drivers have been known to lose their licenses because of tourist complaints. But in Denmark, tourism is not a priority industry and few politicians are enthusiastic about tourism issues. Tourists in Denmark have access to help from the police and other authorities. Chinese tourists who can not speak English, much less Danish, they do not feel protected nor do they have access to assistance when needed. As a Danish official in local government confided, tourists do not receive much attention from political leaders because they do not consider tourists important – "tourists do not vote". While individual tourists come and go, there will always be tourists in the country; they are a constituency in this society (Ooi 2005). Regardless, the Chinese government does involve itself when its citizens are not treated properly.

A Chinese Governments Response: Socialising the Chinese

The Chinese government, as with most other governments, wants to protect its citizens' rights when they travel abroad. The Chinese government, however, seems to go a step further to chastise its citizens for their bad behaviour. The Chinese authorities, including the China National Tourism Administration (CNTA), Ministry of Commerce, Ministry of Construction and the General Administration of civil Aviation of China, have launched a campaign to educate Chinese outbound tourists (*The Straits Times*, 3 September 2006). According to the Spiritual Civilisation Steering Committee, certain widespread complaints about Chinese tourists have hurt the image of China as a civilised country and they have generated negative attention. These complaints include how Chinese tourists clear their throats loudly, how they squat and smoke in public places, how they remove their shoes aboard planes and trains and how they jump queues (*The Straits Times*, 3 September 2006). Such complaints are found in many international media reports, including "Ugly China tourists: Why are they like that?" which presents several accounts of bad social behaviour of Chinese tourists (*The Straits Times*, 31 July 2005). For example, about 200 Chinese tourists were upset because their flight was delayed in Bangkok because of a technical glitch. As a result, they had to miss the day tour in Singapore. The passengers refused to disembark and the airline (Cathay Pacific) must promise to compensate them with US$50 each before they would agree to leave the plane. Hotels also complained about Chinese tourists spitting on the floor in rooms and leaving burn holes in beds and blankets. In interviews with Chinese tourists in the report, one tourist said that such behaviour is true and particularly stark from "backward areas". Although the report ended by suggesting that service staff in Singapore should not misunderstand the Chinese, the Chinese authorities want to get rid of the ugly Chinese tourist perception.

The Deputy Director of the Spiritual Civilisation Steering Committee, Zhai Weihua, claims, "[t]he behaviour of some Chinese travellers is not compatible with the nation's economic strength and its growing international status" (*The Straits Times*, 3 September 2006). As a result, the CNTA is issuing a guide book to Chinese outbound tourists when they purchase tickets from travel agencies. Picking up international social conventions and etiquette is considered good for China's image and a way to self-improvement for the Chinese (*The Straits Times*, 3 September 2006). This so-called educational campaign will run until the Beijing Olympics in 2008. The Chinese authorities also demand that travel agencies educate and guide their customers. If these agencies fail to do so, they will be "criticised, educated and ordered to reform" (*The Straits Times*, 26 August 2006).

Discussions

The beginning of this chapter presented four intrinsic characteristics of tourism: the destination is a playground for tourists, the destination is a site for consumption, local residents may not be welcoming of tourists and tourism offers resources for local development. The literature on tourism impact research tends to emphasise on how tourists have come to exploit, impose and corrupt the host society. There is also a prominent view that the developed world – via tourism – influences and dominates the tourist-receiving third world. The issues raised above present a more complex picture – Denmark is a first world country that wants to please third world China; tourists do not get "their way" in many instances, and in the case of Chinese tourists, their government wants to reform and socialise them into the global tourism culture. The direction of influence is thus not only from guest to host. Let us evaluate the empirical and theoretical issues.

Denmark, like many other countries, is repackaging and re-branding itself to attract tourists. Danes decided to make use of Chinese preconceptions of Denmark to sell their country. The new cool and trendy brand identity had to be re-packaged vis à vis classical images which the authorities wanted to marginalise and forget. Some products that many Danes want to eradicate are popular with Chinese – and other tourists. While such destination problems are not unique to Denmark, they show that the Danish tourism authorities do not have the power to push for a definitive direction for branding the country. There is also limited coordination between different governmental agencies; the celebration of H.C. Andersen's 200th birthday was lauded but some Danish tourism officials were baffled because Andersen is not a major item in the new branding campaign. Regardless, resources were made available for the celebrations and the tourism authorities naturally wanted to tap into those resources. While the Chinese tourists seem to "get their way" in wanting more H.C. Andersen in branding Denmark, they did not succeed in other – and significant – ways: for instance, in visa procurement. Denmark usually has a minority government. Policy formulations and implementations are subjected to negotiation among many political parties. The divergence of interests and policies among political parties often result in the inconveniences of democracy, which may delay efforts in bringing about intended actions. As tourists do not vote, few Danish politicians champion for them. As a result, catching illegal immigrants (a populist political stance) takes precedence over offering a seamless visa application process to welcome potential Chinese tourists.

While some Chinese tourists are cheated without their knowledge, many Chinese tourists complain too, especially when they perceive they have been cheated and treated unfairly. As in the case with the video clip in Malaysia, the Chinese government demanded appropriate actions from the Malaysian government. Possibly rather unique to the Chinese government's obsession with how China is perceived in the world, Chinese tourists are now being socialized into the global tourism culture. Many guest societies have to endure and tolerate unpleasant tourist behaviour, such as those of the brutish British football hooligans, noisy Swedish teenage drunkards and arrogant rich guests from different parts of the world. The Chinese government takes the responsibility for its citizens and wants them to behave in a more gracious manner – according to "global standards". Complaints from various destinations have spurred the Chinese government into action. Tourists may have the economic power to demand services, but they are also subjected to demands by the host society and possibly by their own governments.

The interactions between tourists and hosts are dynamic and complex. The direction of influence does not just come from the first world to the third world or just from tourists to hosts. The economic and social impact of tourism has been well researched, but as we can see above, tourism has political and international relations dimensions, as well. Mapping out the web of interplay amongst individual tourists, different industry actors and state authorities would demonstrate how international tourism has enriched the social life of the guest society, how it has generated local political concerns and how it has entrenched global tourism behaviour in individual tourists.

In the next few years, when the China outbound tourism market expands further, tourism researchers will need to develop new views and theories on power relations in tourism. The social impact of the Chinese on a host society may be significant, but the Chinese themselves would be trained and socialized for the global tourism industry.

Conclusions

Chinese tourists have a prevalent complaint in Europe. They prefer to visit Chinese restaurants, but they find the Chinese food is not "authentic" enough (*People's Daily*, 3 October 2004). With the influx of Chinese tourists to Denmark, perhaps Danes will experience an increased quality of Chinese restaurants in the future. While this case have a positive influence on European Chinese restaurants, researchers have argued whether tourism can be seen as a form of domination. Tourists' preconceptions must be considered when promoting the destination and when selling tourism products. As for the Chinese tourists visiting Denmark, H.C. Andersen, romantic Copenhagen and the sleazy bits of the country are offered because of tourist demands. This chapter has shown that Denmark – as a developed country – is subjected to the demands of the China tourism inbound market, even though China is still a developing country. Thus, earlier tourism studies which have concentrated on how the developed world has affected the developing world through tourism should be re-evaluated. There is a rising affluent class of consumers in the developing world that will bring their demands and wealth into the global tourism industry.

Also, in all tourism studies, the tourist is assumed to be a powerful group of individuals that can devastate, enrich and impose upon a host society; we can see that is not necessarily the case. The Chinese government is concerned with how its citizens behave abroad; effectively, the relatively inexperienced Chinese tourist is being socialised into the global tourism culture. In other words, new tourists have to learn how to be good guests.

Acknowledgement

I would like to thank the Danish Strategic Research Agency for the research grant that enabled the completion of this chapter.

References

Allerton, C. 2003. 'Authentic housing, authentic culture? Transforming a village into a 'tourist site' in Manggarai, Eastern Indonesia'. *Indonesia and the Malay World* 31(89): 119-128.

Burns, P. M. 2004. 'Tourism planning: A Third Way?'. *Annals of Tourism Research* 31(1): 24-43.

Cai, L. A., Lehto, X. Y. and J. O'Leary 2001. 'Profiling the U.S.-bound Chinese travellers by purpose of trip'. *Journal of Hospitality and Leisure Marketing* 7(4): 3-36.

Chang, T. C. 1997. 'From 'instant Asia' to 'multi-faceted jewel': Urban imaging strategies and tourism development in Singapore'. *Urban Geography* 18(6): 542-562.

Cohen, E. 2002. 'Authenticity, equity and sustainability in tourism'. *Journal of Sustainable Tourism* 10(4): 267-276.

Cohen, E. 1988. 'Authenticity and commoditisation in tourism'. *Annals of Tourism Research* 15: 371-386.

Echtner, C. M. and P. Prasad 2003. 'The context of third world tourism marketing'. *Annals of Tourism Research* 30(3): 660-682.

Elliot, J. 1983. 'Politics, power, and tourism in Thailand'. *Annals of Tourism Research* 10(3): 377-393.

Goldberg, A. 1983. 'Identity and experience in Haitian voodoo shows'. *Annals of Tourism Research* 10: 479-495.

Jenkins, C. L. 1997. 'Impacts of the development of international tourism in the Asian region'. In F. M. Go and C. L. Jenkins (eds). *Tourism and Economic Development in Asia and Australasia*. London: Cassell 1997: 48-64.

Leheny, D. 1995. 'A political economy of Asian sex tourism'. *Annals of Tourism Research* 22(2): 367-384.

MacCannell, D. 1976. *The Tourist: A New Theory of the Leisure Class*. London: MacMillan.

Mathews, H. G. 1975. 'International Tourism and Political Science Research'. *Annals of Tourism Research* 2(4): 195-203.

McLean, F. and S. Cooke 2003. 'Constructing the identity of a nation: The tourist gaze at the Museum of Scotland'. *Tourism, Culture and Communication* 4: 153-162.

Morgan, N. and A. Pritchard 1998. *Tourism Promotion and Power: Creating Images, Creating Identities*. New York: John Wiley and Sons.

Møller, J. 2004. Presentation by Global Refund at the "Chinese is ready but are we?" Conference. Copenhagen, 29 October

Newby, P. T. 1994. 'Tourism: Support or threat to heritage?'. In G. J. Ashworth and P. J. Larkham (eds). *Building a New Heritage: Tourism, Culture and Identity in the New Europe*. London: Routledge 1994: 206-228.

Ooi, C.-S. 2002. *Cultural Tourism and Tourism Cultures: The Business of Mediating Experiences in Copenhagen and Singapore*. Copenhagen: Copenhagen Business School Press.

Ooi, C.-S. 2004a. 'Brand Singapore: The hub of New Asia'. In N. Morgan, A. Pritchard and R. Pride (eds). *Destination Branding: Creating the Unique Destination Proposition*: London: Elsevier Butterworth Heinemann 2004: 242-262.

Ooi, C.-S. 2004b. 'Poetics and politics of destination branding: Denmark'. *Scandinavian Journal of Hospitality and Tourism* 4(2): 107-128.

Ooi, C.-S. 2005. 'Sate-civil society relations and tourism: Singaporeanizing tourists, touristifying Singapore'. *Sojourn – Journal of Social Issues in Southeast Asia* 20(2): 249-272.

Ooi, C.-S., Kristensen, T. P. and Z. L. Pedersen 2004. 'Re-Imag(in)ing Place: From Czechoslovakia to the Czech Republic and Slovakia'. *Tourism* 52(2): 151-163.

Pan, G. W. and E. Laws 2002. 'Tourism marketing opportunities for Australia in China'. *Journal of Vacational Marketing* 8(1): 39-48.

Pearce, D. 1997. 'Tourism and the autonomous communities in Spain'. *Annals of Tourism Research* 24(1): 156-177.

People's Daily 2004. 'China to further regulate outbound tourism market', 1 October

People's Daily 2004. 'Chinese flock to European tours', 3 October

People's Daily 2004. 'Tourism chiefs pledge to shake up travel sector', 9 September

People's Daily 2007. 'Chinese travelers changing the world's tourism pattern', 15 June

Prentice, R. 2004. 'Tourist familiarity and imagery'. *Annals of Tourism Research* 31(4): 923-945.

Prentice, R. and V. Andersen 2000. 'Evoking Ireland: Modeling tourism propensity'. *Annals of Tourism Research* 27(2): 490-516.

Richter, L. K. 1985. 'Fragmented politics of US tourism'. *Tourism Management* 6(3): 162-173.

Ryan, C. and X. Mo 2002. 'Chinese visitors to New Zealand: Demographics and perceptions'. *Journal of Vacational Marketing* 8(1): 13-27.

Seattle Post-Intelligencer 2007. 'U.S. targets China as next tourism ticket', 3 June

Selwyn, T. 1996. *The Tourist Image: Myths and Myth Making in Tourism*. Chichester: John Wiley and Sons.

Shenhav-Keller, S. 1995. 'The Jewish pilgrim and the purchase of a souvenir in Israel'. In M.-F. Lanfant, J. B. Allcock and E. M. Bruner (eds). *International Tourism: Identity and Change*. London: SAGE 1995: 143-158.

Silver, I. 1993. 'Marketing authenticity in third world countries'. *Annals of Tourism Research* 20(2): 302-318.

Teo, P. and B. S. A. Yeoh 1997. 'Remaking local heritage for tourism'. *Annals of Tourism Research* 24(1): 192-213.

The Straits Times 2005. '50 000 China visitors gone missing: KL paper', 22 November

The Straits Times 2005. 'Abdullah apologises to China for strip-search clip', 29 November

The Straits Times 2005. 'Chinese welcome, Abdullah tells Wen', 17 December

The Straits Times 2005. 'Malaysia cruel? Then go home, foreigners told', 30 November

The Straits Times 2005. 'Minister says sorry for 'cruel' remark', 1 December

The Straits Times 2005. 'Ugly China tourists: Why are they like that?', 31 July

The Straits Times 2006. 'Tour guides told to rein in rude Chinese tourists', 26 August

The Straits Times 2006. 'Beijing tells Chinese traveling overseas', 3 September

van der Borg, J., Costa, P. and G. Gotti 1996. 'Tourism in European heritage cities'. *Annals of Tourism Research* 23(2): 306-321.

Wanhill, S. R. C. 1987. 'UK – politics and tourism'. *Tourism Management* 8(1): 54-58.

Wonderful Copenhagen 2004a. *Being Chinese in Copenhagen II: Quantitative Survey on Chinese Tourists in Copenhagen 2004*. Copenhagen: Wonderful Copenhagen.

Wonderful Copenhagen 2004b. *Being Chinese in Copenhagen I: Group Interviews with Chinese Tourists in Copenhagen 2004*. Copenhagen: Wonderful Copenhagen.

World Tourism Organisation 2003. *Chinese Outbound Tourism*. Madrid: World Tourism Organisation.

Wu, T. 2005. *Branding Denmark and Stakeholders' Role: China Market*. Master Thesis (Cand. merc INT), Copenhagen Business School.

Yu, X., Weiler, B. and S. Ham 2002. 'Intercultural communication and mediation: A framework for analysing the intercultural competence of Chinese tour guides'. *Journal of Vacational Marketing* 8(1): 75-87. Zhang, G. R. 2006. *China's outbound tourism: An overview*. London: WTM-China Contact Conference

Zhang, H. Q. and V. C. S. Heung 2002. 'The emergence of themainland Chinese outbound travel market and its implications for tourism marketing'. *Journal of Vacational Marketing* 8(1): 7-12.

About the Authors

Mette Bjorn-Hansen graduated from the Copenhagen Business School in 2006 with a Masters degree in International Business. Her thesis concerned Guanxi and multinational pharmaceuticals in China. She has since then worked in the pharmaceutical industry within sales and marketing and is currently Product Manager at Coloplast.

Kjeld Erik Brødsgaard is Professor of International Business in Asia/China and Director of the Asia Research Centre at Copenhagen Business School. He has held visiting appointments in the USA, China, Singapore and Taiwan and is a non-resident Research Associate at the East Asian Institute, National University of Singapore. His most recent books include *Hainan: State, Society and Business in a Chinese Province* (2008), *The Chinese Communist Party in Reform* (2006) and *Bringing the State Back In: How China is Governed* (2004). He is currently engaged in a major research project on State, Party and the Changing Business Environment in China.

Jens Gammelgaard is Associate Professor of International Business at the Department of International Economics and Management at the Copenhagen Business School. His main research interest is knowledge management practices of multinational corporations, international mergers and acquisitions, and subsidiary development. His work has been widely published in journals like *Journal of International Management*, *Journal of Knowledge Management*, and edited volumes.

Peter Gammeltoft is Associate Professor at the Department of International Economics and Management, Copenhagen Business School. His research focuses on innovation, high-tech industries, and emerging economies, especially in East Asia. He wrote his Ph.D. (cum laude) in Economic Geography on development of technological capabilities in the Asian electronics industry. Prior to pursuing a Ph.D. he was senior consultant with Accenture.

Bersant Hobdari is Assistant Professor at the Department of International Economics and Management at Copenhagen Business School. He has a Ph.D. in Business and Economics. His areas of specialization are corporate governance, corporate finance, emerging markets, industrial organization and applied econometrics.

Michael Jacobsen is Associate Professor at the Asia Research Centre (ARC) at Copenhagen Business School. Prior to that Senior Researcher at the Nordic Institute of Asian Studies (NIAS) in Copenhagen, Denmark, Research Fellow at the Southeast Asia Research Centre at City University of Hong Kong, researcher at Centre for Development Research in Copenhagen, Denmark, and Nordic-Netherlands Research Fellow at the International Institute for Asian Studies in Leiden, The Netherlands. He has published widely on ethnicity and politics in contemporary Indonesia, the Chinese Diasporas and entrepreneurship in Indonesia and Malaysia.

Julie Marie Kjersem is International Marketing Product Manager at Novo Nordisk. She carried out research on the internationalisation of R&D as part of her master's thesis in International Business.

Niels Mygind has been a researcher/teacher at Copenhagen Business School since 1980; from 2004 Professor of Corporate Governance and Restructuring in Eastern Europe. Since 1996 he has been director of the Center for East European Studies. He has published in international journals on the effects of different ownership structures, the economic transition and privatization, corporate governance and enterprise restructuring. He is teaching topics such as economics, corporate governance, transition in Eastern Europe and China, and institutional change in emerging markets.

Can-Seng Ooi is Associate Professor at the Department of International Economics and Management, Copenhagen Business School. Besides being the Director of the MSc (International Business) Programme, he is the Editor of the *Copenhagen Journal of Asian Studies*. His research interests include international tourism, the global art industry, place branding and cross-cultural management. His research projects often compare Denmark, Singapore and China.

Marina Papanastassiou is Director of the Centre for International Business and Innovation (CIBI) at the Department of International Management and Economics at Copenhagen Business School. She holds a Ph.D. in International Business from the University of Reading, United Kingdom. Her research interests focus on the internationalisation process of R&D within Multinational Corporations (MNCs) and the evolution of the roles of overseas subsidiaries in MNCs. In 2002 she served as the President of the European International Business Academy (EIBA).

Evis Sinani is an Assistant Professor at the Department of International Economics and Management at Copenhagen Business School. She has a Ph.D. in Business and Economics. Her areas of specialization are foreign direct investment, corporate governance, applied econometrics and emerging markets.

Verner Worm is Professor of Chinese Business and Development at the Department of International Economics and Management and Director of the Copenhagen Business Confucius Institute. He has published extensively in journals such as *International Journal of Human Research Management*, *International Journal of Conflict Management*, *Organizational Dynamics*. His research interest is cross-cultural management focusing on China and China Business Studies in general.